# TRAILS & TRIALS

# TRAILS & TRIALS

## Markets and Land Use in the
## Alberta Beef Cattle Industry 1881–1948

### Max Foran

UNIVERSITY OF
CALGARY
PRESS

University of Calgary Press
2500 University Drive NW
Calgary, Alberta
Canada T2N 1N4
www.uofcpress.com

**National Library of Canada Cataloguing in Publication Data**
Foran, Max
Trails & trials: markets and land use in the Alberta beef cattle industry, 1881–1948
/ Max Foran.
Includes bibliographical references and index.

ISBN 1–55238–089–0

1. Cattle trade—Alberta—History. 2. Beef industry—Alberta—History.
3. Land use, Rural—Alberta—History. I. Title. II. Title: Trails and trials.

SFI96.C2F668 2003      338.1'762'0097123      C2003–910563–6


The University of Calgary Press acknowledges the financial support of the International Council
for Canadian Studies through its Publication Fund.

 We acknowledge the financial support of the Government of
Canada through the Book Publishing Industry Development
Program (BPIDIP) for our publishing activities.

 Canada Council    Conseil des Arts
for the Arts    du Canada

Printed and bound in Canada by AGMV Marquis

♾ This book is printed on acid-free paper.

Cover photo by Dave Brown; furs from *Buckskin Fur & Leather Company*, Calgary, Alberta
Cover design by Mieka West, *The University of Calgary Press*, Calgary, Alberta
Interior design by Jeremy Drought, *Last Impression Publishing Service*, Calgary, Alberta
Photographs by permission of the *Glenbow Museum Archives*, Calgary, Alberta

# Dedication

*to Grant MacEwan*
*agriculturalist, historian, father-in-law, mentor, friend*

...

# Table of Contents

## THREE
# Mixed Blessings 1914 – 20

## FOUR
# Change Out of Necessity 1921 – 30

## FIVE
# The Depression Years 1930 – 39

## SIX
# Extraordinary Times 1938 – 48

- Tables:

- Maps:

- Notes:

- Select Bibliography

- Index

...

# Introduction

THE BEEF CATTLE INDUSTRY HAS ALWAYS BEEN IMPORTANT TO THE ALBERTA ECONOMY. At the close of the twentieth century, beef cattle production led Alberta's agricultural sector. Anchored by a significant feeding industry that fed around 64 percent of Canadian cattle, the Alberta beef cattle industry provided over $2 billion in annual farm receipts and 39 percent of total farm cash income. Meat packing was the province's second largest manufacturing industry employing six thousand people and paying out $167 million in wages and salaries. When the multiplier effect is taken into consideration, the Alberta beef cattle industry was worth around $8.5 billion to the province's economy in the year 2000.

These impressive statistics belie that fact that the road to maturity has been anything but easy. The uncertainties that beset earlier beef producers persist. For example, the unpredictable export market remains vital to the industry. Statistics vary but anywhere from 25 to 40 percent of Canada's cattle leave the country for the United States, a much higher figure than during the period under discussion in this book. Moreover, beef consumption is down significantly from the peak year of 1976. Declining interest in red meat, the vagaries of climate, and the unpredictability of feed cost and availability are as real today as they were one hundred years ago.

Yet in many ways, the modern, integrated beef cattle industry bears little resemblance to its antecedents. Up to the end of the Second World War, the industry was not integrated into a regional feeding and finishing system. It did not produce "good Alberta beef," certainly not for the average Canadian.

Range management was not an important component of livestock management. It is the aim of this study to show the underlying causes which support and explain the above statements.

This book attempts to trace the development of the beef cattle industry in Alberta from its inception in the late nineteenth century up to the dawn of the modern era in 1948 by examining how land issues and markets affected cattle producers. The relationship between production costs and selling prices determined survival for ranchers and stockmen, and involved important decisions for the mixed farmer. Profit margins, or the difference between production costs and selling prices, drove producers to secure leasehold tenure at reasonable rates (cheap grass), and to sell their animals in the more lucrative export market. The interplay between these two factors and their implications through time provide the basis of this study. In response to changing times and conditions, beef producers focused their attention on these two variables. Very cheap grass justified an inherently unstable British market in the open range period. Security of leasehold tenure was the logical response to the changes brought by commercial agriculture after 1906. In the 1930s, the stockmen concentrated on securing reduced leasehold rental rates. The benefits of an open American export market, affirmed between 1914 and 1920 and threatened over the next twenty-eight years, dominated stockmen's dialogue both within and outside the industry.

The narrative ignores other important formative forces within the industry. For example, breeding programmes and animal health issues are dealt with only within their relationship to the two main themes of markets and land use. The cumulative contributions of individual stockmen are not discussed. Their different strategies and their individual responses to the complexities of their environments are not analyzed. However, despite these omissions, this study breaks new ground in terms of both time frame and emphasis. It moves away from the traditional focus on the socio-economic and cultural aspects of ranching and the cattle mystique, and tries to explain the industry in terms of its two most crucial variables. It will also demonstrate the paradox that while the beef cattle industry after 1906 was about much more than ranching, it was guided and shaped by ranching principles.

The beef cattle industry was Alberta's first agrarian-based commercial enterprise. In the last quarter of the nineteenth century, open-range ranching in Alberta was Canada's best example of the North American Western frontier experience. It was a factor in the ongoing debate over the nature of the Canadian and American frontiers, and arguably has been the main focus in differentiating their mythologies.[1] Yet despite its significance to the Alberta economy, the cattle industry beyond 1912 has received scant attention from academics and other writers. The chief focus has been on early ranching period between 1881 and 1912. Commencing with Leroy Kelly's *The Range Men*, an excellent contemporary account published in 1913, the romance and appeal of ranching has been pursued by many writers including Grant MacEwan, Shelagh Jameson and Bill Gold. Academic historians like Lewis G. Thomas, and later David Breen in his superb study, *The Ranching Frontier in Western Canada* (1981), laid out the foundations of what has become the standard interpretation of the ranching experience. Breen associated the Canadian ranching frontier with dominant metropolitan forces that distinguished it from its counterpart in the United States. Interest in this ranching period has remained high. In a recent challenge to Breen's interpretation, Warren Elofson in *Cowboys, Gentlemen and Cattle Thieves: Ranching in the Western Frontier* (2000) argues that powerful continental and environmental factors were crucial influences on early ranching practices and society in western Canada. Geographer Simon Evans has also written extensively on several aspects of the ranching period including spatial distribution patterns and American influences.[2]

The most significant contributions to the post-1912 era include a recent collection of essays edited by Simon Evans, Sarah Carter, and Bill Yeo, *Cowboys, Ranchers and the Cattle Business: Cross-Border Perspectives on Ranching History* (2000), and Ian MacLachlan's excellent study of the Canadian meat packing industry, *Kill and Chill: Restructuring Canada's Beef Commodity Chain* (2001). Sherm Ewing's *The Range* (1990) and *The Ranch: A Modern History of the North American Cattle Industry* (1995) are informative, often first-hand accounts of developments in the modern cattle industry. The process by which open range ranching was consolidated into more diverse beef producing enterprises between 1912 and 1950 has, however, been largely neglected.

This transformation is expressed in this narrative through the responses of beef producers to changing market and land use factors. Two major and several minor themes emerge. The role of live cattle exports is a primary issue. Their effect on domestic consumption and their impact on the development of a feeding industry are crucial market-related factors. The subservient place of cattle to King wheat dominates land use priorities. Leasehold tenure and the slow recognition of range management principles are related issues.

The export market guided the way the industry developed by entrenching particular marketing practices. The ranchers and stock farmers concentrated on the export market with their quality animals. The domestic market was dominated by farmers whose numerical strength had given them the vast majority of the cattle but not the quality. Producers argued that the export market, by clearing surpluses, acted as a price-setter for domestic beef. They never considered the implications of the fact that only 10 percent of production left the country, or the possibility that they might be wrong. The primacy of the export market detracted from an integrated feeding industry both regionally and nationally. Feeding was helpful but not essential to the export market. As for the domestic market, producers always maintained that it was not prepared to pay top prices for finished beef. A feeding industry was therefore neither necessary nor worthwhile. Finally, the battle over exports demonstrated the ongoing antagonisms between the stockmen and the federal government over the proper place of beef cattle in national agricultural policies.

The predominance of the wheat economy prejudiced beef cattle raising up to the 1940s. Cattle raising was more inelastic and capital-intensive than wheat production. Not only was the capital outlay higher for beef cattle, but they also took longer to turn a profit than wheat. For most of this period a producer could make more money from wheat than from beef. Beef prices were even more volatile than the weather, and for most of this period they were low. Much of the 1890s, the first decade of the twentieth century, and most of the 1920s and 1930s were not good times to be raising beef cattle. In fact, during the years under discussion, the cattlemen enjoyed really high prices only in 1918/19, and even then prices were diluted by general inflation.

The emphasis on wheat production delayed a proper recognition of the place of beef cattle in Alberta's land use patterns. By moving into semi-arid areas, wheat acreage threatened leasehold tenure and induced range degradation. Single cereal crop agriculture also retarded mixed farming as a versatile use of the land. It was only in response to the demands of the Second World War that fundamental changes in land use practices began to outline the future demographic face of the modern beef cattle industry. The importance of beef cattle in Alberta's land use priorities was directly linked to a forced decline in wheat acreage, and to the emergence of barley as a premier grain crop.

The producers' long battle to secure leasehold security provides one of the most persistent themes over the whole period. It is also argued that the majority of stockmen often displayed as much self-interest as concern for the range they leased. This point is further evidenced in the emergence of range management principles during this period. Though the stockmen may have been the first to express concern by blaming the farmers for land deterioration, they were not blameless. Ultimately, it was the heavy hand of government that set the rules for managing the range.

The emphasis on wheat growing, and the low popularity of beef cattle in mixed farming operations, elevated the importance of the ranchers. The arrival of the farming frontier is popularly associated with the death of ranching, and it is true that by the first decade of the twentieth century the big open-range leases were largely curtailed. Ranching, however, did not disappear. On the contrary, and despite their declining share of beef cattle numbers in the province, the ranchers retained their privileged position and remained the most powerful force in the industry. Ranchers were dominant in the influential Western Stock Growers' Association, and the strong lobbies it pursued after 1920 always favoured ranching interests. Of more significance is the fact that the evolving beef cattle industry continued to reflect ranching practices.

The interdependence of market factors and land use priorities defined the road taken by the Alberta cattle industry up to 1949. The fact that wheat was more profitable than livestock militated against intensive high-quality beef cattle operations in the agricultural belt. The successful cattlemen were those who utilized relatively cheap leaseholds on non-agricultural land to produce the type of animal wanted by the export market. Outside the semi-arid range areas, land use in Alberta was a response to the wheat economy and to a domestic market unable to pay for plentiful, quality beef. Though the search for stability was far from over by 1949, changing land use patterns, under the influence of higher domestic beef demand and producer prices, indicated that the Alberta cattle industry was entering the modern era.

# ONE

# The Legacy of the Ranching Era 1881–1907

*We believe that we have there the garden of the world.*
CHARLES TUPPER, 1879

THE ALBERTA CATTLE INDUSTRY BEGAN AS AN OPEN RANGE RANCHING ENTERPRISE, fuelled by eastern Canadian and British capital, and supported by untested beliefs about the western Canadian environment. For over twenty years it provided beef to local and regional consumers, and most importantly to a profitable export market in Great Britain. However, by 1908 environmental factors, agricultural land pressures, and international competition in the export market had imposed significant modifications on the ranching industry. Yet ranching did not die. Moreover, the transformed livestock enterprises that had emerged in former ranching areas continued to reflect attitudes and practices forged during this early period.

The Canadian ranching experience was a northerly extension of the American cattle industry. Ranching began in the Alberta foothills area and gradually expanded to the lower plains and brown soil zones to the east. The period before 1896 was dominated by open-range practices and was Canada's closest counterpart to the romanticized American western frontier. Although commercial cattle raising in Alberta actually began in the late 1870s, the ranching era in western Canada owed its formal origins to the leasehold system of land usage instituted in 1881. When compared to American practices, the leasehold system provides a major difference between the two frontiers. Formal leaseholds precluded rangeland violence in western Canada. Also in sharp contrast to the American experience, the survival of the leasehold system helped consolidate the ranchers' privileged position.[1]

The early cattle operators in Alberta shared three assumptions. They presumed that the grasslands were exclusive to pastoral activities, and that the climate was amenable to cheap beef production. They also believed that range cattle could be always marketed profitably. Both the demise of the open-range ranching era and the rise of the more diversified cattle industry that supplanted it should be seen through the interplay of these misplaced assumptions.

## Land Tenure Factors

The promise of low production costs and big profits brought the big cattle operators to the Alberta foothills. The American experience had shown that cheap grass meant excellent beef profits, particularly in a region considered unsuitable for agriculture. From both the ranchers' and the government's viewpoints, leasehold tenure provided the best answer, one mutually beneficial to both parties. This belief contrasted sharply with the American experience.

The negative perceptions of western Canada's agricultural potential had been reinforced historically in reports by Captain John Palliser (1857–60), Henry Youle Hind (1859), and Captain W. F. Butler (1870).[2] On the other hand, commercial cattle raising was seen as the ideal land use for most of the Canadian west. Reports by botanist John Macoun and geologist John Mercer Dawson in the mid-1870s had noted that western Canada was ideally suited to pastoral activity. Dawson, who was attached to the Boundary Commission in 1873–74, referred to the southern plains as "a great area well suited for pastoral occupation and stock farming." Macoun told the House of Commons Select Committee on Agriculture and Colonization in 1876 that "the Canadian portion of the American desert had a better climate and was suited to stock raising."[3] In referring to the breaking up of rangelands in the United States, Professor W. Brown of the Ontario Agricultural College informed the Farmers' Club in Markham in December 1881 that the Canadian ranges, on the other hand, were limitless, and "waiting to be taken up and occupied."[4] These positive comments reinforced the belief that ranching in the Canadian west was a logical parallel to the current westward movement of cattle-based enterprises in the United States.

*Cattle grazing on the Bar U ranch near Longview. The Bar U is one of the most recognized early ranch names. Operated for years by the visionary George Lane, the ranch was set in unparalleled scenic grazing country. Following Lane's death in 1925, the ranch became part of a multi-ranch cattle operation owned by Pat Burns. In 1950, the ranch lands were sold to other ranchers. Today, the Bar U Ranch is a National Historic site of Canada, occupying 148.43 hectares and containing thirty-five buildings (ND 8-67).*

Like their American counterparts, Canadian and British investors were drawn to the prime grasslands in the lee of the Rocky Mountains by the promise of big profits. General J. S. Brisbin's enormously popular book, *Beef Bonanza: or, How to Get Rich on the Plains* (1882), guaranteed profit margins of between 25 and 50 percent on cattle operations in the Great Plains. These grand predictions influenced investors, who genuinely believed that all the factors were in place to make cattle operations in western Canada even superior to those in the United States. The merits of a leasehold system were advanced vigorously in Ottawa by Quebec stock breeder Senator Matthew Cochrane, who argued that with the Plains Indians now on reservations, the time was ripe for commercial cattle ranching enterprises in the West. In the fall of 1881, a federally controlled leasehold system set the stage for an open-range cattle industry in the Alberta foothills.

*Cattle on Highwood River (ND 8-107).*

This system clearly favoured the big operators and showed the predisposition of a federal government desperate for investment in its uninhabited North-West. Leases of up to one hundred thousand acres were granted at a nominal cost of one cent per acre per year for a period of twenty-one years. This lease system ushered in a brief and monopolistic era for the big ranches. In 1884 two-thirds of stocked land in southwestern Alberta was controlled by four companies backed by Canadian and British capitalists.[5] By 1887 the formalization of the cattle industry under these generous land terms was fully established. In that year over 4.4 million acres were under lease in the North-West Territories. Sixteen leases were for one hundred thousand acres and more, while another twenty covered leases of fifty thousand acres. Large-scale leasehold land usage in Alberta was at its height.[6]

The big leaseholders assumed that their monopoly over the rangelands of southern Alberta would go unchallenged. They felt that the two-year cancellation clause in the 1881 grazing regulations protected their interests since no incoming homesteader would be prepared to wait that long. They

4

*Cattle in corrals, Drowning Pond area north of Medicine Hat, circa early 1900s. The ranching areas of southeastern Alberta and southwestern Saskatchewan were later additions to the original enterprises in the Alberta foothills and were characterized by more American influence and money (NA 2003-3).*

were wrong. The huge size of the leaseholds worked against them. Incoming settlers gravitated towards the foothill slopes adjacent to established centres like Calgary and Fort Macleod, and soon began applying political pressure to modify or break up the big leaseholds.[7] In 1883 they called for an end to the two-year cancellation clause in favour of immediate pre-emption. Two years later an Order in Council abolished this clause and made land under lease available to homesteads or pre-emption for prospective settlers. The lease rental rate was also raised from one cent to two cents an acre. A year later the even-numbered sections in the lease were thrown open to homestead entry, and in 1889 all grazing on public lands was prohibited without the consent of the Minister of the Interior. In 1892 the ranchers' access to school land leaseholds was restricted to five years and set at a high rental rate of four cents an acre. In the same year, notice was given that all leases which did not provide for homestead entry or for railway purposes would be terminated on 31 December 1896. By the end of that year only 257,983 acres were under lease in western Canada. The largest lease a year later was 7,500 acres.

The assault on leasehold land tenure for grazing purposes continued into the twentieth century. Those big leaseholders who wanted to remain in ranching were allowed to purchase 10 percent of their lease at $1.25 per acre, a practice which allowed many ranchers to consolidate their holdings on both deeded and leased land. Several ranchers secured leases from the owners of railway land grants, especially the Calgary and Edmonton Company. Others ran their cattle on unwanted homestead lands in more marginal areas. Some simply went east and continued operations on open crown or Canadian Pacific Railroad land. A few used their political influence to secure twenty-one-year closed leases from the Minister of the Interior, Clifford Sifton.[8] In November 1905, new lease regulations were issued under Frank Oliver, a less sympathetic Minister of the Interior. They showed that western Canada was no longer viewed officially as grazing country. Sifton's preferential policy was abandoned. Any long-term lease had to be in country deemed unsuitable for agriculture and was subject to a two-year cancellation clause. The new system was a blueprint for failure. The stocking rates were set at one animal to twenty acres within three years, an impossible figure, justifiable only in the best areas of the foothills. The two-year cancellation clause removed any chance of long-range planning and herd build-up.[9] The 1905 regulations, promulgated by a government unsympathetic to ranching interests, represented the death knell of the ranching industry as it had existed since 1881.

However, the demise of the big leaseholds did not mean that they disappeared. Prospective homesteaders were not inclined to take out leases in sub-marginal country with inadequate water and soil resources, or far from a railroad or town. Thus, while large leases in prime grazing areas were seen as discriminatory and as evidence of political favouritism, their presence in non-agricultural areas was less threatening.[10] In the early 1900s American cattle companies took up leaseholds in the shortgrass country of southeastern Alberta. By 1903 twelve American leaseholders controlled over six hundred thousand acres in southern Alberta, where they established, according to one scholar, "a robust variation of the American cattle kingdom."[11] The famed Matador Ranch in Saskatchewan was one of the lucky few that secured a closed twenty-one-year lease from Clifford Sifton.

Despite restrictions on their tenure, location and deployment, smaller leases remained very popular, growing in terms of numbers and gross acreage. Homesteaders were encouraged to take out leases of less than four sections

(2,560 acres).[12] Between 1900 and 1905 lease acreage quadrupled, and by 1907 Alberta's share of federal leased lands totalled over 1.5 million acres. In 1903 the 908 leases in the North-West Territories averaged fourteen hundred acres as compared with sixteen years earlier when 167 leases averaged over twenty-six thousand acres each.[13] The point is that while changes in leasehold tenure provisions were restricting factors, the concept remained ingrained. A commitment to leaseholds became an article of faith among Alberta stock growers. This was made abundantly clear in the long struggle after 1908 over leasehold consolidation. Furthermore, the continuing availability of cheap leases for stock raising ensured the survival of practices consistent with ranching. The ongoing role of the horse, the importance of roping and herding skills, the group round-ups and branding activities, and even the survival of stock watering reserves beyond the open-range era were all closely associated with the leasehold system of grazing.

## Climatic Variables and Ranching Practices

The nature of ranching in Canada took its example from the more climatically temperate United States, and presupposed animal thrift in an untended, outdoor environment.[14] The pioneering ranching operators believed that cattle could live and thrive as well as the buffalo they had replaced.[15] The plains bison, however, had evolved through centuries of enduring northern latitude winters and were equipped to cope with cold and deprivation, migrating large distances and subsisting on marginal forage. They would also paw through snow to reach food, something cattle would not do. Cattle were nowhere as resilient, especially the original longhorn strains imported from the United States.

Misconceptions about western Canada's climate lulled many potential investors into a false sense of security. Many ranchers arrived in the West completely ignorant of the harsh realities of a mid-latitude continental climate. As one observer wrote in the *Montreal Gazette* in 1881, "For the purposes of the stock raiser it suffices to know that for a great part of the winter much of the surface is free from snow and that it seldom or never attains the depth sufficient to prevent animals from feeding."[16] Prospective British investors were encouraged by newspaper accounts that referred to chinook winds dissipating snowfalls so quickly that wheeled vehicles were in vogue year round. Amenable winters made converts out of some early settlers. One wrote to the

*Mowing prairie grass, Bird's Hill, Manitoba, 1884. The original winter hay on the Alberta leaseholds was cut from native grass, and was one of the earliest "non-cowboy"-type activities associated with the Alberta ranching experience (NA 33-17).*

*Toronto Globe* in 1881 extolling the Fort Macleod area as "the garden of Canada," and dismissing winter's threat by referring to chinooks that melted two feet of snow an hour.[17]

This optimism was based on a sequence of mild winters in the late 1870s, a phenomenon consistent with western Canadian climatic patterns over short periods of time.[18] Amid the wetter conditions of the 1870s, the prevalence and intensity of the chinooks lulled residents and visitors into believing that cold weather in the foothills came in intense short snaps, producing minor personal discomfort and little distress to hardy grazing animals. As late as 1903, an editor with a short memory wrote in the *Nanton News* about local open-range cattle going to market fatter than those from the American corn belt.[19]

Experience soon showed otherwise. The years that allowed year-round grazing were more than offset by winters that reduced forage availability and which sapped life-supporting energies. Several severe winters between 1882 and 1907 brought high death tolls, severe financial losses, and the gradual realization that the expense involved in providing winter hay was well worth it; that is, if it could be done. Provision for proper winter feeding required about one ton per head.[20] A herd of five hundred head, therefore, needed five hundred tons of hay each winter, often from ranges that could not supply that amount. In 1893, for example, during a bitter cold spell which brought minus-forty-degree temperatures and intermittent storms, the 76 Ranch deployed its entire winter feed supply in two weeks.[21] When factored into the problems of distribution over leases of up to one hundred thousand acres, the impossibility of adequate winter feeding on the large leaseholds becomes apparent. The much-discussed catastrophic winter of 1906 – 07, while it marked a watershed for the cattle industry, also reinforced the fact that large-scale open-range ranching may never have been as viable as romance would have it. Simply put, the climate was too severe for the scope and type of operations embarked upon in 1881. Indeed, one is led to wonder if the big cattle companies would have come to the Alberta foothills country in the 1880s had they been aware of the realities of cattle survival on the open range.[22]

## Mixed Farming Operations

Climatic extremes and predators, plus the steady curtailment of the big leaseholds, led to smaller ranching operations and mixed farming enterprises. A smaller herd enabled closer monitoring and less risk of crippling losses. As early as 1888, immigration agents were commenting on the number of incoming homesteading families who were including livestock in their operations.[23] Clifford Sifton's leasehold revisions, proposed but never implemented in 1905, gave priority for smaller leases in grazing areas.[24]

The high appeal of beef cattle in this period is reflected in the philosophy of the typical mixed farmer. Unlike their counterparts in later years, the mixed farming operations of the late nineteenth and early twentieth century stressed livestock over grain, a situation exacerbated by the rising cost of farm implements and falling prices for grain products in the 1880s and 1890s. Frank and John Copithorne gave up mixed farming in Cochrane west of Calgary in 1899 only when they thought they could make it on their own with cattle.[25] Similarly, Frank and Charles Houcher, who had set up a mixed farming operation south of Wetaskiwin in 1895, moved to more remote Czar four years later because grain farmers were restricting their cattle operations.[26] Dick Bradshaw reluctantly broke prime grazing land near Lethbridge in 1902 so that he could grow oats for cattle feed.[27] Most of these mixed farmers survived by supplying larger operations with feed oats and hay for their horses, and the slaughterhouses with mixed cattle. They also undercut the larger operations

*Haystack and cattle. The proximity of the haystack to the ranch buildings was a clear indication that successful ranching operations were forced to concentrate their feeding during winter months (NA 4198-2).*

by peddling their meat at cheaper prices in urban centres like Calgary.[28] By 1901, 69 percent of Alberta farms were under two hundred acres and the average size of all farms was only 288 acres.[29] Territorial figures for the same year showed an average of 19.1 head of cattle on each farm.[30]

Some big leaseholders also realized the value of mixed farming. George Lane, the American-born cowboy whose business acumen and vision led him from ranch foreman for the North-West Cattle Company to the ultimate ownership of the famous Bar U Ranch south of Longview, was an early proponent of mixed farming. Once quoted as saying that in his experience he did not know of four men who had gone broke mixed farming, Lane was experimenting with irrigation in the 1880s. He was convinced of the merits of growing alfalfa for feed long before it became the staple of production in the Lethbridge and Bow River irrigation districts. Over the years he continued to build extensive grain operations in addition to his livestock enterprises. Though popularly recognized for his Percheron horses, his friendship with the Prince of Wales, and for his role as one of the Calgary Stampede's "Big Four," George Lane ought to be better remembered as the practical visionary who made the first on-site statements about Alberta's optimum agricultural land use.

# Feeding and Finishing

The integration of grazing with more intensive feeding practices was an accepted tradition in Great Britain. Fat animals brought better prices, and while grass alone was sufficient to put on flesh through time, a grain diet prior to slaughter ensured a better finished animal. The practice of combining grazing with feeding had its best North American example in the United States where Midwestern corn belt farmers fattened animals bred on the Western and Southwestern range states. In western Canada, Alberta was ideally suited to fill this role. The primary ranching areas of the South were not far away from the more fertile parkland grain belt. However, this integration did not occur, and the failure of Alberta (or Canada for that matter) to develop a feeding tradition was an area of recurring concern for livestock experts. While the reasons were in part related to production costs as well as market distance and density, they had their roots in attitudes developed in this period.

The merit of grain feeding cattle was recognized early. A few mixed farmers constructed the necessary facilities and began grain feeding their animals, mostly for the discerning export market or for show or fat stock sale. In 1882 Joseph McFarlane combined his three-hundred-head operation near Fort Macleod with feed grain growing on one thousand fenced acres.[31] Bob Newbolt grew oats on his mixed farm near the Bow River, north of Fort Macleod, so he could provide feed for his livestock.[32] In 1895, Claude Gardiner used rye, barley, oats and wheat grown on his ranch in the Porcupine Hills as feed for his 170 cattle.[33] In the same year, Frederick Godsal adopted irrigation methods on 280 acres to produce hay for his thousand head of cattle in the Lethbridge area.[34] From its inception in 1905, the *Farm and Ranch Review* was consistent in publishing articles praising the value-added factor of feeding home-grown grains to cattle.[35] The federal government was an early proponent of grain feeding. William Pearce, Dominion Superintendent of Lands and Mines and influential supporter of livestock interests, was outspoken in his support of livestock feeding.[36] Some far-sighted operators took him seriously. The Knight Sugar Company at Raymond, for example, was feeding beet pulp to five hundred head as early as 1905.[37]

However, despite encouragement and example, there seemed little inclination to abandon traditional practices that equated good livestock management with the provision of adequate winter hay supplies. Grain feeding was far more the exception than the rule. Frequent references to the reluctance of cattle owners to grain feed their animals evinced a frustration over a resistance to change, and led one expert to quote in 1905 that "only spasmodic efforts are made to fatten animals."[38] The *Farm and Ranch Review* castigated its readers for failing to take the feeding of stock seriously. Phrases like the "time being ripe for western Canada to devote more attention to the feeding of livestock," and the "surprising number of people who rough their stock through winter" were far more prevalent than those attesting to the contrary.[39]

The reasons for this reluctance were associated with the newness of ranching and its corresponding lack of consensus over optimum land utilization. The western Canadian ranching industry had no precedent in terms of climatic variables and in these early years even experts differed as to how the land should be best utilized to raise livestock. William Pearce, for example, was adamant in his belief that the western Canadian rangelands should serve as a finishing area for cattle bred elsewhere. He felt that the climate was too harsh to allow for quality breeding operations but that the area's potential for feed production was limitless.[40] On the other hand, Dr Duncan MacEachran, Dominion Veterinarian and part owner of the Walrond Ranch, was equally convinced of the opposite. He thought that cattle should be bred in the West but finished elsewhere, perhaps in eastern Canada or even in the American corn belt.[41] In 1882 he had doubted the viability of exporting western Canadian cattle to Great Britain because the plains did not allow finishing.[42] This disagreement between high-placed, influential and outspoken experts in the two government departments most concerned with western Canadian cattle operations exemplifies the uncertainty surrounding the best way to manage livestock on the new frontier.

This uncertainty bred attitudes that were hard to dislodge. First, and most important, many were convinced that grain feeding was unnecessary, and that cattle could be profitably marketed off grass. The essence of ranching precluded grain finishing programmes. Contemporary markets demanded weight more than finish, and over a four-year period it was possible for range animals to reach impressive weights. Twelve- to fifteen-hundred-pound animals became the norm. In 1902 three carloads of cattle, wintered on nothing but grass in the Pole Hole area near Lethbridge, averaged 1,800 pounds with the heaviest steer topping the scales at 2,175 pounds.[43] Heavy weights were not confined to isolated animals or smaller batches. In 1906 a Pat Burns herd of two thousand

*A 2165-pound steer from the H2 Ranch, 1920. Owner Walter McHugh bet ten dollars that that his steer weighed more than a ton (NA 217-39).*

head weighed an average of 1,540 pounds.[44] Three years later a 3,500-pound steer raised in the Rosebud Creek area was taken to the Alaska-Yukon Exposition to show the possibilities of Alberta's natural grasslands.[45] This conviction that Alberta cattle were most profitable when marketed off grass supplemented by winter hay was to be a recurring legacy of the ranching era.[46]

In this period, the economics of the export market favoured heavy grass-fed cattle. Heavy animals could withstand shrinkage and still net a healthy return. For the above-mentioned reasons, grain feeding was not an option, especially on the big leaseholds that dominated the export market. There was no point in spending money to finish animals when the inevitable weight loss would put them at a distinct disadvantage when set against finished British cattle in the upper end of the market.

The belief that that a good feeding programme required indoor facilities was a further dissuading factor. The most accepted method of feeding involved containing the animal in an indoor stall over the winter months. Even if this method was feasible in western Canada, few producers could afford the three thousand dollars expended by a Manitoba stockman in 1905 to build a large stone barn in which to winter feed his cattle.[47] Corn was the ideal feed grain and its scarcity even in Ontario, let alone the more arid West, made cattle finishing too expensive.[48] Feeding experiments in eastern Canada between 1890 and 1902 had shown that corn ensilage was easily the most profitable feed in terms of gain and cost to gain.[49] The association of corn with proper feeding died hard among stockmen, as was evidenced by the slow growth of barley as a feed grain.

Expert opinion rightly held that the lack of scientific knowledge on feeding methods led to inefficient practices. The Fifth Annual Report of the Territorial Cattle Breeders Association in 1905, commented that "very little scientific work has been done in the country on the feeding of cattle."[50] Another expert referred to meagre information in a field that "was practically unexplored."[51] The experimental farms at the time provided little leadership. The editor of the *Farm and Ranch Review* criticized them in 1905 for their feeding experiments that were "lacking in continuity and confined in volume."[52] In 1908, A senior official in the Department of Agriculture described previous federal experiments as "desultory." A year earlier, a spokesman from the Ontario Agriculture College in Guelph said that profit margins indicated that "there was something wrong with the current standards laid down for fattening steers."[53]

Grain feeding was not economically viable. Too often the price received did not warrant the effort of intensive feeding, particularly in the 1890s when cattle were sold locally for thirty-five to forty dollars per head regardless of age or condition.[54] In 1906, the *Farm and Ranch Review* complained that feeding was being discouraged by the narrow margin between rough and grain-finished stock.[55] As a case in point, the price paid in Calgary for all grain-fed beef in 1906 was 4.5 cents per pound, scarcely more than the average price overall and not enough to cover even the cost of feed, which was at least 0.8 cents per pound of gain.[56] Statistics are unavailable as to the cost per day of grain feeding in Alberta, but it was not likely to be lower than the 14.05 cents established during a federal government experiment in eastern Canada in 1902.[57] Even careful winter hay feeding was expensive, particularly in older animals where feeding costs might be as high as 85 percent more for a three-year-old than a two-year-old steer.[58]

While it is impossible to secure figures on grain-fed versus grass-fed animals on the smaller operations during this period, the producers' inability to meet specific demands indicate that well-fed cattle were the exception rather than the rule. Grain-fed cattle could be marketed year-round. The demand existed from British Columbia urban and mining areas. Alberta cattle, however, could not fill it. Efforts to establish a dressed meat or "dead meat" trade, as it was called in those years, were inhibited by the fact that consistent supplies of quality beef were impossible to provide. In January 1891, the manager of the 76 Ranch informed his employer in Britain that there were not enough available cattle to meet the request from Vancouver meat dealers to supply them with a carload of dressed beef a week for five months.[59]

The time-honoured practice of marketing grass-fed animals only in the fall was to last well beyond this period. The increasing inferiority of Canadian export cattle in the British marketplace was due primarily to their lack of finish, a situation which led some Scottish graziers to assume that Canadian conditions precluded proper feeding.[60] The poor appearance of many Western steers when set beside their American or Scottish counterparts was a ongoing source of embarrassment to Canadian officials in Birkenhead or the Smithfield Market in London.[61] One buyer in 1905 was appalled at the "sorry looking specimens" and observed that "western Canadian cattle were not a credit to this country."[62] As late as 1908, the livestock agent for the Canadian Pacific Railway referred to Canadian cattle at British stockyards as "thin and gaunt" compared to American cattle, and that he was "positively ashamed to see [them] on the hooks beside American corn fed steers."[63]

The point to note is that, even at this early stage, the merits of proper feeding were being widely advertised. The reluctance to integrate optimal feeding practices into stock raising methods was to carry over into succeeding years. When mixed farmers in the subsequent agricultural era continued to favour grain as a marketable commodity rather than as feed for their cattle, they mirrored precedents established in this early ranching era.

## Markets

Like all businessmen, the early ranchers needed to market their product profitably. For most of this period, cattle prices were more consistent than for other agricultural products.[64] One expert, using 250 cows as a base, estimated an elevenfold increase in their value in five years.[65] As David Breen has shown, these profits were substantial enough to justify lavish lifestyles and surplus funds for investment elsewhere.[66] What is of interest for the purposes of this discussion is not the level of profitability either generally or individually,

15

although evidence seems to suggest that the golden years were over by 1902. More relevant is the nature of the market, its declining stability and the implications it had in terms of attitudes carried over into subsequent phases of the industry.

Good prices and production costs were necessary to sustain a viable ranching industry. The first problem was one of transportation. Railroad facilities were often inadequate to handle the traffic. Many shipments were delayed, and often ranchers had to return their cattle to the range after finding that railroad cars were unavailable. Freight rates to Toronto and Montreal from Calgary were ninety cents per hundredweight or, at 1900 prices, about 25 percent of the market price. Shrinkage in transit was another problem. In 1906 one rancher complained that cattle which were weighed in at Fort Macleod on Sunday showed a two-hundred-pound shrinkage when weighed again at Winnipeg on the following Tuesday.[67] Ranchers believed that the CPR was both inefficient and greedy. It was common for over thirty head to be packed into a thirty-six-foot railway stock car for forty hours without food nor drink.[68] George Lane accused the railroad company of cruelty because of its refusal to detrain animals for feeding and watering purposes.[69] In referring to poorly-built loading corrals and to stock yards that put cattle up to their knees in mud, D. H. Andrews of the 76 Ranch wrote in 1891 that he would drive his stock three hundred miles to a U.S. rail point rather than ship them on the CPR.[70] Maintaining that "the CPR was putting [them] out of business," angry stockmen met at Medicine Hat in October 1901 and protested the delays and inadequate care in transporting their animals.[71] The situation was worse for the export cattle whose condition and health deteriorated in the appalling conditions in which they were forced to travel. Often supervised by untrained and disinterested returning immigrants, many cattle arrived in Britain in pitiful condition.[72] Accusations of trafficking were levelled at monopolistic shipping companies whose charges often ran to as high as thirty dollars a head, a figure which ate deeply into profit margins.

Thus, during this period, most cattle marketed in Canada were done so locally. The original livestock enterprises that operated in Alberta in the late 1870s supplied the Mounted Police with beef. The local market was expanded in the 1890s and 1900s by increasing urban settlement, the mining districts of the Crowsnest Pass, and the demand created by the various Plains Indian bands, all of which had been removed to reserves by 1877. Railroad construction

*Stockyards at Alix, circa 1910. Small stockyards along the various railway lines were often the first marketing point for small batches of cattle from surrounding area farms and ranches (NA 205-21).*

provided another important market during the period 1880 – 1900 and enabled the rise of Pat Burns, western Canada's first home-grown millionaire. His slaughterhouse and packing facilities plus other livestock-related manufacturing enterprises such as soap works, tanneries and cold storage plants in Calgary was proof positive of that city's early role as a true cattle town.

The significance of this local market lay not so much in its ability to absorb the bulk of production but rather in its domination by a couple of individuals. For example, William Roper Hull, the first major cattle buyer in Alberta, used his profits to become a prosperous businessman and one of the builders of early Calgary. The method of marketing cattle locally was through individual buyers who set prices on site for ranch cattle. Usually only one buyer visited a ranch, and by the early 1900s he invariably worked for Pat Burns. Shrewd enough to be called "half oracle, half Sphinx" and to buy and feed cattle year round, Burns had become the dominant force in the Alberta meat trade by the end of this period.[73] His monopoly frustrated ranchers. Prominent rancher E. H. Maunsell felt the only alternative was co-operative marketing in the form of a chilled meat trade.[74] One rancher complained of the ridiculously low price offered to him by Burns for his first-prize winner at the Fat Stock Show. After grain feeding his winning entry for six months he

*Five hundred steers arriving at Dawson City, Yukon Territory, October 1901. The animals, which were raised and bought in the Cochrane area, realized between sixty and seventy cents per pound in the Yukon (NA 25-31).*

netted scarcely more than Burns's standard price.[75] In 1907, a prominent Chicago livestock man called Alberta's industry "a one man power operation."[76] A year earlier an Alberta rancher summed up the situation succinctly when he commented that Burns had the perfect monopoly in that he set both wholesale and retail prices.[77] According to the 1907 Beef Commission, integrated operators like Burns could reap a profit of 46 percent on cattle that had netted their producers a minimal profit or even a loss.[78] This level of price control exerted by Burns dissuaded cattle finishing for the local market and reflected itself in the indifferent quality of beef offered for sale.

The beef marketing problems were severe enough for the four western provinces to issue joint orders in council in 1906 authorizing the establishment of a Beef Commission "primarily to investigate whether there is a combine affecting the price of cattle and meat."[79] The three-man commission that opened its inquiry in June 1907 heard a battery of criticisms from farmers and ranchers.[80] A rancher of seventeen years' experience lamented that even after buying the best Shorthorn bulls, he could still make no money out of ranching.

A newly arrived farmer bluntly told the Commission that he had "never come into contact with such a bunch of pirates in my life." The facts supported their contentions. The Commission received evidence to the effect that a producer was actually losing $5.80 on a grain-fed bull. Yet on the same bull, the abattoir dealer made $23.20, and the retail butcher a further $13.60.[81] One country butcher told the Commission that his normal profit on beef was 25 percent.[82] Given the prevailing price after 1902 of around $3.00 per hundredweight, producers stood to gain very little by selling cattle locally.[83] Burns laconically defended his monopoly by telling the Commission that if he closed down, "in ten days the people of this country would be starving." The Commission's findings released later the same year confirmed that monopolistic trade practices were retarding the industry, but that these were related to the chaotic nature of the business, and that there was no evidence of combines in restraint of trade. The Commission's recommendations included the establishment of experimental farms and provision for provincial livestock commissioners.

## The Export Market

In this early period, the best Canadian market outlet outside Alberta was in British Columbia. Both live animals and dressed beef made their way in increasing numbers after 1890 to Vancouver and the Kootenay mining regions, reaching the equivalent of 9,563 head in 1902.[84] There were also efforts by Pat Burns to supply the Klondike gold mining camps with Alberta meat. The problem with the British Columbia market in this period, however, was maintaining a steady supply in winter, a situation that led to the first experiments with frozen beef and grain feeding.

When compared to countries like Argentina, Australia and even the United States, Canada's international beef export trade was small. This early period was significant because it was the only time Canada shipped live cattle overseas in any quantity. In the long run, she could not compete with stronger competitors like Argentina, Australia or the Irish Free State which wielded distinct advantages in terms of low production costs and/or market distance. At its height, Canada's exportable surplus approximated a quarter of a million head, and for most of the period covered by this narrative averaged between 100,000 and 150,000.

*Pat Burns's residence, Calgary, circa 1911. Situated on Fourth Street SW, between Twelfth and Thirteenth Avenues. A former homesteader and cattle buyer, Burns got his real start filling railway construction meat contracts in the late 1880s and 1890s. His integrated meat-related businesses, ranging from ranches to retail outlets, made him one of western Canada's wealthiest citizens. In 1928 he sold his meat packing interests to Dominion Securities for $9.7 million. He was elevated to the Senate in 1931 and died in 1937 (NA 3918-5).*

However, the small international export market assumed an importance far beyond its impact in gross numbers. In 1890 cattle exports comprised almost 20 percent of Canada's export trade with Great Britain.[85] Equally significant was the tremendous impact of exports on domestic prices. Conforming to contemporary economic theory, producers and experts believed that the exportable 10–15 percent of Canadian beef production fixed the domestic prices at profitable levels. This assumption, entrenched during the ranching era, continued to be the most dominant force behind the overall development of the cattle industry during the first half of the twentieth century. As late as 1942, the Chairman of the Wartime Beef Advisory Committee used the words "strange but true" to encapsulate an assumption that had underlain beef marketing practices for over fifty years.[86]

Throughout the entire period under discussion there were only two export markets for Canadian cattle: Great Britain and the United States. In the years 1882–1907, this export market lay exclusively in Great Britain. Trade with the United States was sporadic and while it did increase after the lifting of quarantine regulations in 1897, it remained largely confined to eastern Canada, and was discouraged by the high 27.5 percent tariff.[87]

The British export market in the late 1880s was important to the infant western Canadian industry.[88] Enabled by the completion of the Canadian Pacific Railway and by the British embargo on U.S. cattle on the grounds of pleuropneumonia in American herds, a steady flow of cattle from the Alberta leaseholds made their way to Great Britain. Mostly mature range cattle and a few stockers or feeders, the animals were shipped by train to Montreal and then by cattle boat to Liverpool or Dundee. The feeder cattle were sold to Scottish graziers, while the fat animals were marketed in Smithfield in competition with British cattle and other finished animals from Europe. In the ten years 1880–90, the number of Canadian live cattle entering Great Britain increased from 32,680 to 66,965. In 1891 the figure stood at an all-time high of 107,689 and realized a total value of almost $9 million. Between 1887 and 1906 an average of 115,000 head were exported annually, reaching a peak of 163,994 in 1906.[89] Of these numbers, the western Canadian share grew from around 10 percent in 1892 to over 33 percent after 1895.[90] Western Canada's growing importance as an exporter was reflected in the virtual control wielded by the Winnipeg-based buyers, Gordon, Ironsides and Fares. With ranches in western Canada and Mexico, extended operations in Chicago, and working in close collusion with the CPR, Gordon, Ironsides and Fares concentrated entirely on the live cattle export trade.

As long as prices remained high enough to offset the expense and rigours of transportation, the British market was the mainstay of the ranching industry. It also justified the economics of allowing steers to reach weights of upwards of fifteen hundred pounds through four years on range grasses.[91] Offering profits as high as $40.00 per head, the British market filled the ranchers' needs. However, after 1902 prices in Britain plummeted and continued to decline.

The reasons were linked to competition and in particular to chilled beef. The rise of Argentina with its cheap production costs and highly efficient chilling processes put the rough Canadian product at a crippling disadvantage. Prior to Argentinean competition, Alberta exporters had yielded the high end of the British market to Scottish grain-fed beef and had relied on quantity demand at lower prices. Competition from Argentina, and to a lesser extent Australia, combined to threaten that niche. Argentinean chilled beef was virtually undistinguishable from the fresh product, and effectively ended Canada's tenure as a major player in the British market.[92] Live cattle constituted about 50 percent of British beef imports in 1900. By 1910 the corresponding figure was 17 percent.[93] While this process had not been completed in 1907, the faltering British market was affecting producers as early as 1904. Although export numbers remained high, dramatically falling prices undermined producer confidence.

In the few short years it had been in operation, the British export market established two premises that were to guide cattlemen for the next fifty years. First was the crucial role of the export market as a safety valve to protect domestic prices. This reliance on export sales as a domestic price setter was so important that the matter of quality in the domestic market place was irrelevant. Even the British Columbia market during this period was for second-class animals unfit for export to Britain. The policy of the McIntyre Ranch south of Lethbridge was typical. The best steers went to Britain; the cows to the local market.[94] The dynamics of home demand were never a consideration until forced much later by widespread and crippling constrictions in the export market.

Second, the export market became associated with quality. Only the best cattle were considered for export, particularly after 1892 when the British, after claiming to have detected pleuropneumonia in two animals from Canadian ships, placed an embargo on Canadian cattle that required them to be slaughtered at their ports of entry. There were two further reasons for this concentration on quality in the export market. The better the animal the more chance it had of realizing a good price despite shrinkage during transport. Also, higher prices, especially in the later American market, influenced domestic price levels. Before grading came into effect in the late 1920s, export quality denoted the highest grade of Canadian cattle.

Set against the above factors, the decline in the British market's profitability after 1904 prompted reactions among cattlemen that were to be repeated later in similar circumstances. Scapegoats were sought and alternatives explored which had had little relevance as long as the export market was healthy.

Any emphasis on grain feeding in the first years of the twentieth century represented more a reaction to a declining British market than it did a desire to produce a superior product for general consumption. The initiatives to develop a chilled meat trade in Canada were meant to counter Argentina's

*Shipping cattle in Calgary. Cattle shipped to eastern Canada or for export travelled in thirty-six-foot livestock cars with twenty to thirty-two head per car. Since cattle could not be held without food and water for more than forty hours, stockyards were built at White River on the Canadian Shield between Winnipeg and Toronto where the animals could be detrained, fed and watered (NA 2407-5).*

threat in a favoured market. Although little had been done by 1907, serious thought was being given to the possibilities.

The attention to herd quality was always directly proportional to the current health of the export market. The system of big leaseholds had allowed mixed breeding and by the 1890s the quality of western Canadian herds was being questioned.[95] Little was done, however, until prices began to fall. The Calgary Bull Sale in 1901 was a direct reaction to the falling competitiveness of western Canadian animals in the export sale ring. However, despite these ongoing sales, the problem of indifferent quality in western Canadian cattle herds was to endure as another legacy of the early ranching industry.

Finally, there was the question of the British embargo on Canadian cattle. Imposed in 1892, it was partly in retaliation by British agricultural interests to the threat of foreign competition, and revealed the hand of politics in animal health issues. Yet in spite of its vilification by eastern Canadian stock and shipping interests, the embargo remained unimportant to western Canadian cattlemen for a dozen years, and only loomed as an issue after 1905 when the future of the export market seemed in jeopardy.

## The British Embargo on Canadian Store Cattle

In late October 1892, the *Huronia* and the *Monkseaton*, two cattle boats out of Montreal, landed twelve hundred head of Canadian store cattle at the Scottish port of Dundee.[96] Within days the animals were sold and relocated to seventy-nine places in several Scottish Counties including Aberdeen, Fife, Forfar, Kincardine and Elgin. A week later contagious pleuropneumonia was detected in one of the animals landed by the *Monkseaton*, as well as in some infected home-bred animals.[97] All animals that had been on the two steamers were immediately slaughtered, and within a week the British Board of Agriculture announced that Canadian cattle were to be scheduled effective 21 November 1892. Essentially this meant that all Canadian export cattle had to be slaughtered at the port of entry instead of being allowed to move inland for fattening purposes.

More alarmed than surprised, Canadian interests were quick to react, even though the British had attempted initially to ameliorate matters through reference to the embargo's temporary nature. Canada's Prime Minister, Sir John Abbott, expressed his concern a few days before the scheduling notice when he told John Carling, Canada's Minister of Agriculture, that "if once scheduled the consequences will be serious and lasting."[98] Accordingly, senior Canadian officials proceeded to exhaust every diplomatic avenue in an effort to persuade the British to change their minds. The Canadian case was based on the absence of the disease in Canada and on the exhaustive measures immediately undertaken to prove same.[99] Certainly the Canadians believed, initially at least, that matters would be righted if the British could be persuaded to delay their decision until completion of a thorough Canadian herd inspection.[100] As a last resort, the Canadians offered to finance a British inspection of Canadian herds in return for delaying the embargo. The offer was refused. Ultimately it did not matter that the resulting inspection detected no evidence of the disease in Canada. Britain's mind was made up.

Whether or not the Canadian cattle did have pleuropneumonia seems to be beside the point, given Britain's sensitivity over potential disease threats to its herds.[101] Indeed, the practice of importing any live animals flew in the face of an expensive ongoing programme in Britain to eradicate pleuropneumonia. Also, the depressed agricultural conditions prevalent in Britain in 1892 probably stiffened the British official resolve to back the conclusions of its veterinarians.

Whether or not British decision-makers overreacted, basing their decision on tenuous grounds, their actions attest to a seriousness of intent, and to the mood of the powerful agricultural lobby. The British simply did in 1892 what they felt they should have done in 1879 when they scheduled American cattle. The embargo represented the last step towards a universal policy of exclusion based ostensibly on animal health principles. Yet, despite the underlying fear of disease endemic in British conservative rural thinking since the 1870s, the concomitant commercial advantages of excluding Canadian fat and feeder (store) cattle also appeared as an indirect benefit. The embargo's maintenance was to be a direct result of this belief.

Despite some rumblings in the British House of Commons, mainly from members representing grazing areas in Scotland, the embargo's status remained unchanged.[102] According to Board of Agriculture President, Walter Long, in 1895, several instances of pleuropneumonia had subsequently been found in the lungs of slaughtered Canadian cattle.[103] Confident that they could build up their supply of store cattle and that consumer prices would not be threatened, the British gave permanency to the embargo through the Importation of Animals Act, passed in 1896.

Definitely, this embargo impacted negatively on eastern Canadian producers, who had found the store trade profitable. Western Canadian cattlemen, however, were not adversely affected. William Pearce noted amid the embargo debate in 1892 that "scheduling would not be disastrous. In fact it might be of benefit to us."[104] A year later he appeared vindicated. "As far as ranching interests are concerned, the scheduling of cattle has not hurt the same ... more cattle have been shipped in this year than any other."[105]

By closing the market for eastern Canadian stores, the embargo enabled the ranches of the West to become a viable replacement. After 1892, western Canadian herds were augmented by eastern Canadian cattle which would ordinarily have been bound for Britain.[106] The embargo reduced Canada's export potential by 20 percent, a percentage almost precisely matched within four years by the number of store cattle from eastern Canada to the ranches and leases of the North-West Territories.[107] In 1896, the number of cattle shipped to Great Britain from the North-West Territories totalled 17,935. In the same year 16,000 stockers were shipped to the West from Eastern farms.

Store cattle did not figure in the western Canadian cattle trade, which was confined to mature grass-finished animals. The fact that their long trip affected their selling price was a moot point, for while they doubtless would have sold at a higher price if taken inland for fattening, these four-year-old steers were just too wild to handle and virtually had to be slaughtered at the point of entry. Stories abounded about terrified Canadian steers "on being unloaded from the boat stampeding the yards and jumping into the River Clyde."[108] Giving evidence before the 1891 inquiry on the treatment of cattle, one exporter noted that cattle from the North-West had to be loaded directly from the train to the boat since "North-West cattle will not stand any fooling…. If they do not have the proper arrangements made, they will break away and it is no easy task to recover them."[109] In the same inquiry, William F. Cochrane, Manager of the Cochrane Ranche, explained that "we had to kill our cattle when they landed there because they are so wild that we could not take them out of the lairs."[110]

Yet, regardless of its impact on the western Canadian cattle industry, the embargo of 1892 clearly demonstrated for the first time the unpredictability of the export market and the dangers it posed to those who relied on it. The embargo remained a factor in the industry for thirty years before being lifted in 1923, and became a barometer for the health of the Canadian export trade. When export markets were sound, the embargo was inconsequential. During the debate on the embargo in the Canadian House of Commons, Alberta's lone representative, rancher D. W. Davis, was silent. Later, when the Western Stock Growers' Association was formed in 1896, the embargo did not figure in its original goals, nor was it mentioned in subsequent meetings. However, whenever the export market was constricted, the embargo issue emerged as a solution. Between 1905 and 1908, agitation from Alberta stockmen to lift the embargo, though unsuccessful, revealed a much different attitude than that which had existed in the more prosperous times.[111]

# Conclusion

Large-scale open range cattle ranching in Alberta lasted about twenty-five years. It was gone by 1908. The reasons for this short duration were rooted in land and market factors. When the big cattle companies claimed their hundred thousand acres under the federal government's leasehold system of 1881, their owners had already been caught up in myth. They assumed that cattle could survive as well as the buffalo they had replaced. They thought that their ranges would remain limitless areas of cheap grass. Finally, they firmly believed that they could sell all the beef they produced at a profit. By 1907 these myths were shattered and those who wanted to raise cattle in Alberta were forced to modify their pure ranching enterprises into smaller livestock operations based loosely on mixed farming practices. The prime movers behind the industry's establishment had all been disproved. The notion that Alberta's climate allowed minimal human interference in the management of cattle, the original belief that grazing lands were both extensive and uncontested by agriculture, and the conviction that there always would be a profitable market for beef were rebutted by bankruptcies, herd liquidation and new economies and realizations. By 1908 the cattle industry as it had existed since 1881 was in full retreat. It would never again advance in the same formation.

As if in evidence of the above, three brief items in the *Farm and Ranch Review* appeared within a few months of each other in 1906–07. In one, reference was made to cattle mortalities through starvation and cold. A second documented the sale of the famous Walrond herd because of leasehold constraints. The third lamented the deplorable state of the cattle industry because of sustained depressed prices and narrow profit margins.[112]

The ranching era, however, had left legacies beyond its association with the Western frontier experience and the romantic foundations of a major industry. It established practices and attitudes towards livestock raising which were to last for at least two more generations. Though open range ranching may have been constricted, the notion of cheap grass remained entrenched. This early period established leaseholds as integral to effective livestock practices. Finally, it identified the export market as the prime influencing factor in determining cattle quality and price. The interplay of these factors was to explain the subsequent evolution of the industry as it sought to consolidate itself in the land and in the marketplace.

# TWO

# The Agricultural Frontier, 1900 – 13

*Ranching has become only a memory.*
J.G. RUTHERFORD, 1910

THE DETERMINATION OF THE RANCHING AREAS OCCURRED DURING THIS PERIOD in response to land pressures and changing attitudes. The cattle industry suffered as wheat and other cereal crops defined new land use patterns. Ranching was sustained in areas generally unsuited to agriculture, while more intensive livestock operations emerged in the grain belt. The implications of this transformation were observable by the end of the period with the consolidation of ranching through security of leasehold tenure and in the advent of crop-based mixed farming enterprises. The opening of the American market in late 1913 provided the most significant market development in the history of the industry.

## Agriculture and Its Impact on the Cattle Industry

The arrival of large-scale agriculture affected the cattle industry in several ways. Cattle raising became secondary to cereal crop agriculture. Farming forged new attitudes towards land use. Ranching was forced into its more natural geographic domain. The new emphasis on land use brought the issue of leasehold tenure to the forefront.

It is difficult to understate the enormous impact of the agricultural frontier; it changed the nature of the Canadian economy. One source has estimated that the wheat boom of this period accounted for 50 percent of the gain in per capita income.[1] It epitomized a time when panaceas were associated with reality, when visions of universal prosperity were as real as the wheat fields that were changing the face of the western landscape. In western Canada, cereal crop agriculture and its accompanying mythology swept all before it in an inexorable tide. Supported by a policy of cheap land, rising grain prices, extensive railroad construction, and a cycle of favourable climatic conditions, cash crop farming quickly changed the demographic face of western Canada. In the period 1900 to 1912, over 370,000 homestead entries were taken out in western Canada. In Alberta, 187,618 acres were in field crops in 1901. By 1910 the figure was 2.1 million acres and a year later had reached 3.37 million acres. Between 1900 and 1910, Alberta wheat acreage jumped from 43,062 acres to 879,756 acres, oats went from 117,745 acres to 783,074 acres, and barley from 11,055 acres to 121,435 acres. Crop yields were equally impressive. Approximate increases over the same ten-year period amounted to 1200 percent for wheat, 500 percent for oats and 1000 percent for barley. Yields of forty bushels per acre for wheat and over one hundred bushels per acre for oats were not unusual. And because cash crop farming meant money and prosperity, its appeal was self-generating. Between 1901 and 1911 the average value of crop per acre rose from $12.69 to $28.37 whereas the average value of livestock per acre dropped from $5.57 to $4.79.

A decreasing interest in raising cattle during this period was directly related to the high appeal of cash crop farming, and accounts for the tremendous pressure on grazing leases. The new agricultural order was considered superior to the haphazard and wasteful practice of assigning large tracts of good land to grazing. "Slavish unpleasant work" was how one observer put it in 1911.[2] The amended Dominion Lands Act in 1908 removed cattle raising as an option in securing a homestead patent. By predicating it solely on land breaking requirements, even in those less fertile areas defined by the new homestead purchase option, the new act clearly showed the official preference for agriculture over stock raising. This change was especially noticeable in new farming areas where cattle were clearly not an option.[3] Moreover, the financial returns from cattle raising suffered in comparison with grain. Even when cattle prices were rising in 1909, Alberta stockmen maintained that the high price of grain and the small margin for grain-fed cattle kept many from feeding.[4] The result was an enduring conviction throughout most of this period that stock raising was both risky and unprofitable.

The agricultural land rush was indiscriminate in terms of homestead selection, and clearly ignored the importance of livestock. Alberta's soil zones and climate generally require interdependence between livestock raising and agriculture. One expert warned as early as 1907 that cash crop farming would deplete the soil if the fertilizing properties of livestock were not present.[5] The false assumptions surrounding the universality and profitability of field crops affected the cattle industry during this period.

The fallacies were twofold. First was the belief that the market demand for grain crops, especially wheat, was limitless. It was widely believed that rising urban populations in both Europe and North America would continue to demand more and more grain from Western farms. Wheat exports to Great Britain from Canada more than doubled in the decade 1902–12. Cash crop farming therefore guaranteed ongoing prosperity. Yields from the 1906 crop season reached twenty dollars per acre.[6] Second, rising wheat prices fuelled the optimism—it seemed they would never drop. Wheat prices in Winnipeg rose from eighty-three cents per bushel in July 1909 to over $1.10 a year later.[7] As one real estate agent commented in 1909, "it is not often that money comes the farmer's way and if it is wheat and land one cannot blame him."[8] As long as wheat prices exceeded production costs, crop acreage expanded to the detriment of livestock. An article in the *High River Times* in 1908 enthused over the limitless productivity of the surrounding area, but admitted that "the cattle industry is being disregarded."[9]

Aside from its potential for profits, cash crop farming was seen as more desirable than ranching because it raised the value of the land. As early as 1906, prices for land devoted to cattle raising versus crop land varied from as much as twelve dollars per acre in the High River district.[10] Many prospective settlers became farmers because they could realize a more substantial profit when they sold out.[11] Land was a good investment if it was farmed. When leased or even owned for cattle grazing it promised a much lower reward.

The universality of single cash crop farming was established during these years. The newness of the North American farming frontier led to Utopian associations. Unprecedented volume production, and a simplistic view of global food supply and demand factors elevated King Wheat to a lofty and permanent throne The gospel of western Canada's limitless cereal crop potential was preached loudly and widely. *The High River Times* wrote of district yields that had grown from zero bushels in 1904 to 99,800 in 1905, and which would

*Prospective settler camped at Grouard Land Office, 1913. He waited three days in order to file for his homestead (NB 15-59).*

total more than 600,000 bushels in 1906.[12] By 1909–10, High River was the largest grain shipping point in western Canada. The *High River Times* noted the transformation with satisfaction. "Six years ago, the centre of the cattle ranching industry in the central section of southern Alberta. Last year, the largest individual grain shipment point in Western Canada. [This] is in short the history of the transformation that has taken place in the High River district." The *Farm and Ranch Review* informed prospective farmers in 1909 that grain yields in the Calgary district were over double the U.S. averages.[13] With scarcely a thought to factors of soil fertility or to long-range precipitation cycles, the most knowledgeable fell captive to the appeal of wheat. According to Hon. George Harcourt, the provincial Deputy Minister of Agriculture, in 1910, "an all wise providence is holding lands in reserve for land hungry immigrants for a thousand miles from the Red River to the Rockies."[14] It was argued that soil quality was less important than cultivation methods in achieving high yields.[15] The Minister of the Interior, Hon. Frank Oliver, instructed his ranch inspectors not to recognize climatic factors when deciding whether or not land was suitable for agricultural purposes.[16] Only land that was gravelly, sandy, or stony was to be excluded from the farmer's plough.

Against this type of euphoria and confidence, pastoral land use was sinful and mindless, probably in that order of demerit.

The appetite for land was insatiable. One farmer waited for eleven days outside a land office in Saskatchewan to secure a homestead.[17] Ed Gould, in his book *Ranching in Western Canada,* used his grandparents as an example of the land fever. Sight unseen they chose a homestead in the Drumheller area only to discover it was "as dry as a Depression banker's smile."[18] In 1910, the Lethbridge Land Office received more than one thousand homestead registrations in a single day.[19] Others took anything they could get. The *Farm and Ranch Review* captured the mood of the times in an editorial: "Out on the prairie 100 miles from a railroad and 25 miles from a chance of getting one, men have frantically jumped on a quarter section of sandhills and coulees consoling themselves with the false conviction that it is this or nothing … even men on well established farms past the meridian of life have joined the merry scramble for more land."[20] It seemed not to matter to either expert or farming neophyte that the brown soil zones of southern and eastern Alberta were lacking in both moisture and organic content, or that the luvisolic soils which covered most of the province were acidic and nitrogen deficient. The assumption that a quarter section near Manyberries or Rocky Mountain House was as productive as one near Red Deer led thousands of settlers to break land with equal confidence.

The rhetoric was hard to resist when it was accompanied by official approval. In 1908 at the Canadian National Exhibition in Toronto, the Alberta Department of Agriculture graphically displayed its priorities through a three-dimensional exhibit that depicted ranching in retreat from farmers. In the same year the Fort Macleod Board of Trade sent a public letter of censure to Hon. George Harcourt for remarks which had suggested that the Macleod area was not pure grain country.[21] While the Board admitted that the area had long been advertised as ranching country, it was quick to point out that "fortunately that erroneous impression is being removed." No less an authority than Dr. Charles Saunders, Director of Experimental Farms, following a tour of Alberta in 1905, said that he had seen "wheat growing on farms hitherto fit only for grazing." His detailed report published in 1906 contained not a single reference to livestock raising or forage crops.[22] In that year the federal experimental farms in Alberta experimented solely with grains. The provincial government was even more inclined to support the farming impetus since it

Poster advertising Dominion Exhibition, Calgary, 1908. The message is quite clear. The caption "Another Trail Shut Off," the sign about expendable Indians—and presumably, cowboys—and the rancher coming up against a barbed wire fence beyond which he faces luxuriant wheat fields is meant to convey the coming of a new and better era (NA 1473-1).

Harvesting near Medicine Hat, 1912. Yields like this made it difficult to convince settlers that the heyday of grain farming may be limited (NA 4061-7).

meant higher population influx and greater revenues. It promoted the agricultural potential of Alberta in U.S. magazines and newspapers and sponsored lectures throughout southern Alberta by American dry farming experts. A good example was F. W. Campbell of Lincoln, Nebraska, who in 1908 under the auspices of the provincial government gave a series of twelve lectures in southern Alberta on "Scientific Soil Culture and What It Means to the Great West."

The most extreme manifestation of the agricultural myth concerned dryland farming practices. Deriving its impetus from the United States, and aided by a sustained period of favourable moisture, dry farming employed new tillage and soil cultivation methods to extend the farming frontier into the semi-arid areas of southeastern Alberta.[23] Concentrating mainly on fall or winter wheat, dryland farmers maintained that "every foot of the province could be utilized for agriculture."[24] In 1909, the *Farm and Ranch Review* referred to yields of thirty to forty bushels per acre, and editorialized that "the value of lands for farming hitherto considered dry and unsuitable are only beginning to be realized. Dryland farming has neutralized the effects of drought and hot winds. It should be an encouragement to those contemplating opening up for cultivation and establishing homes in those parts of our province hitherto avoided."[25] At the Fourth Annual Dry Farming Congress held in Billings, Montana in 1910, three presentations from Alberta, including one by W. H. Fairfield, Superintendent of the Lethbridge Federal Research Station, endorsed the merits of dry farming.[26] The Alberta government also promoted the "new agriculture" through international advertising and by sponsoring lectures by dry farming experts. Given these endorsements, it is not surprising to find that the population of Alberta's dry belt jumped from 4,415 in 1901 to over 100,000 fifteen years later. The number of farms went from 2,000 to 30,883, many on "arid lands once considered fit only for the coyote."[27] By 1917, this had translated into an increase in areas under crops from 80,000 acres to 2,690,230 acres.[28]

## Impact on the Livestock Industry

Cereal crop agriculture had a considerable effect on the cattle industry. The fragile system of leasehold tenure was further undermined. Fences discouraged the movement of cattle between leases. As early as 1902, fences in the Macleod area had severely disrupted the traditional spring and fall roundups.[29] Furthermore, herd law stipulations did not allow cattle to graze in areas that had pockets of unprotected grain.[30] The *Macleod Advertiser* blamed the government for forcing farmers to use their marginal lands solely for grain instead of allowing them to run a few head of cattle.[31] Cut off from summer ranges and with their leaseholdings constricted, many ranchers were forced to overgraze. Railway construction further restricted cattle operations since leases could not be granted within twenty-five miles of an existing or prospective railroad.

Farming affected livestock operations in other ways. Dryland farms dislocated ranching areas. Since they were seen as a superior substitute to stock raising, they were allowed to disrupt the leaseholders, who had retreated into the last bastions of cattle country. By 1906 most of those engaged in the raising of cattle in other areas were forced to do so on their own deeded land. Those with large leases often had to buy their own stock watering reserves. The intrusion of crops, the lack of certainty of leasehold tenure even in marginal areas, and the fragmentary effects of dryland farming were reflected in the

*Casualties from the winter of 1906 – 07, Shaddock Ranch, Langdon. Generally accepted as the worst winter in the history of ranching, the winter of 1906 – 07 wrought catastrophic stock losses. For example, the Two Bar Ranch near Gleichen lost eleven thousand of its herd of thirteen thousand. The winter sent scores of ranchers into bankruptcy and has been seen as the most tangible indicator of the end of the old ranching order (NA 1631-1).*

activities of the Western Stock Growers' Association. By 1911 it was considering disbandment.[32]

Ranchers found themselves hemmed in on all sides by homesteads and, denied access to leased land beyond their own fences, many simply sold out. A few retaliated by ignoring herd law stipulations and stampeding their cattle over ripening crops.[33] Others transformed their operations and provided horses for farm power. Although a few left the country altogether most simply capitulated to the new ethos. They became farmers. In 1909 the *High River Times* referred to the many former ranchers who had gone into wheat farming.[34] Rancher and farmer Lachlin McKinnon wrote about his neighbours east of Calgary: "Some of the ranchers like Shaddock and Strange sold out and left the area.... Billy Bannister ran a few horses but went into grain farming.... Moorhouse started farming too and ceased his range cattle operations."[35]

Set against these variables, the catastrophic winter of 1906/07 could be viewed as a poignant demonstration of livestock's inappropriate place in the new agricultural order. Its staggering death tolls dealt the range industry a telling blow. According to one conservative estimate, half the capital invested in the range industry was liquidated.[36] Scores of ranchers were ruined. Ironically, the subsequent herd liquidations occurred at a time when the cattle cycle had begun to turn in the stockmen's favour. After 1907, the rush to farming intensified, and included former mixed farmers. It is a mistake to consider the winter of 1906–07 as the worst in Alberta's history; there were others equally sustained and extreme. In terms of timing, however, its impact was incalculable in that its ghastly statistics simply justified the rhetoric of the times. Not only was wheat more profitable, it was safer.

## Cattle Feeding

The popularity of grain, combined with the disarray of the ranching industry, negated any opportunity for regional integration within the industry. Since grain farming was paramount, the result was a step backwards for cattle feeding in the new agricultural areas. Just as the logistics of the ranching industry negated any growth in cattle finishing during the earlier period, so did the appeal of cash crop farming obviate any necessity to pursue feeding as a worthwhile venture.

The wintering of stock on farms remained haphazard. Commenting on the wintering practices of most farmers, the *Farm and Ranch Review* editorialized in 1913 that "wintering as far as we know consists of letting the cattle get to just enough feed to keep them from starving to death."[37] In 1912 an advertisement sponsored by the provincial government advised prospective settlers that they could make money out of a four-year-old steer that "has never been under a roof, nor fed a pound of grain or a ton of hay."[38] Furthermore, the demerits of feeding were linked to a lack of public appreciation for anything except range-fed beef.[39]

Thus the legacy of the ranching period was carried over. Most farmers and ranchers still felt that extensive grain feeding except for the export market was simply not profitable. A good example was provided by an experiment carried out by the provincial government at its Stony Plain Experimental Farm from July 1913 to July 1914. A total of twenty-four steers increased their average weight by three hundred pounds on a diet of oats, barley, green feed, and hay for a net profit of only $1.87 per animal.[40] The belief still lingered that western Canada lacked the climate to properly finish cattle consistently on a large-scale basis. Corn was still considered the primary feed grain, and much of the

*Last big round-up at Cochrane Lake near Cochrane, 1908. This round-up probably reflected the herd liquidations that followed the winter of 1906 – 07 (NA 381-1).*

debate about feeding during this period hinged on the feasibility of growing corn in Alberta.

Nevertheless, cattle feeding was increasing throughout this period. In 1908 several ranchers established an outdoor feedlot near Alix, and fed 190 specially selected cattle on a ration of 1.5 oat sheaves per day.[41] The grain-dominated diet of a prizewinning Shorthorn from Priddis in 1911 included several daily rations of oat chop, linseed cake and boiled barley.[42] Pat Burns was finishing cattle on fine ground oats and barley from self-feeders in three feedlots in 1913.[43] Advice on how to grain feed cattle was promoted in the agricultural press in line with increasing knowledge about rations and different nutrient values. Government experimental farms began work with alfalfa, hay, and forage crops towards the end of this period, while the first experiments were carried out in steer feeding at federal and provincial experimental farms. The CPR funded feeding competitions in the irrigation block as early as 1912.

For the most part, however, beef cattle feeding was haphazard and incidental and was seen primarily as a useful adjunct to the real business of grain farming.

The most common argument supporting livestock feeding on farms was based on their utility in disposing of frozen or marginal grain.[44] This belief militated against cattle on the mixed farm because hogs and dairy stock were more cost-efficient than beef cattle. It also showed the switch in the mixed farm philosophy from the early period. They were now crop- rather than cattle-intensive.

One direct result of grain feeding was the change to selling live cattle by the hundredweight instead of by the head. Effective feeding became associated solely with fattening, a belief that was to last until after the Second World War.[45] This belief ignored evidence to the contrary and assumed that fat animals on the hoof translated into dressed beef of commensurate weight and quality. Reinforced over the years by the show ring, the notion that meat quality and quantity bore a direct relationship to live weight remained unchallenged.

## Markets

Unprofitable markets compounded the cattle industry's plight during this period. First, the export market virtually vanished. The traditional British market collapsed during this period and was never to emerge again as a viable outlet for Canadian live cattle. The high transportation costs precluded competition with chilled beef from South America. For example, between 1906 and 1913 the boat rate per head from Canada to Britain was almost double the animal's market price in Toronto.[46] British prices could not absorb these costs. George Lane told the Beef Commission in 1907 that the British butchers in Liverpool had beaten the Canadian rancher down to the point that the butchers "had their own way."[47] One rancher complained in 1912 that "It is impossible to raise two steers on the farm in Alberta for the price of one on London's Smithfield market."[48] Another visiting Canadian expert commented that the bulk of Canadian cattle actually brought less than chilled beef from other countries.[49] Statistics support the dominance of chilled beef. In 1904 Britain imported 210,000 quarters of beef in the form of live cattle. By 1912 the number was down to 24,000. In the same year South America sent 427,000 quarters of chilled beef.[50] By 1912 there was no British market for Canadian cattle.

Yet it was this sombre period in the industry which first revealed the potential of western Canada's second export market in the United States. Historically, the United States had not been a viable market for Canadian export cattle. Indeed, if anything, the movement seemed to be the other way; American cattle were largely responsible for stocking the western Canadian leaseholds in the 1880s. Both countries were in direct competition for the British market,[51] and in the mid-1890s were two of only three countries exporting live cattle to Great Britain.[52] Both Canada and the United States guarded this lucrative market zealously. Each subjected the other's cattle to a ninety-day quarantine to satisfy British concerns over the introduction of contagious pleuropneumonia into English herds. Canada quarantined American cattle in 1879 after the British scheduled the United States because of pleuropneumonia. Thirteen years later, the Americans subjected Canadian cattle to quarantine restrictions for the same reason.[53] Reciprocal tariffs, however, were the greatest barriers to trade between the two countries. In 1886 Canada imposed a conditional 20 percent tariff on American cattle entering the country.[54] This rate matched the corresponding U.S. levy on Canadian cattle.[55] It was seen not so much as a barrier to trade but as inhibiting local herd buildup.[56] Then, in 1897, the Americans increased this levy to a more prohibitive 27.5 percent.[57]

Yet, despite this heavier tariff, Canadian live cattle exports to the United States increased with the removal of the ninety-day quarantine on both sides of the border in 1897.[58] The Canadian Department of Agriculture enthused in 1898 over the emergence of "a profitable outlet for cattle not suitable in size for exportation to Great Britain."[59] Duncan MacEachran, Canada's Veterinary General, wrote in the same year that "the rapid development of the cattle trade between the United States and Canada especially in the class of feeding purposes has been much beyond expectations."[60] In 1896, live cattle exports to the United States totalled 1,646 head. When the quarantine was lifted in 1897, the number jumped to over 35,000, and over the next five years averaged over 85,000 head annually.[61] This new trade was so brisk that the Canadian Department of Agriculture had to add two permanent officers in 1901 to handle the mandatory TB Testing.[62] Generally these exports of cattle to the United States were one- and two-year-old stockers and feeders shipped from eastern Canada, and between 1898 and 1901 realized a profit of between five and eight dollars a head in spite of the heavy tariff.[63] The new trade, however, was short lived. Falling prices after 1902 reduced U.S. shipments, and for the next decade they contributed only about 5 percent of the value of Canadian live cattle exports. The western Canadian industry, being still oriented towards

*Texas longhorns in Union Stockyards, Chicago, 1896. The presence of mixed cattle of widely varying quality in the premier market in the U.S. no doubt explains some of the success enjoyed by Alberta ranchers who always shipped only their best animals (NA 1741-1).*

raising big four-year-old range-finished animals for immediate slaughter was never an active participant in this surge in exports to the United States between 1897 and 1902.

Favourable prices and the growing instability of the British market led to the first cattle exports from Alberta to the United States in 1907. A few venturesome cattlemen in the Red Deer District risked the tariff, the nine and a half day trip, and a freight rate that was almost double that to Montreal for a chance at the lucrative Chicago market.[64] It was an arduous undertaking for the animals that had to be detrained, fed, and rested on three separate occasions. High prices for the top-end cattle justified the effort. The best animals sold for $85.18 per head, a price well above that of the Winnipeg market. In 1912 George Lane increased his profit margin by one dollar per animal by selling choice steers on the American instead of the Canadian market.[65] Increasingly, a small but steady stream of prime cattle made their way annually to Chicago and other Midwest points where they were sold as fat range animals or "grassers."[66] Some ranchers bought their calves in the United States and took advantage of the tariff exemptions applicable to American-bred cattle that had been on Canadian grass for two years.[67] By 1910 American buyers, usually representing the big packing houses, were in Alberta selecting batches of quality animals for shipment south. The finer, less fat Canadian cattle were preferred by American buyers for their taste and often brought higher prices.[68] Though their numbers were small, Canadian cattle during these years established a solid reputation among Chicago buyers. In 1912, for example, George Lane topped the market in Chicago with three hundred head shipped from Brooks. His price of $10.25 per hundredweight eclipsed the Chicago record for grass-fed steers by fifty cents per hundredweight.[69] The same year and again in 1913, steers owned by Brandon rancher J. G. McGregor won the Fat Steer Championship at the prestigious Chicago International Exposition.[70] These initial forays into the American market between 1907 and 1913 were significant in terms of potential rather than volume, for as long as the high 27.5 percent tariff on Canadian cattle remained, profits were restricted to prime animals only. Since the best money was to be made in shipping whole carloads of cattle, the advantage of the large ranchers over the small operators partly explains their domination of the American market.

The feasibility and appeal of the new American market was reflected in the ranchers' advocacy of reciprocity during the federal election campaign of 1911. In a letter to the Hon. Frank Oliver, George Lane summed up the cattlemen's argument for freer trade:

You are aware of how the cattle interests have suffered in this country in the past twenty years. You certainly have got the greatest mixed farming country in the Dominion and probably there are none better in the United States. You have not half the cattle in this country than you had ten years ago. What is the reason? The high tariff on the American side [and] high rail and steamship rates is what has caused the reduction of cattle in this country. You have got the country to raise them but not the market…. We thought the only danger of the agreement not going through would come from the United States, and now we find it coming from some of our own people.[71]

Although the Liberals and reciprocity were defeated in the election of 1911, the possibility of free trade in cattle with the United States remained, and was reinforced by expert predictions that the United States would soon be a beef importer. Over the next two years it was touted in the agricultural press as a solution to the stockmen's problems. The Fort Macleod *Advertiser's* comment that "those who voted against reciprocity obviously were not interested in a share of that market" reflected a growing sentiment.[72]

The emergence of the American market reinforced a belief nurtured during the earlier ranching period. The discerning British market between 1887 and 1900 had established the premise that export standard was the yardstick of quality. An equally discriminating market in Chicago sustained this belief. Only the very best animals were sent to Chicago. Fort Macleod rancher E. H. Maunsell made that point very clear to his fellow ranchers upon a return from Chicago in 1913.[73] His advice to send only the very best to Chicago simply reaffirmed the obvious. If export standard was a belief in the 1890s, it was an article of faith by 1913. Maunsell's accompanying statement that rough and inferior stock should be reserved for the local market completed the twin axioms characteristic of cattle marketing for the whole period under discussion.

The slump in British exports was not counterbalanced by the rise in American outlets during this period. As a venue for beef sales, eastern Canada did not provide an unlimited market for western Canadian surplus cattle. Low prices and high transportation costs were crucial factors preventing the national integration of the cattle industry. In 1908 the number of cattle shipped east from western Canadian farms and ranches totalled less than 8 percent of total marketings.[74] Often it was cheaper for Eastern buyers to secure their cattle from the American Midwest than from western Canada.[75]

The loss of markets outside Alberta put pressure on local demand. Yet while the influx of population into the West during this period increased the size and importance of the local market, it was not translated into respectable profits for producers. Part of the reason was the glut of low-quality animals in the fall. Packers would simply buy low and freeze their inventories for future sale at higher prices. Prices paid to producers throughout this period

*Interior of Pat Burns's Packing Plant in Calgary, early 1900s. As early as 1898, Burns's packing plant was processing 150 head of cattle per week. This plant was probably his second in Calgary. The first burned down in 1892 and the second in 1913. The third was operated until 1984 (NA 2351-4).*

were inelastic. According to Dalmead rancher Lachlin McKinnon, they did not change from year to year. Furthermore, quality was not considered in price setting.[76] One southern Alberta rancher wrote in 1909 that "the buyers were largely responsible for the general apathy towards stock raising. They will offer so much for a bunch with the privilege of cutting them out without even looking at them. This is no encouragement for the man who keeps stock."[77] Small wonder that ranchers referred to the packing houses as "the Trust."[78] Believing that they were better off even after paying a commission, some ranchers began consigning their stock to commission houses and bypassing the buyers altogether.[79] According to Alberta Livestock Commissioner W. F. Stevens, the primary remedy for beef marketing problems lay in securing more buyers from outside the province.[80] The Canadian Council of Agriculture blamed monopolists in 1911 for retarding the beef industry.[81] The packers who employed the buyers defended themselves against

45

charges of price fixing and monopoly by attributing the stockmen's low profit margins on price-setting mechanisms associated with the limited local consumer market. They claimed that the lack of year-round beef supplies forced them to keep large frozen inventories for extensive time periods, and therefore they had little control over the difference between producer and retail price.[82]

## The Chilled Beef Initiatives

The attempt to establish a chilled meat export industry during this period was a direct response to these marketing problems. It was correctly assumed that the long journey precluded Canadian live cattle from competing in the British market. It was estimated that a dressed beef trade to Britain would net western Canadian producers ten dollars more per animal.[83] Furthermore, year-round beef supplies were necessary if Canadian producers were to achieve stability of price and supply. Reacting to the success of U.S. and Argentinean chilled meat in Britain, and to the increasing presence of chilled meats on Canadian tables, Canadian stock interests took up an initiative that dated to the early 1890s when dressed meat from Alberta ranches found a ready outlet in Vancouver.

In spring 1908, E. G. Palmer, a cold storage expert, was asked to address the annual meeting of the Alberta Cattle Breeders' Association on the subject of chilled meat.[84] Palmer extolled the superiority of chilled beef to its frozen counterpart. He also pointed out that Chicago had sent fifty million pounds of chilled meat to Britain in the first three months of the year. Loud applause greeted his rousing statement that Canada should "take the place in the business now occupied by the States." Yet, after discussing cost and profitability factors, Palmer concluded that government involvement was necessary to expedite a national chilled beef trade.

Matters took a step further in July at the Dominion Exhibition in Calgary when a meeting of stockmen chaired by Hon W. F. Finlay, Alberta Minister of Agriculture, endorsed the notion of a chilled meat trade as the best way of stabilizing the industry.[85] Finlay's presence was not surprising. He had gone on record a few months earlier as favouring a chilled meat industry, but felt that it should be a federal initiative. A committee of inquiry was struck to prepare recommendations for Finlay to take to the federal government.[86]

Over the next few months the committee, which included representatives from various livestock associations, a cold storage expert, and W. F. Stevens, gathered information from South American and British experts. They began selling the idea of a chilled meat trade to the livestock community. Stevens addressed the Central Alberta Stock Growers' Association meeting in December 1908. Loud applause followed his presentation. The *Farm and Ranch Review* reported that "a settled conviction seems to at last have taken hold of the minds of producers that the time has arrived to take practical steps to provide another method of marketing the surplus stock of this country."[87]

In February 1909 the committee's recommendations were submitted to the federal government. In a comprehensive report, the committee condemned stagnant Canadian marketing practices, and suggested that the reform measures taken in other beef-exporting countries should be applied to Canada. Its recommendations were accompanied by approximate costs to the government. The proposal called for the establishment of thirty small feedlots across western and central Canada, five central depots for slaughtering and chilling, two cold storage waterfront facilities, five hundred refrigerated cars, and one hundred retail outlets in Great Britain.[88] The committee concluded by suggesting that the government fund all or part of the $4,915,000 necessary to implement the project.

The Liberal government registered its lack of interest by delaying its reply. Arguably, it had good reason. First, the cost estimates were likely closer to $8 million, a 60 percent increase on original estimates. Second, the market had already been secured by cost-efficient competitors with big cattle inventories, and given the time needed to establish the industry on a secure footing it was felt that Canada could never gain parity. Argentina's highly refined and efficient chilling methods provided a sobering case in point. Beef chilling was a sensitive process. The constant temperature of 31 – 32 degrees Fahrenheit was almost impossible to maintain in railway cars, especially in those coming from the Canadian prairies in winter. Finally, there were strong doubts that Canada could produce the numbers to consistently supply the export market. One estimate called for 375,000 head annually, a figure well above Canada's best export year to date. It was also true that the big players in the cattle industry during this period were simply not interested. The major exporting company, Gordon, Ironsides and Fares, was not prepared to abandon its reliance on the live cattle trade. Neither was the CPR interested in building refrigerated cars when it was earning large profits from the transport of live cattle.[89]

In early 1910 a private company, Meat Exports Limited, submitted a more modest proposal to establish meat chilling operations in western Canada. The federal government was asked to guarantee the $2 million necessary to begin production.[90] Like the first proposal, it was rejected on the grounds that it was too expensive and elaborate.[91] In all likelihood, the proposals were never seriously entertained. The Department of Agriculture did not lend its support, nor was the subject discussed in the House of Commons. The government was clearly not interested. The problems inherent in establishing a chilled beef industry could have been addressed through an experiment involving seaboard facilities and a limited number of cattle. However, important though the cattle industry was to Alberta, it did not figure high in federal trade policies. The emergence of the big beef producers in the Southern Hemisphere foreordained Canada's role as a minor player on the British export stage. Increasingly, beef fell behind wheat, and later pork, as one of Canada's major food exports. Nowhere was this more evidenced than in the federal government's lack of co-operation in helping cattlemen solve export problems deemed crucial to the growth of their industry. Just as it had not maintained an ongoing campaign against the British embargo after 1892, the federal government remained indifferent to the merits of the chilled meat export trade between 1908 and 1910. Unfortunately, it was an official position destined to be repeated again in the 1920s and 1940s.

By 1910, the cattle industry in Alberta had reached its nadir. The British export market had vanished and there was no adequate replacement in sight. Inferior classes in the various show rings and bull sales reflected diminishing herd quality. One rancher complained in 1908 that purebred bulls were bringing less in Calgary than were steers in Chicago.[92] Herd depletion continued in ranching areas as producers liquidated their female stock. In 1909, 65 percent of the stock handled by Pat Burns's company in Calgary were female. One cattle buyer commented in 1910 that "nothing persuades farmers to keep their young heifers."[93] A year later Pat Burns commented that the excessive marketing of young cows and spayed heifers was putting the industry in dire jeopardy.[94] It was noted in 1912 that far too many calves were killed for veal.[95] Herd depletions resulted in a temporary but chronic shortage in traditional cattle-raising areas. Cattle had to be imported from the East to meet consumer demands, and in 1913 several thousand mixed longhorns were imported from the United States to bolster depleted herds.[96] In the same year the superintendent of the Dominion Research Station summed up the situation in a single sentence when he said "cattle disappeared from the plains much as the dew from the early morning sun."[97]

# Land Use

This period saw a marked change in the demographics of the cattle industry. On the one hand, leaseholds, particularly in more arid southern and eastern Alberta, increased in size and scope. In 1901 leases averaging 847 acres were distributed among 715 leaseholders. By 1911, 1,166 leaseholders controlled an average of 2,824 acres per lease.[98] These leases, however, contained proportionately fewer cattle than in the earlier period. By 1912 only one-third, or 165,000 head, of Alberta's cattle were on grazing leases. After the winter of 1906–07, 85 percent of leasehold cattle numbers were held in herds under five hundred.

The permanent distribution pattern of cattle numbers throughout the province was established during this period. Over the ensuing forty years, the seventeen census districts in Alberta showed little proportional variation in numbers. The heart of the ranching areas in the four census districts of southern Alberta supported about 30 percent of the cattle population in 1911. More farms carried fewer cattle. The average number of cattle per farm in Alberta dropped from 29.2 in 1901 to 9.6 in 1911. The vast majority of Alberta's beef cattle were concentrated in central Alberta between Calgary and Edmonton, and after 1910, cattle shipments from points north of Calgary were greater than those from the old ranching areas to the south.[99]

In spite of leasehold uncertainty and the appeal of agriculture, cattle numbers rose during this period. The Census of Canada shows an increase of over 350,000 beef cattle in Alberta from 1901 to 1911. Also, Alberta's share of the nation's cattle numbers doubled in the same period. These increasing numbers and the changing demographics of the cattle industry meant that ranching now coexisted with more intensive farming operations that happened to include cattle. However, integration of the industry still did not occur.

The increase in cattle numbers during this period was not accompanied by any general awareness about optimum land use. Rather, it reflected the belief by many farmers that a few head of livestock were useful addenda to grain farming. They were not crucial components in the overall marketing equation, as witness the wide discrepancies between cattle and grain returns. In 1911 Alberta's farmers received about $14 million from grain sales. In contrast, the value of livestock slaughtered the same year was only $658,712. So while the permanent demographics of the cattle industry in Alberta had been established by 1912, the ranching and the farming areas remained distinct entities. The economics of complementary land use were simply not realized.

The leaseholders' problems contributed to further uncertainty. As long as ranchers were denied leasehold security, the ranching industry could not consolidate itself. Leased land adjacent to homesteads in both good and marginal farming areas disappeared. In 1908, when the federal government threw open all remaining even- and odd-numbered sections for pre-emption or homestead entry at three dollars per acre, some twenty-eight million acres of potential grazing land were lost.[100] The two-year cancellation clause ruined many. One leaseholder was left with six thousand head on his deeded quarter section following cancellation.[101] Aggressive real estate agents who secured grazing lands kept them for farmers.[102] As a result, disillusioned ranchers often declined to bid on leased grazing land when it did become available.[103] Farmers who leased land near their farms for grazing purposes were faced with rising production costs when their leases were cancelled. As one rancher put it in 1909, "We cannot raise 3 and 4 year old steers for $45.00 on land worth from $15.00– 30.00 per acre that we used to rent for 2¢ per acre."[104] Provincial taxes on leased land doubled the cost. In 1907 the education tax of 1.5 cents per acre on all lands not organized into school districts was clearly aimed at leaseholders.

The overall result by 1912 was the random presence of beef cattle on farms. Many farmers were committed to self-sufficiency, which meant rudimentary animal husbandry in association with cereal crop agriculture. Indeed, many incoming settlers and former farmers from the East or the United States arrived in Alberta with their own animals. Animals were part of a farmer's stock in trade and could not be related to land use priorities. Dryland farms and tenuous leasehold provisions undermined land use patterns in the shortgrass grazing country. The lowest point in land use rationalization had been reached.

## Mixed Farming

While some form of mixed farming had existed in Alberta since the 1870s, this period marked the first official interest in it as a viable land use alternative.

*Typical homestead yard, Viking area, 1908 (NA 3543-59).*

Commencing around 1912, the promotion of mixed farming began in earnest. In Ottawa, the strongest official proponent was Veterinary Director General and Livestock Commissioner Dr. J. G Rutherford. In his widely published report, "The Cattle Trade in Western Canada," released in early 1910, Rutherford dismissed the ranching industry's passage as "a cause for no deep or lasting regret," and focused his attention on the boundless merits of mixed farming.[105] Later, the recommendations of the Ranching Commission in 1913 gave lease preference to those who were interested in winter feeding in order to encourage mixed farming.[106] The provincial government endorsed these initiatives. In 1913 Livestock Commissioner W. F. Stevens told the Hazelmere Stock Association that mixed farming practices could help control 560 of the 600 noxious weeds in Alberta.[107] "Mixed Farm" trains sponsored by the government and the CPR toured the West, and by stressing security over profit tried to persuade single-crop farmers to create agriculture's best natural order by diversifying with livestock.

51

Certainly, there were some favourable responses. The *Farm and Ranch Review* sarcastically editorialized in 1911 that those who refused to take mixed farming seriously wanted their lands to last no more than ten years and seemed determined to exterminate the beef trust by starving it to death.[108] In 1912 George Lane told the National Livestock Convention that mixed farming was the only way to maximize western Canada's agricultural potential.[109] Farmers' associations were formed to purchase cattle and in 1913 the Macleod Board of Trade fostered urban-rural co-operation when it brought in a carload of cattle to be bought by farmers at discounted prices.[110] In 1911, the Pincher Creek Chamber of Commerce chose mixed farming as the theme of its promotional brochure.[111] The Alberta Produce Association was formed in Red Deer in 1913 to combat the regrettable fact that more attention had not been paid to mixed farming.[112] The first mixed farming convention in Alberta was held in Lethbridge in 1913. Over four thousand invitations were sent to Alberta farmers exhorting them to attend. Appropriately, J. G. Rutherford delivered the keynote address. Rutherford left the government for the CPR, where he began a much more intensive and hands-on operation to encourage mixed farming on the CPR's irrigated lands.

The chief reasons favouring mixed farming stressed risk-reduction rather than optimum land use. It was promoted not as a land use practice but as an economically viable and profitable farming alternative. The profitability of wheat was set against the shortness of the growing season and the impact of capricious weather. It was held that livestock could dispose of any spoiled or frozen grain, thus turning a certain loss into a potential profit. According to one mill owner in 1912, the poor quality of grain in certain areas was a sound reason for a conversion to livestock-based enterprises.[113]

Yet despite all the promotion, the bandwagon of mixed farming was not overcrowded. First, the proponents of mixed farming ignored reality by presuming an easy transition from one agricultural practice to another. Even then it was more risky than believed. The Edmonton branch of the United Farmers of Alberta censured the provincial government in 1913 for providing misleading information about mixed farming, noting that every bushel raised [for mixed farming] is "raised at a loss."[114]

Furthermore, mixed farming downplayed some distinct advantages associated with a single-crop economy. Wheat would not spoil and tolerated delays in marketing far more than did cattle. Moreover, of all the livestock components in mixed farming, beef cattle, while promising the most profit, were also the most expensive and risky.

Despite the rhetoric promoting mixed farming after 1912, the cattle industry did not consolidate itself in the grain growing districts as a powerful complement to the ranching areas. Cash crop farming pushed cattle raising into second-class status; it was most common in farming areas containing non-arable pasture or where oats and barley represented the ideal grain crop. The romantic ideal of grain growing died hard. In 1913 the *Macleod Spectator* wondered why mixed farming was being promoted in an area already noted for unparalleled prizewinning grains.

## Recovery

A combination of four factors after 1912 resurrected the fortunes of the cattle industry. Rising beef prices and the first falterings of the wheat economy began putting beef cattle in a more favourable light. Indeed, it could be argued that the official promotion of mixed farming reflected these contemporary realities. Equally important was the ranchers' success in achieving a measure of leasehold security. Finally, the opening of a free American market began a redefinition of the Alberta beef cattle industry.

The wheat boom received its first setbacks in 1910 when the southern Alberta crop suffered from drought. One Tongue Creek farmer referred to the 1910 crop year as the driest season he had ever experienced in the West in thirty years. Estimates for the High River area predicted a harvest of 75 percent below expectations.[115] The following year was similar. Described as "the most trying crop season in the history of the country," the 1911 crop year was beset with belated spring rains, drought, hail and early frosts, all of which contributed to a great deal of frozen or inferior grain.[116]

Land deterioration in dryland farming areas was also becoming evident. Speakers at the 1912 Livestock Convention referred to excessive soil deterioration on grain farms, while J. G. Rutherford warned that Alberta would soon follow Manitoba, where grain yields had fallen dramatically—in some areas from forty bushels per acre to barely fifteen.[117] One year later, an agricultural expert noted that "with few exceptions, dry farming has not been a glowing success in this country."[118] These first signs of vulnerability in the new wheat economy were not lost on the bankers who had been advancing money to farmers to expand their operations. By 1912 farmers were feeling the pinch from bankers reluctant to support their grain operations.[119] In the wake of rising cattle prices, many believed that their credit rating would improve if they had a few livestock to add as collateral.

The downward pressure on beef prices occasioned by the cattle cycle, diminished exports, and herd liquidations had begun to reverse itself by the end of the decade. Rising prices for beef began changing attitudes towards stock raising. Cattle that were selling in Winnipeg in 1908 for $3.53 per hundredweight were bringing over $7.00 per hundredweight in Calgary by 1913. Prices in Chicago were appreciably higher. Fall cattle in the same year were fetching as high as $8.50 per hundredweight, with the top prices for grain-fed cattle being well over $11.00 per hundredweight. By 1913 the *Farm and Ranch Review* was noting that "anything with meat under its hide is selling at fair prices and cattle in some condition are in brisk demand."[120]

The prospect of leasehold tenure reform had seemed impossible under the federal Liberal government. In 1909 the Western Stock Growers' Association had unsuccessfully petitioned the government to convert all uncancelled leases to closed leases and allow stockmen the right to purchase 10 percent of their current leaseholdings. The situation changed dramatically with the election of a more sympathetic Conservative government in 1911. A few weeks after the election in late 1911, a committee of the WSGA prevailed on Robert Hugh Borden, the new Prime Minister, and the Minister of the Interior, Robert Rogers, for assistance in saving the ranching industry. When Rogers visited Calgary a few months later the stockmen presented him abundant evidence of their plight and urged him to prevent homestead entry in lands suitable only for grazing in order to preserve the industry from becoming "only a memory."

The result was the appointment of the Ranching and Grazing Investigative Commission to investigate the ranching industry and to recommend on the means by which it might be rejuvenated. It was also charged with deciding what lands should be withdrawn from homestead entry and be reserved for leases. The Commission, which included Medicine Hat rancher Walter Huckvale, took evidence from hundreds of cattle operators in thirteen ranching centres across the West.

The Commission's report, released in January 1913 and made law several months later, concluded that the ranching industry's 75 percent decline in five years was due in large part to a lack of leasehold security. Its recommendations provided for new grazing regulations, which granted ten-year closed leases of up to twelve thousand acres in designated areas at a rental rate of two cents per acre per year.[121] The large leaseholds were confined to areas where fitness for agriculture did not exceed 25 percent. The leases were to be fenced and stocked at a rate of thirty acres per animal. Leaseholders could cut but not sell hay on their leases which had to be inspected upon application to ensure that they were not in an area suitable for agriculture.

The new regulations did not meet all the stockmen's wishes. They had wanted larger and longer-term leases plus an option to buy up to 10 percent of the lease for personal feeding-related use. Still, they had at last achieved some security of tenure, and had registered the first successful if modest counter to the farming frontier.[122] In fact, it was opposition from farming interests that had caused the Commission to modify its original intent for leases of twenty-four thousand acres. In addition, the new regulations encouraged farmers to secure grazing leases adjacent to their homesteads where possible. The impact of the new regulations was reflected in the number of leases and total leased acreage. In 1910, 2.77 million acres were held by 971 leaseholders in western Canada. Two years after the new lease regulations, 3,352 leaseholders were in control of over 5.21 million acres.[123]

Circumstances in the United States also worked in the Alberta cattlemen's favour. In the period 1904–13, the population of the United States had increased by twenty-one million. U.S. cattle numbers, on the other hand, had dropped by seven million head.[124] Faced with a 96 percent decline in cattle exports and upward pressure on consumer prices, the United States enacted the Underwood Tariff in October 1913, allowing Canadian cattle free entry to American markets.[125] This meant that a new market much closer and larger than its British counterpart was there for the having. It was like a dream come true. Stockmen were elated. The second "golden age" of the industry had begun.

## Conclusion

The period 1907–13 began on a low and ended on a high note. First, the beleaguered ranching industry became consolidated. The leasehold regulations of 1913 provided ranchers with a giant victory. Their industry was stabilized, their survival and influence assured. The tenuous movement towards mixed farming had positive though distant implications for beef cattle on farms. The ideal export market in the United States had opened up. The comment by *Farm and Ranch Review* Editor, F. S. Jacobs, that "we no longer have to accept prices dictated by a limited consumer market" unwittingly encapsulated the enduring ethos of the Alberta cattle industry: export or starve.[126] For a few years, at least, there would be few hungry cattlemen in western Canada.

On the other hand the period, had done little to remedy deficiencies inherent in the early ranching period. Both the limited British and American markets continued to attract only the best animals, with the result that the export trade was still dominant in marketing practices. The local market was mainly for the low-quality beef that continued to characterize the industry. In many ways nothing much had changed since the early 1890s.

Some regarded the newly won security of leasehold tenure as a respite only. There was also the question of how cattle on farms would integrate with the stabilized ranching operations. It remained to be seen whether the increasing interest in cattle raising on farms was linked to changing attitudes or merely to the immediate advantages associated with rising beef prices. Attitudinally, it would have to be demonstrated that the mixed farming trend would not only sustain itself but also result in greater priority being given to cattle raising and feeding.

# THREE

# Mixed Blessings, 1914 – 20

*Will those days ever return?*
CANADIAN CATTLEMEN, 1939

I N MANY WAYS, the period 1914–20 could be described as the cattlemen's second "golden age." High cattle prices and an assured export market advanced the Alberta cattle industry in terms of both herd production and quality. The period also entrenched ranching as the leading component of the industry. The effects of prosperity, however, were not all positive. First, tensions developed between the ranchers and the livestock farming community. Second, the increased emphasis on the export market impacted negatively on beef quality in the domestic market. The prosperity also reinforced the misplaced belief that Alberta was best suited for breeding stock either to be finished elsewhere, or to be fattened on grass alone. The good times paradoxically stalled the impetus toward mixed farming. If cattle raising was profitable, grain farming was even more so. Finally, the prosperity of the period encouraged profligate land use practices. The results were land degradation and a renewed stockmen's battle over leasehold tenure.

## The Export Market

The most significant change during this period was the shift in export priorities from Great Britain to the United States. Previously, the British market, however deficient, was of primary importance to Alberta exporters. After 1913 it became irrelevant, serving only as a stop-gap measure whenever the American market was curtailed.

## The American Market

The removal of the tariff on Canadian cattle in 1914, together with the high demand in the United States, had an immediate and enormous impact on the Alberta cattle industry. In 1912 Canada exported 9,878 cattle to the United States. After the removal of the tariff in late 1913 the number jumped to 180,383, and over the ensuing six years averaged 220,000 head annually, reaching a peak of 453,606 in 1919.[1] In 1912, Canada's live cattle exports counted for 12 percent of total cattle movements. In 1919 the corresponding figure was 37 percent.[2] The extraordinary demands associated with the war effort sustained high prices well after the cattle cycle had peaked in 1914. Chicago replaced London as the price setter for Canadian beef.[3] The price for choice butcher steers in Montreal in 1914 was $8.40 per hundredweight. It went to over $10.00 per hundredweight in 1917 and hovered near $13.00 per hundredweight in 1919. In the same year the Toronto price exceeded $14.00 per hundredweight.[4] Profits were further increased by the higher prices in Chicago. For example, in 1917 and 1919, Chicago prices exceeded Montreal quotations by $7.90 and $7.30 per hundredweight respectively.[5] Local markets, too, were hungry for beef. Range cattle consistently brought around $100 a head in High River.[6]

Western Canadian range-fed steers were popular among U.S. buyers and consistently outperformed their American counterparts. In 1915 the *Farm and Ranch Review* noted that "western grass fed beef is a scarce commodity this year and the Canadian delegation has been very welcome to the packers in Chicago."[7] A year later Alberta rancher Alfred E. Cross "broke all records" at $10.75 per hundredweight with his four-year-old Hereford Shorthorns fed on "nothing but range grass."[8] An Angus steer from Acme set a new Chicago record in 1917 of $12.00 per hundredweight. In the same year the CPR made a promotional movie depicting a shipment of prime Bar U cattle en route to Chicago.[9] In December 1918, a three-and-a-half-year-old seventeen-hundred-pound Shorthorn Hereford cross from Monitor, Alberta brought $18.75 per hundredweight, the highest price ever paid in Chicago for a range-fed steer.[10] A year later, a shipment of Pat Burns's cattle brought Chicago's highest prices for range-fed steers. The success of Alberta cattle also drew the attention of the large Chicago commission houses whose aggressive marketing strategies served to increase the bargaining power of the big Alberta ranchers.[11]

Yet, dramatic as the Chicago market was for fat steers, the demand in the Midwest for stocker and feeder cattle was more significant. In 1915, 85 percent of all stocker and feeder cattle from the Winnipeg stockyards went to the United States.[12] Six years later, the federal Department of Agriculture reported that the number of U.S.-bound stockers and feeders exceeded those being returned to Canadian farms by a ratio of almost three to one.[13] Their destination was the Midwest corn belt where they afforded farmers an attractive alternative to their usual sources in the range states. This new market for western Canadian cattle represented a major departure from established export practices, which had previously concentrated on fat, mature animals.

Contemporary opinion endorsed the inevitability and the permanence of this new market. The *Farm and Ranch Review* saw a permanent dependent market since "we safely can assume that their current supply is wholly unable to meet their needs."[14] In a like comment four years later, the *Review* noted that American meat consumption was fast approaching its production limits, and that the country's depleted cattle stocks of over ten million in a decade guaranteed high prices for the duration of the war and for several years thereafter.[15] The *Review* argued further that global food production limitations meant that Canada would reap tremendous post-war gains. Referring to an abundance of surplus nutritional grass presently going to waste, the *Review* grandly predicted that "all we have said about paying attention to livestock will prove sound."[16] Individual livestock operators were just as optimistic. One rancher took particular satisfaction in reflecting that "it was only a few years ago that we were almost ashamed to be in a livestock country, but now we have come back and this time we have come back to stay."[17] Brand registrations in 1916 exceeded the previous year by almost one thousand. Several new stock companies were incorporated, including the Janes Real Trading and Ranching Company which was capitalized at two hundred thousand dollars.[18] Rancher George Lane predicted enormous growth in the emerging American market of the Pacific Northwest:

It is my honest conviction that this country will control the markets, particularly in cattle, oats and barley, in Washington and Oregon. All along the Pacific Coast they need these goods and this is the nearest point for them to obtain them. Then we will have St. Paul, Minneapolis and Chicago to fall back on which must be an advantage; and certainly Western Canada can hold the Alaskan trade which is a large one in cattle and is principally controlled from Seattle.[19]

Official government spokesmen echoed the opinion that herd depletions in the United States and wartorn Europe meant permanent prosperity for Canadian livestock operators.[20] Dr. J. G. Rutherford, Canada's former Veterinary Director General, wrote in 1913 that it was unlikely that cattle prices would ever permanently recede from their high levels.[21] In 1919–20 the federal Department of Agriculture reflected the continuing optimism when it commented that "except for the increase during the war, the United States is rapidly approaching the time when its surplus will turn to a deficit necessitating purchases from outside."[22] The Commissioner of Agriculture for Canada was confident that meat prices would remain high after the war, an opinion supported by the Head of the Manitoba College of Agriculture, who predicted better economic times for stockmen over grain growers in the post-war period.[23] In 1918, federal Minister of Agriculture, Hon. T. A. Crerar, spoke positively about cattle operations during the reconstruction period and asked livestock men to maintain their breeding programmes at wartime levels.[24]

Very few voices of caution were raised, and these usually concerned the need to protect the new market from animal health issues. For example, in 1919 when mange was detected in western Canadian cattle, the federal Minister of Agriculture promptly dispatched the Veterinary Director General to Washington to soothe any fears regarding the effectiveness of Canadian containment measures.[25] George Lane was one of the few to appreciate the reality of American politics when he said in 1916 that "the most dangerous thing that stockmen have to fear is a change in administration on the other side of the line that would slap a duty on everything."[26] As in his previous arguments in favour of mixed farming, Lane foretold a reality incongruent with the mood of the times.

## The British Market

The attractiveness of the new market meant that the traditional British cattle trade was completely dismissed during this period, wartime conditions notwithstanding. One casualty was Gordon, Ironsides and Fares, which paid the price for its exclusive concentration on the live cattle export market to Great Britain. Amid severe financial difficulties it was taken over in 1918 by the Toronto-based Harris Abattoir Company.[27]

The best example of the general Canadian indifference over the demise of the British market concerned the debate over the 1892 embargo. The federal government's apathetic stance was not surprising given the low place of export cattle in national agricultural priorities. To the western Canadian cattlemen, the embargo was at worst a nuisance since it limited their export options for younger cattle. In these prosperous years, the embargo was inconsequential. After all, they had everything they wanted on this side of the Atlantic.

Canada's official indifference to the embargo was exhibited during the Imperial War Conference in 1917. When Prime Minister Robert Borden and Minister of Public Works Robert Rogers journeyed to London in the spring of 1917 for the conference, the embargo was on their agenda, but only to dispel the stigma it had attached to Canadian cattle. To them, it was a disease-related matter and no more. At one point during the debate on 26 April, Borden said that as long as the slur was removed, "if it is desired to protect the cattle industry in the United Kingdom, then let it be done."[28]

Doubtless, Borden and Rogers were surprised when the president of the Board of Agriculture, R. E. Prothero (later Lord Ernle) promised much more. Prothero admitted that the embargo was based on erroneous grounds and that the import of Canadian store cattle was desirable given plans for increased arable acreage in Britain after the war, the need to augment depleted British cattle inventories, and the probable reduction in the Irish role in producing store cattle.[29] A subsequent resolution was passed to "remove the embargo on Canadian cattle as soon as possible." According to the Duke of Devonshire, Canada's Governor General at the time, both Borden and Rogers left London convinced beyond all doubt that the embargo, along with the stigma attached to it, would be totally removed after the war.[30]

Borden might have had reason for disquiet had he been aware that the Colonial Secretary, W. H. Long, who had chaired the meeting, had been the President of the Board of Agriculture when the embargo had been made permanent in 1896. He might have picked up on the way Long had taken issue with Prothero during the meeting for admitting that the embargo had been imposed in error, or the manner in which he neatly turned the discussion back to an argument for removal of the stigma. If Borden had noted the above, he would not have been surprised at Long's subsequent turnaround when he stated that Canada should be exempt from the Disease of Animals Act but that it would have to be accompanied by a clause that nothing in the excepting act permitted Canada's cattle to be landed as stores.[31] This statement bolstered an admittance made outright by the Board of Agriculture in 1919 that animal health was not the issue.[32] Reinforced by a resolution in the House of Lords supporting the embargo and by the outspoken support of vested interests like the Royal Ulster Society, the Ulster Farmers Union, the Royal Agricultural Society and other rural organizations worried by the diminished consumer demand for beef,[33] Prothero, now Lord Ernle, issued a public statement in 1920 to the effect that his words at the Imperial Conference in 1917 had been misinterpreted.[34] Inquiries in the British House of Commons from Scottish Members of Parliament about the merits of removing the embargo met with flat refusals from two successive presidents of the Board of Agriculture, Lord Lee of Fareham and Sir Arthur Griffith-Boscawen. The British had clearly drawn their battle lines. At this point, the Canadian government had little interest in the British debate.

As the year 1919 closed, the debate on the embargo's removal was a British affair, with agricultural interests in England pitted against the largely Scottish graziers who wanted Canadian stores. Given the relative disinterest of Canadian cattlemen, basking as they were in the heady atmosphere provided by good prices and a healthy U.S. market, the whole issue of the embargo's removal was a matter of British political preference. In 1918 Canada's niggardly 2 percent share of the British imported beef market was entirely devoted to frozen beef. At the time, no one in Canada cared about Britain as a market for Canadian live cattle—not the federal government, and certainly not the Alberta stockmen. The axiom that the U.S. market was the only crucial variable affecting the success of the western Canadian cattle industry was already well entrenched.

## Positive Impacts

Aside from its profitability, the return to prosperity was positive in other ways. First, and most importantly, it proved the viability of livestock raising in the province. The sudden emergence of a lucrative market, combined with recurring drought conditions, put cattle raising in clearer perspective both commercially and in terms of land use. Gross statistics show the sudden and dramatic impact of the open American market on Alberta. In the three year period 1914 – 17, the value of cattle in the province rose from $28.98 million to $77.70 million.[35] Between 1911 and 1921, the number of beef cattle in Alberta went from 11.3 percent of the nation's total to 16.4 percent.[36] All segments of the industry grew, including purebred breeders, stockyard operations and beef packers. Between April and June 1917, the value of export cattle to the United States from southern Alberta exceeded $1 million.[37] Two years later, a trainload of cattle one-third of a mile long with an animal value of almost one hundred thousand dollars left the Edmonton stockyards under contract bound for North Dakota. In gleefully noting the prices paid in the United States for common cattle, the contractor affirmed that he would be sending two trainloads a month if he could procure the stock.[38]

Attention to breeding reversed a longstanding trend that had resulted in an alarming deterioration of quality in western Canadian herds. In 1916 the *Farm and Ranch Review* reported on the unprecedented demand for purebred stock, or as one breeder noted, "never before in the history of the west have such uniform high prices been paid."[39] The improved quality was reflected in prices paid at the Calgary Bull Sale. In 1911 a total of 104 animals brought an average price of only $96.49.[40] Six years later, 462 head were sold at an average price of $306.00.[41] In referring to this sale as the largest of its kind in North America, the *Farm and Ranch Review* reported on the "complete change from four or five years ago when breeders were afraid to enter their best animals."[42] A year later in 1918, a record 779 purebred animals were sold mostly to local ranchers in what was advertised as the largest bull sale in the world.[43] As prices climbed higher, individual records were set. A Shorthorn bull calf went for $5,000 in 1919, while two years earlier Frank Collicutt of Crossfield had paid $11,900 for Gay Lad 40th, a quality Hereford bull.[44] Also in 1917, Alberta cattle began competing in the Chicago Stock Shows. In that year an Alberta Hereford took third place in what was described as "one of the finest classes of Herefords ever exhibited there."[45]

The growing demand for purebred stock was reflected in 1917 through the establishment of provincial associations for the three major breeds, Shorthorn, Hereford and Aberdeen Angus.[46] Their subsequent role in advancing their breeds brought a greater level of general awareness and preference, and lent credibility to controlled crossbreeding experimentation. This distinct increase

*Frank Collicutt ranch, Crossfield, 1924 (ND 9-98).*

in the number and quality of purebred herds was aided by various government incentives that assisted farmers and ranchers to secure better sires as well as female stock.[47]

The period also saw the emergence of a new type of successful stock grower, one that was neither a rancher nor a grain-oriented mixed farmer. Operating on much smaller land acreage and concentrating on the livestock end of business, the new operators pursued top prices with their quality animals. Typical was Frank Collicutt from Crossfield.[48] A New Brunswick native who arrived in the West as a teenager with his family in 1890 and who later married the daughter of Calgary's first mayor, Collicutt worked first as a range rider before spending six years as a cattle buyer for Pat Burns. Capitalizing on his experience and knowledge of the cattle business, he bought an American-owned purebred Hereford herd in 1912, supplemented it with further purchases in 1914, and then spent huge sums to acquire two high-quality bulls in 1917 and 1919 from Paris and Son of Missouri. These bulls, Gay Lad 40th and Gay Lad 16th, helped consolidate his Willow Springs Hereford Stock Ranch as one of the country's premier breeding operations and the home of what was commonly recognized as the finest Hereford herd in the country.

Another individual to take advantage of the prosperity was Lachlin McKinnon of the LK Ranch in the Dalmead Shepard area east of Calgary.[49] McKinnon had begun ranching in 1894 but with the growing shortage of range grass he had sold the bulk of his cattle by 1914 and had followed the widespread move into grain farming. After 1916, however, under the irresistible influence of favourable market conditions, he began rebuilding his depleted herds. By 1919 he was buying cattle in lots of two hundred and feeding them on surplus grain. By utilizing his own feedlots, he forged a business that would make the LK Ranch one of the most successful and diversified cattle operations in western Canada.

## Mixed Blessings

Despite its benefits, this prosperous period reinforced the industry's heavy export orientation to the detriment of the local market. The traditional belief that the best-quality cattle should always be reserved for the export market was consolidated during this period. Local markets like Calgary and Winnipeg were considered outlets for cattle below export standard.[50] The *Calgary Herald* cautioned ranchers in 1915 to send only their very best to Chicago and referred to the Calgary Stockyards as being best for fat dairy stock and second-grade steers.[51] This relative indifference to the local consumer market also affirmed the belief that high export prices and quotas predetermined domestic consumer levels. Referring to a later crisis in the Canadian beef cattle industry, one senior spokesmen blamed it on "the unpalatability of most of the beef offered for sale, a situation brought about by a traditional reliance on the export market to provide the primary incentive for the improvement and finishing of our cattle."[52] As late as 1942, the editor of the *Lethbridge Herald* noted that "Canadians are not getting now and seldom did get beef of export quality."[53]

The sudden emergence of a ready market for stockers and feeders induced large-scale movement of one- and two-year-old animals to the U.S. Midwest. The higher prices diverted thousands of stockers and feeders from their usual destinations in the finishing areas of Ontario and Quebec and the farms of western Canada to the American corn belt. Alarmed at the domestic implications of so many young unfinished cattle leaving the country, the federal

Department of Agriculture intervened in 1916. Through the Car Lot Policy, farmers purchasing stockers and feeders at western Canadian stockyards could ship their animals back to their farms free of charge.[54] Other government measures to restrict stocker and feeder exports by restricting licences were resisted strenuously. The *Farm and Ranch Review* in arguing for an unrestricted free market appealed to patriotic fervour by insisting that a steer fattened in Iowa would contribute more meat to the war effort than one marketed at a lighter weight in Canada.[55]

The movement of feeder cattle to the United States indirectly vindicated a longstanding belief, first articulated by Duncan MacEachran, that western Canada was not suited to the finishing of beef cattle. The heavy exodus of stocker and feeder cattle to the corn belt was rationalized as not only the best and most logical, but probably the only real solution open to western Canadian cattlemen. The *Calgary Herald* wrote in 1917 that Canada was not equipped to prepare Canadian beef for the market.[56] Two years later, the Alberta Department of Agriculture echoed the consensus by reporting that "the large number of stockers and feeders shipped across the line … has proved very profitable and a good industry is being built up. The importance of this market should be impressed on the breeders of this province and every effort taken to hold it."[57] The belief that the best possible relationship in the industry was between U.S. corn-belt farmers and Alberta breeders was established in this period and maintained well into the modern era.

The good times and the American market removed the need to fatten and finish cattle in large numbers. George Lane believed that Alberta's underutilized feeding potential meant a differential of about 1.4 million head in the province's cattle population.[58] In all likelihood, this period saw proportionally fewer well-finished animals than in the earlier ranching era. The former British market had at least reinforced the need for well-fattened animals. Though some farmers were actually ensiling grain for feeding purposes during this period, they were the exception rather than the rule. Experimental farms concentrated on forage crops, not finishing programmes. Ranchers were encouraged to plant non-native forage crops and, where possible, to explore the possibility of alfalfa production.[59] Any widespread attention to the proper grain-finishing of livestock during this period was usually devoted to swine.

The traditional reasons were given and showed little or no advances from the earlier period. Alberta Livestock Commissioner W. F. Stevens echoed the

*Winnipeg Stockyards. Winnipeg was the largest beef cattle marketing centre in western Canada, a role generally underappreciated because of the city's widespread association with grain (NA 2183-2).*

consensus when he said in 1915 that fattening cattle on grass and hay alone was sufficient.[60] Profitability was stressed in 1917 by the *Calgary Herald* when it observed that it was cheaper to send cattle to the feeding areas of the United States. Mixed farmers endorsed this contention through their tendency to dispose of their entire grain crop for instant cash rather than risk using surpluses to feed and finish their cattle.[61] The *Farmers' Advocate* commented in 1917 on the number of cattle flooding the Winnipeg markets due to the fact that their owners did not want to bother with winter feeding them.[62] It was stated in 1917 that 90 percent of the livestock feed produced in Canada went to the United States.[63] Part of the federal government's rationale in introducing its Car Lot Policy in 1916 was to encourage farmers to utilize their own surplus grain for finishing cattle. Despite experiments with barley, it was not accepted as a suitable replacement for corn.[64] The reluctance to maintain cattle finishing programmes in Alberta was linked to an enduring contrary mentality. In 1916 the editor of the *Farm and Ranch Review* wrote exasperatedly, "the sooner the farmers in Western Canada realize that we have to feed to make our business pay the sooner we will be independent."[65] The tendency so evident by the end of this period to market Alberta cattle in an unfinished condition was to continue into the next decade.[66]

In spite of breeding improvements, the bulk of Western cattle still lacked competitive quality. Though bull prices increased in Canada during this period they still lagged behind U.S. levels with the result that many quality bulls went south.[67] In 1919, Canada's Livestock Commissioner told the Agricultural Committee of the House of Commons that of the 743,250 cattle slaughterings in Canada in 1918 only about 5–10 percent were fit for export.[68] A year earlier, the Alberta Dominion Livestock Representative was quoted as saying that Canada possessed a reputation for producing *cattle*, rather than *quality* cattle.[69] Probably the most telling example of the poor quality of Western cattle came in 1919 when an Argentinean cattle expert toured the West to see if resident herds posed a threat to the Argentinean beef trade. Two months convinced him that Argentina had nothing to worry about. Referring to "the tremendous number of cattle that were not that good," the Argentinean felt that "it will be a good many years before we fear your competition."[70]

## The Dominance of Ranching

Of all groups, the ranchers profited most by the prosperous times. It was they who benefited most by the marketing practices that were established during this period. By the end of the period the ranchers had emerged as the spokesmen for the entire industry in western Canada.

The ranchers' pre-eminence in the export market was consolidated during this period. In the early period they had plied the British market with their four-year-old grass-fed steers. The emergence of the American market gave them an even greater role. With their volume sales often made through American commission agents, the ranchers dominated the lucrative U.S. market. It was they who sent the fat cattle to Chicago, and more importantly, it was they who furnished the quality feeders to the American Midwest. The notion that the growth and survival of the western Canadian cattle industry was predicated on the American feeder cattle market was very much a rancher-dominated philosophy. Accordingly, their breeding programmes, their lobby interests, and their relative disinterest in the development of a feeding industry were associated with an overriding need to maintain the American export market.

The ranchers' need for an organized voice to protect their export interests resulted in the consolidation of the Western Stock Growers' Association as a powerful lobby for ranching interests. The WSGA, although dating to 1896,

*Cattle in dipping vats on the Black Tail and Ross ranches, Milk River, 1920 (NA 3914-20).*

had never been a particularly forceful body.[71] Its main contribution had been in orchestrating early mange control activities and related range matters. Even the lobbying efforts to secure the formation of the Ranch Investigation Committee in 1912 were associated more with private individuals than with the WSGA officially. After 1914 it was virtually moribund, its headquarters in Medicine Hat indicating its ranching priorities. In 1916 its president admitted that "we have come to the parting of the ways, and that unless ... we can demonstrate our usefulness ... we might as well go out of business."[72] The WSGA had difficulty retaining a permanent secretary and as late as 1919–20 no one paid membership fees. The distance between its two main focuses in the foothills area of the Rocky Mountains and in the dryland tracts of southeast Alberta made cohesion more difficult.

It took a threat to the new American market to force the stockmen into strong organizational action. In early 1918, imported cattle infected with mange had alarmed American officials and had resulted in the imposition of a blanket quarantine on southern Alberta and south-west Saskatchewan. The immediate reaction to this threat was the formation of the Cattlemen's Protective Association of Western Canada (changed to the Stock Growers' Protective Association of Western Canada [SPGA] in 1920) to stamp out the disease and to remove the quarantine. Meetings were held between federal officials and local ranchers and a promise secured from the Veterinary Director General that the quarantine would be lifted if cattlemen would co-operate in a veterinary-supervised programme which involved two separate dippings of all cattle in the infected areas. This was carried out with such efficiency in early summer 1920 that the Minister of Agriculture was able to state "it was, it is believed, the first time on record that the department was able to obtain the united co-operation of practically all the livestock owners in the area." The quarantine was lifted in August 1920.[73]

The ranchers' swift and concerted response had shown how important the American market had become. Equally important was the message that only a well-organized and efficient group could hope to gain Ottawa's attention. For instance, the WSGA admitted in 1922 that the main reason Saskatchewan's provincial taxes were lower than those in Alberta was due to the former's stronger organizational voice.[74] In 1921 the more effective SPGA merged with the WSGA to take advantage of the latter's charter that gave it greater power over brand inspections outside Alberta. Operating as the Stock

Growers' Protective Association for a short time, the newly constituted group reverted to the older and more familiar Western Stock Growers' Association in 1923. The merging of the two ranching areas into one organizational voice and the subsequent battles looming over the American tariff both unified and ensured the primacy of ranching interests in western Canada's largest stock association.

While the need to protect the American export market was crucial to the ranchers during this period, they also found themselves beset with other issues. One concerned the collapse of the boom in 1920 and its effects on the industry. Another involved land issues.

## The End of Prosperity

The period of prosperity evaporated as suddenly as it had begun when market factors and land issues combined to send the cattle industry into sharp decline. The sudden collapse in prices in 1920 was compounded by a growing fear of a return to the dreaded tariff promised by the new Republican administration in the United States. Second, the process of land deterioration, while only partly caused by stockholders, had become sufficiently serious to pose major problems for the industry.

The dramatic downturn in livestock prices, which had been supported by the extraordinary wartime economic circumstances, was perhaps inevitable. As the world markets stabilized after the war, agricultural prices dropped, severely affecting countries like the United States and Canada, whose agricultural production had expanded greatly to meet wartime needs. Canada's pre-war cattle numbers were about six million head. By 1918–19 they had swelled to over ten million head, easily the largest proportionate increase of any major cattle-producing country. By 1920 the effects of these inflated inventories began to manifest themselves. The first ripples came in the middle of the year. Cattle prices for good butcher steers in Toronto fell from $15.02 per hundredweight to $14.59 between June and July 1920. The downward spiral continued. By the end of the year they were below $10.00 per hundredweight, and in July 1921 had hit $6.84, falling even further over the later part of the year to close at $5.61 per hundredweight.[75]

The collapse of world agricultural prices together with the stabilizing of wartorn European markets heralded a return to a global policy of protectionism. By 1920 several countries, including Italy, Spain, Belgium, Switzerland, France and Great Britain, were considering extensive tariff revisions.[76] The United States was no exception. Yet, as the tariff threats mounted in the second half of 1920, the WSGA did nothing. The *Farm and Ranch Review* seemed aware of the pending troubles when it wrote in November 1920, "we fiddle while Rome burns." At this stage however, the stockmen's inactivity showed that they believed that their industry and the American market had become interdependent. They were wrong.

# Land Issues

Land issues combined in four ways to produce uncertainty in the cattle industry by the end of this period. First, mixed farming suffered a setback. The accelerated process of land degradation affected leasehold tenure. Farmer and rancher were thrown into conflict. Finally, the costs of land usage rose dramatically following the collapse in beef prices.

The arrival of the agricultural frontier and the consolidation of leasehold tenure in non-agricultural areas resulted in new spatial distribution patterns for beef cattle by 1915. The population focus moved north of the Bow River where it was concentrated in mixed farming enterprises in the Red Deer River area and farther north in the Edmonton districts. To the south and east in the shortgrass country of the brown soil zones, large leaseholds and open CPR and Crown land enabled grazing enterprises. Arable land in the foothills was devoted to grain and mixed farming, while cattle and sheep contested the pastoral uplands of the Southwest.[77]

The rhetoric of mixed farming had begun around 1912 in response to rising beef prices, the first ripples of uncertainty over wheat farming, and the diversification potential associated with irrigation. Typical of the promotional fever was the ready-farm concept developed by mixed farming advocate Dr. J. G. Rutherford, who negotiated with the CPR to have instant mixed farms available on railway lands in the irrigated belt. By 1915 there were seventy such "ready-made farms" on irrigated CPR lands. Farmers wishing to buy livestock from the CPR on credit in 1916 had to plant ten acres of alfalfa as a condition of purchase.[78] The railway company also encouraged the planting of mixed pastures on irrigated lands by donating seed on the condition that an equal area of land would be seeded at the farmer's expense.

The provincial government endorsed mixed farming in 1917 through the Livestock Encouragement Act (also known as the Cow Bill). Under this act, the government guaranteed individual loans of up to five hundred dollars at 6 percent interest to farmers to buy livestock, providing they organized themselves into an association. Hailed as a major breakthrough since it enabled farmers for the first time "to buy stock on no other credit than the livestock itself," the Cow Bill helped an average of 226 associations to buy $1.5 million head of stock between 1917 and 1919.[79] Other government measures to encourage mixed farming included a baby beef competition at the Calgary Fat Stock Show in 1917, and the entrance of an Alberta herd at the Chicago International Stock Show. The federal government maintained its interest in sponsoring mixed farming. Addressing the House of Commons in 1919, Dr. S. F. Tolmie, Chairman of the House Agricultural Committee, cautioned that he "did not know of any greater responsibility that the federal and provincial governments have than the encouragement of mixed farming across the Dominion of Canada."[80]

Yet, despite intense promotion by both the government and the railway company, the popularity of mixed farming did not increase as expected. The main reasons were expense and the continuing allure of wheat farming. Conversion from grain to mixed farming was expensive. Livestock demanded water requirements that grain did not. Well digging or dugout provision was time-consuming, expensive, and often futile. Forage crop seed was costly. For example, Northern Crown alfalfa seed was $26.50 per hundredweight in 1915, while the price for Gold Standard brome seed hit $29.50 per hundredweight in 1920. The need for barns and silos in addition to grain-growing equipment provided further financial burdens. Furthermore, the diversion of potentially profitable wheat fields to a non-marketable commodity like hay or forage for a period of up to five years was a risk many farmers refused to take. One study has postulated that in the ten-year period 1910−19, a farm of 360 acres would have made 20 percent more by staying in grain farming as opposed to turning it in to a mixed farm with ten head of cattle.[81] Other factors were at work dissuading mixed farming. Historian Paul Voisey has argued that farmers lacked the bookkeeping skills to enable them to measure hidden costs like depreciation or to accurately calculate the real profitability of a given farm product such as cattle or hogs as opposed to hay or grain. Furthermore, when set against wheat and other grain crops that did not spoil and could tolerate delays in shipping without loss of quality, livestock marketing presented a much higher risk factor.[82]

The post-war depression hurt the mixed farming initiatives. When their notes came due in 1922, many farmers could not afford to pay back the money they had borrowed under the provisions of the Cow Bill. Eventually the province was to lose $1.4 million, two-thirds of its expenditures made under this bill. In referring to the Cow Bill, the Canadian Pacific Railway Department of Natural Resources felt that it should have applied to dairy stock only. In its opinion, the purchase of beef stock was too risky for most mixed farmers to undertake.[83] Any cautious advances mixed farming might have made after 1912 were negated completely by the depression of the early 1920s when the worth of the more capital-intensive livestock component fell dramatically.

The renewed appeal of agriculture hurt mixed farming, for if cattle did well during this period, grain did even better. The bumper crop of 1915 and a 50 percent increase in the price of wheat led to the conversion of more land to grain. In his report for the year 1916, the Inspector of Ranches reported that "owing to the exceptional crop of 1915, the granting of leases for grazing purposes is getting more difficult to settle satisfactorily as much land that was heretofore looked upon as worthless from an agricultural standpoint is now being entered for that purpose."[84] Statistics bear out this continued reliance on grain farming. Between 1911 and 1921, the number of occupied farms in Alberta rose from sixty thousand to over eighty thousand, and the percentage of the province under farms went from 10.9 to 18.4. The average per-acre value of farm property increased from $28.37 to $33.06.[85] The value of field crops rose by over 800 percent, compared to about 250 percent for cattle.

The appeal of wheat dominated all other factors. After 1915 farmers renewed their familiar confidence in wheat farming. One farmer who had offered his farm for sale for eight hundred dollars in 1914 found it was worth eight thousand dollars after his sixty-three-bushel-per-acre yield in 1915.[86] In his well-documented history of the Upper Oldman River Basin, Barry Potyondi noted that by 1916 many farmers in the area had doubled their money over the previous five years.[87] George Lane threshed two hundred thousand bushels of wheat in the fall of 1917, while in the same year Charles Noble had fourteen thousand acres under wheat at his Nobleford farms.[88] By 1920 wheat acreage in Alberta had tripled over 1911 figures. In that year, wheat had comprised a little over one-third of the total value of field crops. In 1920, at over $92

*Harvesting on Arvid Carlson's farm north of Bow Island, 1915 (NA 4046-3).*

million, wheat values stood higher than 65 percent. The corresponding drop in the proportional value of both oats and barley indicated that while cattle were profitable, the best profits were in wheat. As the *High River Times* gleefully noted in 1917, "When did the old term 'as good as wheat' mean as much as it does now? Never!"[89]

In their enthusiasm for wheat, wartime farmers broke land everywhere they could. Dorsey McDaniel, who utilized open range country north of Wayne to sustain a profitable beef cattle operation, was forced to yield to homesteaders set on growing wheat in what was clearly sub-marginal agricultural land. The Alberta government aided the rush to wheat growing. Using the short-term rationale that newly broken land was initially up to three times as productive as older farmlands, Alberta Department of Agriculture officials followed a policy of increased wheat acreage in the province. In 1918 Alberta was divided into sixteen districts under the control of supervisors whose task was to see that land breaking was carried out to the fullest extent.[90]

The predictable result of these agricultural incursions into pure grazing country was the ongoing land degradation that gripped southern and southeastern Alberta after 1916. A decade of intermittent droughts devastated the dry belt areas of southern and southeastern Alberta. The dust bowls that marked former farms were, to quote one author, "the baneful results of the repetitive tearing and rendering of the soil."[91] On many of these grain farms, the long-range implications of groundbreaking in arid areas clearly had not been realized. A government official in 1915 had commented on a patch of ground that had been broken in 1885 as having "never grown back to its natural state."[92] William Pearce had preached against the practice since the 1890s. The first to feel the effects were the dryland areas of eastern Alberta. Many of the 30,888 mixed and grain farming enterprises in the dryland areas began suffering mightily from the recurring droughts. In 1918 a CPR sale of twenty thousand acres of farm lands south of Brooks and Tilley to settlers from North Dakota was cancelled due to the drought.[93] Although the farm abandonment catastrophes belonged properly to the next decade, the foundations were being laid in the beginnings of drier years after 1916. Distance was another factor. The annual convention of the WSGA in 1916 referred to farmers simply giving up and leaving because they were too far from a railroad to market their crops profitably.[94] The result was abandoned and ruined land.

The larger stock growers on leaseholds suffered also. First, many were overgrazing. The stipulations on stocking rates in grazing regulations reflected official interest in securing maximum usage of the land. The concept of range carrying capacity was little-understood as witness the fact that grass conditions were not a factor in assessing leasehold stocking rates. After 1914 it was a maximum of thirty acres per animal regardless of location—a ridiculously low number, as time was to prove. Accustomed to an extended period of favourable grazing conditions, ranchers, too, seemed to accept the notion of unlimited grass. Indeed, when A. E. Cross was asked by the Minister of the Interior to comment on the 1914 grazing regulations prior to their issuance, he argued that the stocking rate of thirty acres per animal, while quite satisfactory for dryland areas, was far too stringent for the foothills region.[95] In fact, according to the regulations the Minister could compel a leaseholder to stock more cattle if he deemed it necessary. In 1919, for example, a leading official in the Department of the Interior felt that grazing lands in southern Alberta should be stocked more heavily.[96] Most certainly, the period of favourable prices encouraged stock growers to overstock their ranges and leases.

Thus they were caught unawares by the unprecedented and sustained period of drought, a situation compounded by the harsh winter of 1919–20 which

*Burying dead cattle on Bill Chaffin's ranch in the Blackie area following the infamous May blizzard of 1919 (NA 2245-1).*

depleted stocks and forced several ranchers into bankruptcy. Already burdened with lower feed stocks following a dry summer, ranchers faced a cold, snowy fall with intermittent chinooks that left a deep crusty blanket of snow on the ground. A three-day late-spring blizzard decimated the already weakened animals. Stock and financial losses were catastrophic. One Milk River rancher with a herd of twelve thousand worth one hundred dollars per head lost three thousand animals to the winter, only to find that the remaining nine thousand were worth only fifty dollars per head a year later.[97] Under government emergency policies over one hundred thousand tons of feed had to shipped in from the north, while 31,350 head of cattle were freighted free of charge to feeding areas north of Edmonton.[98] Old-time rancher Bert Sheppard recalled that those who had borrowed heavily for adequate feed supplies during the winter found themselves bankrupted by high prices in the fall a year later.[99] In comparing that winter to its fearsome predecessor of 1906–07, one rancher estimated that because of the greater investment in cattle, the winter of 1919–20 really dealt the industry a more severe blow.[100] Another long-time rancher later reminisced that "no one in the business ever quite recovered from that year."[101]

The chronic feed shortage of 1919 persisted through the early 1920s. Any available feed became prohibitively expensive. Hay that cost the McIntyre ranch five dollars per ton in the fall of 1919 jumped to over thirty dollars per ton a few months later. A carload of hay from Ontario sold in High River during the winter of 1919–20 for eighty dollars a ton. It was estimated that the cost of feeding an animal through the winter was at least 50 percent of the value of the animal, even before the severe drop in cattle prices. The formation of associations to take advantage of government aid to bring hay supplies from the Peace River country were desperate responses to extreme times.

The federal government reacted to these worsening conditions in two ways. Displaced farmers were encouraged to relocate north and become ranchers. An amendment to the 1914 grazing regulations granted twenty-year leases on land north of the North Saskatchewan River and allowed flexibility respecting size and stocking numbers. This incentive failed through lack of interest. A dry-belt MLA told the Legislature in 1922 that "you would have to take shot guns as well as railway cars to move the people of Alberta out of the dry belt."

The federal government's next move was more ominous. The three-year cancellation clause was reintroduced into the existing grazing regulations in 1920, a measure which sent shudders of alarm through the leaseholders.[102] While it could be argued that the reason for federal wariness over solidifying long-term leases was related to an Alberta initiative to secure control over natural resources, the government's rationale in again threatening security of leasehold tenure was also linked to a lingering antipathy towards large-scale leasehold operations.[103] The limit of twelve thousand acres per lease in the regulations of 1914 was designed to encourage smaller operations, and in particular mixed farming.[104] Yet there were also leases issued under previous regulations encompassing much larger acreage. Ranchers were given no preference when a cancelled or expired lease became available. The system of bidding gave preference to adjoining farmers, and in cases of multiple bids for the same lease, the inspector of ranches had the prerogative of dividing the lease up or turning it into community pastures.[105]

This threat to long-term leasehold tenure emphasized the growing friction between the ranching and farming communities over grazing land deployment. The emerging issue of community pastures was a good example of these differences of opinion in the cattle raising community. Community pastures were essentially grazing leases in sub-marginal areas under the control of the surrounding farmers. They were hailed as a logical extension of the mixed farming philosophy in that they enabled bona fide grazing within areas primarily used for crops. The idea of community pastures in lieu of leaseholds had been touted as early as 1914 but had not gained much political credence, probably due to the favourable economic conditions and to the recovery of the new grazing regulations. Its re-emergence towards the end of the decade in southern Alberta was not surprising given the worsening impact of drought conditions. In 1918 two Alberta MLAs petitioned the federal government to cancel all leases in the foothills area and turn it into a community pasture.[106] The United Farmers of Alberta went on record in asking that no lease be renewed until farmers in the immediate area had had an opportunity to organize for a group application. Both governments were convinced that community pastures provided a possible solution to the problems of ruined grain farmers in dryland areas.

The move towards community pastures was greeted with dismay by the big leaseholders, who saw them as a retrograde step far worse than the unrestricted open range practices of the 1880s. To them it increased straying and rustling and led to diminished herd quality. It also necessitated cross-fencing and encouraged overstocking and land degradation.

Added to the uncertainty over leasehold tenure was the growing financial burden on both leased and deeded lands. As long as beef prices ensured a reasonable profit margin, lease rental costs and taxes were accepted as necessary evils.[107] Since the late 1880s, annual rental rates on crown land were stabilized at two cents an acre, a figure based on an arbitrary assessment of all Western grazing land at twenty-five cents an acre with 8 percent interest.[108] The doubling of the rate in February 1919 to new leaseholders was an official reaction to prosperous times.[109] Other rental rates increased during this period. Leases on school lands were raised from six cents to ten cents per acre in 1919, while grazing rights in forest reserves cost the rancher eight cents per animal per month for a seasonal permit.

Provincial land taxes on leased lands were more contentious. Stock growers contested the province's right to tax federally leased lands, via court actions and the formation of associations like the Medicine Hat Stock Growers' Association in 1913. Ultimately unsuccessful, they had to face the inevitability of provincial taxes, which varied according to municipal district but for the most part averaged from two to four cents per acre per year.

If the rentals and taxes on leased lands were becoming excessive, the taxes on deeded land were even worse. The differentials between taxes on leased and deeded land were considerable. In 1922 A. E. Cross paid $5.20 tax on a

*Western Stock Growers' Association Annual Convention, Palliser Hotel, Calgary (NA 2928-25).*

quarter section of leased land. A deeded quarter in the same township cost him $26.34 in taxes.[110] One stock grower who ranched only on deeded land told the Southern Alberta Survey Board in 1921 that he paid roughly fifteen cents per acre in all taxes on deeded land, whereas leaseholders in the same area were only remitting 5.75 cents per acre.[111] In 1921, it cost $67.50 to raise a five-and-a-half-year-old steer on leased land. It cost $96.00 to raise a similar animal on deeded land.[112] The increasing financial hardships impacted heavily on leaseholders as well, since their operations included both deeded and leased land. In fact, the building restrictions on leased lands virtually precluded leasehold-only operations.

In many ways the "golden era" mirrored its ranching era predecessor and was more a negative than a positive factor in terms of the overall growth of the beef cattle industry in western Canada. The post-war depression had underscored, yet again, the high vulnerability of the livestock industry. The economics of the cattle cycle had made its impact felt as never before. Security of land tenure had been eroded, and the enduring appeal of cash crop farming continued to militate against responsible land use in many areas of the province.

Moreover, the prosperous years 1914 – 19 reinforced traditional notions about how the industry should be best managed. The export market was more important than ever, with a better American version simply replacing the British one. The appeal of wheat, and a ranching philosophy that equated industry success with supplying quality feeders to the U.S. market, delayed cattle feeding in the province. The Alberta cattle industry had become inextricably bound to the U.S. market.

The chief differences with the ranching period lay in a growing awareness of land degradation and an early identification with the principles of range management. Also, the new times had seen the birth of a true organized voice for the stockmen, one that was prepared to deal with wider issues rather than with day-to-day range-related problems. That these wider issues emphasized the ranchers' dependence on the export market was to become abundantly clear during the next decade.

FOUR

# Change Out of Necessity, 1921 – 30

*A traditional reliance on the export market provides the primary
incentive for the improvement and finishing of our cattle.*
R. S. HAMER, 1928

THE 1920S WERE A WATERSHED IN THE DEVELOPMENT of the Alberta cattle
industry. First, the sustained period of market instability, particularly in
the vital export sphere, modified the traditional attitudes of beef
producers. Second, rangeland vulnerability was recognized for the first time.
Finally, the collective voice of the WSGA denoted a willingness by stockmen
to become involved in the promotion of their industry.

## Markets

Statistics reveal the dramatic downturn in the cattle industry everywhere in
the country. Between 1920 and 1930, the value of cattle sold off Canada's
farms declined by 40 percent. The number of packing plants dropped from
eighty-six to seventy-six and sales fell by more than $76 million during the
same decade. An animal worth seventy dollars in 1918 was valued at thirty
dollars in 1924.[1] Good-quality bulls sold for as low as fifty dollars at the Calgary
Bull Sale in 1923.[2] The best year for cattle exports between 1920 and 1930 was
1920, and throughout the decade the annual value of beef exports did not
reach one-third of the 1919 figure. Alberta's share of the nation's cattle dropped
from 16.4 percent to 14.1 percent between 1921 and 1931 and by a total of four

hundred thousand in the years 1921–25. One telling example of the woes of the industry was the Canada Land and Irrigation Co. Ltd.'s sale of a herd of 751 head in 1924. The 300 wet cows, 400 steers and heifers, and 18 bulls brought an average price of $2.84 per hundredweight.[3] Lamenting on the number of maturing bank notes facing hundreds of farmers and ranchers in 1921, the *High River Times* called the cattle industry "a hollow-eyed weakened ghost of its former self."[4]

These declines were related to two broad factors. First were the global economic difficulties which accompanied the stabilization of the world's markets after World War I. Countries like Canada that had vastly increased their agricultural production during the war years were particularly affected. More specific in terms of the Alberta cattle industry were restrictions in the all-important export market, a situation exacerbated by increased cattle inventories between 1914 and 1920. In the peak years 1918–19, Alberta contributed about 9–10 percent of total marketings. In 1921 the corresponding figure was 13.25 percent.[5]

# The Export Market

The export market continued to be the most dominant force in the Alberta cattle industry, or to quote one contemporary expert, "Canada is irrevocably wedded to a live cattle export trade."[6] In this period, curtailment in the export market forced changes in the industry. The severe restriction of the American market, the inadequacy of the replacement British market, and the failure of the experimental Oriental market all combined to place the Alberta cattle industry at a crossroads by 1927–28.

## The American Market

As has been seen, the presence of a free American market had become the most important constant around which the Alberta cattle industry had organized itself after 1913. It functioned both as a safety valve supporting domestic prices, and allowed the type of beef cattle operations considered most suited to Alberta conditions. The best fat four-year-old range-fed cattle went to Chicago, a venue described in 1922 as the end of the line for every major shipper in Alberta. The bulk, however, were lighter, younger animals destined for the feeding areas of the Midwest. Since these feeders represented around 90 percent of Alberta's beef cattle sales in 1922, an outlet for them was the mainstay of the industry. John Reid, Secretary of the Canadian Livestock Exchange, remarked in 1922 that "nothing is so important to Western Canada, not even the embargo, as free entry into the U.S. of range cattle in feeder shape."[7] Three years later, C. W. Peterson editorialized in the *Farm and Ranch Review* that "if I were to be offered the fulfilment of one solitary wish in the interests of western agriculture, I should without hesitation name the free admission of lighter cattle to the United States."[8]

The closure of the American market took more than a year to take permanent effect. True to its promise, the newly elected Republican administration in the United States lost little time in amending the tariff. Live cattle were targeted by American tariff proponents, who felt that Canadian cattle imports in the post-war period contributed to the collapse of prices in 1920–21.[9] In May 1921 the Young Emergency Tariff became law. Under this tariff live cattle from Canada were subject to a prohibitive levy of 30 percent or three cents per pound. The *Farm and Ranch Review* summed up the tariff's impact with the statement, "Cattlemen are going down for the last time."[10] Then on 9 September 1922 President Warren Harding signed the Fordney-McCumber Tariff Bill which imposed a levy of 1.5 cents per pound on cattle weighing less than 1,050 pounds and two cents per pound on those weighing over 1,050 lb. Though less severe than the Young Emergency measure, the Fordney-McCumber tariff was a daunting levy.

The restricted American market affected the industry in several ways. First, it added to the economic depression in Alberta. The wholesale price index for animal products fell from 149.9 to 95.1 between 1920 and 1923. Overall, the value of cattle shipments out of the country dropped from $21 million to $3 million following the Young Emergency Tariff. Alberta cattle prices that were $10.75 per hundredweight in 1918 were $3.88 per hundredweight in 1922, and by 1925 had risen to only $5.11 per hundredweight. It was said that the price of cattle in the province dropped $15.00 a head following the imposition of the tariff.[11] One Calgary sale in August 1921 returned the owner a total of $110.00 for twenty-three head. Rising costs of production compounded a worsening situation. In 1924 the tariff was blamed on market conditions that saw feeders and stockers bringing less than the cost of production.[12] In the worst years 1921–22, rancher A. E. Cross figured that it cost him $114.74 to raise a four-

and-a-half-year-old steer, and that the imposition of the tariff meant a loss of $30.34 per head.[13] Under these appalling circumstances, many cattle operators went out of business. As herd liquidations climbed to over two hundred thousand, rural newspapers carried full-page listings of tax sales for farm lands heavily in arrears.[14] Some ranchers were forced to mortgage everything they owned.[15] Those who stayed afloat by borrowing heavily against a lifetime of investment in cattle and land faced the most harrowing times in the history of the industry. Many were refused financial assistance. Responding to an allegation in the Alberta Legislature that the banks were "squeezing stockmen," Agricultural Minister George Hoadley agreed that the financial institutions had not treated the cattlemen with the best of consideration.[16]

### Battling the Tariff

The importance of the American market to the Alberta cattlemen was demonstrated in the sustained efforts by the WSGA to have the tariff lifted. The nine-year battle tested the strength of the stockmen and solidified their organized voice. It also revealed that the federal government had different priorities on how the beef export industry should proceed than did the stockmen.

The WSGA was initially slow to respond to the threat of a reimposed tariff, believing that it would be a temporary measure. A. E. Cross's Chicago stock agent advised him that inside sources in Washington believed that the tariff was likely to be postponed indefinitely.[17] The WSGA's initial response was a bland caution to the federal government not to announce reprisals.[18] While several letters were sent to federal cabinet ministers in 1920–21 urging them to counter any American tariff measures, their tone indicated that the WSGA considered that the issue would be concluded amicably through political channels.[19] Even after the temporary tariff was extended indefinitely in November 1921, the WSGA still seemed content with encouraging the federal government to act on the stockmen's behalf. As late as 20 January 1922, the president of the WSGA expressed optimism that "given the feelings of U.S. statesmen, arrangements can be made between the federal government and the United States."[20] Certainly Charles W. Peterson, editor of the *Farm and Ranch Review*, believed that the tariff would not last. "I cannot bring myself to seriously believe that a trade agreement will not be entered into with our neighbours.... I cannot contemplate the possibility of any government failing to take such a step."[21] Peterson was voicing the consensus among stockmen that the tariff on Canadian cattle would be waived through some reciprocal concessions on the part of the Canadian government.

By the spring of 1922, it became clear that the Americans were intent on instituting permanent tariff legislation. It was only then that the WSGA became more proactive. Its first reaction was a strongly worded message to Ottawa calling for the government to act on the stockmen's behalf, and to effect "the only practical relief possible of attainment which this association believes can permanently save our industry."[22] Four weeks later, it amended its total opposition to the tariff, and asked that it be excluded only from feeder cattle.[23] In the same month a seven-man committee was struck to spearhead an anti-tariff campaign. This committee engaged Theodore Knappen, a well-known professional Washington lobbyist.[24] Knappen had close contacts with the president of the American Farm Bureau Federation, through whom he hoped to solicit the support of bureaus outside the Midwestern corn belt. He felt that he could use the differences of opinion between the House of Representatives and the Senate to advantage and secure a lower recommended levy of one cent per pound. Above all, he was of the opinion that success was contingent upon a change in public opinion.[25]

Aside from the hiring of Knappen, the WSGA's campaign to overthrow the tariff took several forms. A barrage of appeals to the federal government was maintained. Several Chicago livestock commission houses that had a lot to lose and nothing to gain through tariff legislation were persuaded to lobby Washington politicians. They also furnished the names and addresses of thousands of corn belt farmers.[26] Letters asking for support were sent to various livestock associations and to prominent individuals in the United States. In its most active measure, the WSGA circularized thirty thousand farmers in the corn belt requesting them to press their respective organizations and representatives for free entry of Canadian feeders.[27] Finally, the agitation was coalesced in Canada through the support of the press, and of livestock and business organizations.

The WSGA was fortunate in having a very able spokesman in Jack Dillon, its honorary secretary. The Irish-born Dillon had spent his teenage years in Chicago, and had attended the University of Chicago. He had cultivated extensive contacts in the American cattle business through his work as a cattle buyer in the Dakotas. He had been a livestock commission agent in Iowa and a rancher in Montana before arriving in Alberta in 1918 to manage the OH

Ranch west of High River.[28] An active member of the Liberal party, Dillon was also well-known in Canadian political circles.

The Canadians based their case for tariff redress on four main grounds. First, they argued that Canadian cattle made very little impact on American production, contributing less than 1 percent of marketing receipts, and while this figure was minuscule in U.S. terms it meant a loss of fifteen dollars per head on the Canadian side.[29] Second, it was pointed out that deprived of the American market, Canadian exporters would simply send more cattle to Britain where they would be in direct competition with American beef. Third, Canadian stockmen pressed the fact that their production costs were no lower than those in the United States and therefore should be exempt from the levelling intent of the tariff.[30] Fourth, it was held that the Canadian trade helped the Midwest farmer because Alberta feeders, being from a harsher climate, tended to fatten faster and more efficiently on surplus corn than similar cattle from the Southwestern states.

The WSGA and its allies continued to be optimistic right through the summer of 1922. Chicago commission agent Charles Robinson felt that the wrangling over the tariff would go on until a "duty satisfactory to all can be arranged."[31] On 18 July Knappen informed the WSGA that when the House of Representatives returned from vacation they would react to public opposition to the tariff and press the Senate privately to recast the bill.[32] Ten days later, the WSGA told the Canadian Bankers' Association that five hundred letters had been sent to Washington from corn belt farmers and that "we are led to believe that our campaign can have good results."[33] A. E. Cross was told by his commission agent that a prominent railroad man and "a great wire puller" knew a Senator who was going to effect an amendment to the bill allowing free entry of Canadian cattle.[34]

As it turned out, the anti-tariff campaign began too late to gain significant grassroots support. Theodore Knappen felt that action should have been initiated months before when the bill was still in its early stages—especially when it was before the Ways and Means Committee.[35] Once the bill had reached the pro-tariff Senate, there was little hope for any downward revision. By early September, just days after the circulars went out, the WSGA knew it had all been for nothing. Explicit comments from American-based sources showed clearly the pro-tariff mood in Washington. The Chicago commission houses on which the WSGA had relied on so heavily for help and that had lent their private support were loath to make their views public. "We are hesitant about placing the matter in front of our customers as we do not wish to antagonize any one of them whose business means money to us and whose views on the subject are radically different." When providing the list of corn belt farmers to the WSGA, the same sentiments were expressed: "Do not mention our name."[36] When Cross asked his commission agent to support the Canadian cause at the National Livestock Association Convention in Denver, he demurred on the grounds that despite his personal position "it would be slow suicide for me to go on record re admitting Canadian cattle free of duty."[37]

Potential supporters in Washington were just as nervous. One American stock agent said that politicians in Washington were afraid to support the Canadians. He referred to friends "entertaining fifteen Senators for lunch, all afraid to go on record as being in favour of allowing Canadian cattle to come in free of duty as they thought it might prevent them from coming back to Washington."[38] One Washington lobbyist said that politicians were as "afraid of bucking the tariff as they were of a polecat."[39] The signing of the Fordney-McCumber Tariff Bill in September 1922 devastated western Canadian cattlemen. Their main hope of redress lay in an option which, if recommended by the newly-formed Permanent Tariff Commission, gave the President the power to effect a 50 percent reduction in the tariff of any item.

The WSGA's response to the tariff was announced in the *Lethbridge Herald* on 14 October 1922 in the form of a renewed lobbying campaign in the U.S. corn belt for the 50 percent reduction.[40] In November the WSGA approached the banks, the Canadian Pacific Railway and the Canadian government asking for financial assistance. By the end of the year the banks had donated twenty-two hundred dollars and the CPR five hundred dollars. Another six thousand dollars would soon be added unofficially by the federal government.[41] Further support was solicited from the United Farmers of Alberta, the Western Canada Livestock Union, the United Grain Growers, the stock growers' associations in Saskatchewan and the British Columbia Interior, and various city boards of trade. Circulars were sent south calling for support for the 50 percent reduction. WSGA delegates attended the American Farm Bureau Federation Annual Convention in December and were successful in having the Illinois Farm Bureau file for the reduction.[42] Delegations attended other livestock association meetings. Other futile measures showed the desperation with which the WSGA pursued its goal. It tried unsuccessfully to arrange a meeting with

Vice President Coolidge during his visit to Vancouver in the spring of 1923. In March 1924, the association attempted to use a current proposal to bring dairy stock into Canada from Wisconsin under the tariff as a lever to secure reciprocal arrangements for Canadian beef cattle. In May 1924 the WSGA asked C. W. Peterson to press the Canadian case on his forthcoming trip to England with the American Agricultural Editors' Association. At an International Livestock Convention in Calgary in July 1924, several Canadian speakers regaled their audiences, which included hundreds of American representatives, on the importance of a healthy cattle trade between the two countries. Despite these efforts, however, the tariff remained and the WSGA opted to wait until its application for the 50 percent reduction was considered by the Permanent Tariff Commission.

The WSGA renewed the battle again in 1925, its confidence buoyed by falling cattle inventories and rising prices in the United States, the surfeit of corn in the Midwest, and by President Coolidge's announcement in late 1924 of a special committee to investigate agricultural conditions. The WSGA again marshalled local and regional support. The federal government was provided with biographical information on Coolidge's agricultural committee along with each member's position regarding the tariff.[43] The circular route was pursued in the Midwest states, this time with specific support being sought among the various farm bureaus in Iowa, Illinois, Indiana, Ohio, Pennsylvania, Wisconsin, Minnesota, Kansas, Nebraska, and Missouri. In this circular, the WSGA backed off its earlier plea for tariff abolition in favour of temporary suspensions in the fall.[44] Theodore Knappen was rehired. Invitations were extended to American stockmen to visit Alberta and see the quality feeders available to them.[45] The big Chicago packing houses were wooed with the argument that Canadian cattle now being sent to England were negatively affecting their beef exports.[46] In spite of these efforts, however, the WSGA had to be content with only a small measure of success. In December 1925, the Permanent Tariff Commission requested statistics on western Canadian cattle numbers, the available supply of feeders and the number of purebred breeders.[47] Yet three months later, Knappen advised the WSGA that no hope could be held in the Tariff Commission and that the only measure of success lay in a highly unlikely joint resolution by Congress.[48]

The Americans raised a glimmer of hope in the beginning of 1928 when R. A. Wright, president of the Western Canadian Livestock Union, was invited

*Rancher and Senator, Dan Riley. Born in Prince Edward Island, Dan Riley came west to Calgary in 1883. After working as a cowboy and with William Roper Hull on the 25 Ranch, he acquired his own land on Willow Creek in the Porcupine Hills where he became a successful rancher and farmer. A longtime president of the WSGA, he enhanced the association's influence with his elevation to the Senate in 1927. Fondly remembered for his comment, "the more I see of Ottawa the more I like High River," Riley died in 1948 (NA 67-2).*

to Washington to present his views on the cattle situation in western Canada.[49] Later that year, two representatives of the Permanent Tariff Commission visited Alberta to inquire into costs of cattle production in western Canada.[50] The Canadian stockmen were both surprised and confused by the implications of the visit. To C. W. Peterson, the visitors' real intent was to prove lower production costs in Canada as a reason for raising the tariff still further.[51] The WSGA felt, however, that their purpose was to lower the tariff and that "the pendulum was swinging in [their] favour."[52]

If the WSGA was surprised by the sudden interest of the Permanent Tariff Commission, it was devastated by the later news that "powerful interests were likely to compel the Administration to increase the present tariff rate, 100%"[53] At a special Directors' meeting on 15 January 1929, a new committee borrowed five thousand dollars to mount a campaign designed not to lower or remove the tariff, but to maintain it at its present level. Jack Dillon and WSGA president Dan Riley were sent to Washington to meet with sympathetic parties. Forty-three hundred pamphlets, "Does the Tariff Help the Livestock Industry?"

and another thousand, "Do U.S. Manufacturers Want Canadian Business?" were distributed throughout the United States. Arrangements were made to have the Canadian case published in several newspapers in the Southwestern states where the move for the tariff increase on cattle was the strongest.[54] Other stock organizations became involved. The Western Canadian Livestock Union began active negotiations in Washington, and a month later the Winnipeg Livestock Exchange sent its own representatives to Washington. Further assistance in lobbying the Americans was obtained from the Canadian Chamber of Commerce and from senior American railway officials.[55]

The Canadians were hopeful. The *Farm and Ranch Review* reported in June 1929 that "it may now be taken for granted that the duty on feeder cattle will remain unchanged."[56] As late as September, Dan Riley wrote to Prime Minister Mackenzie King informing him that a fellow Alberta Senator had heard it from tariff proponent Senator Smoot that Smoot was not pressing for any increase on live cattle.[57] A month later A. E. Cross's Chicago commission agent, referring to the tariff debate as "a cat and dog fight," was hopeful that the debate might prove so protracted that the tariff would ultimately be left the way it was.[58]

The Canadian efforts were all in vain. Herbert Hoover's commitment to tariff increases had been anticipated by the House Ways and Means Committee, which had already begun work on a new tariff bill before he made it official during his first months in office. Typically, the work of this committee was towards upward tariff revision.[59] When President Hoover ultimately signed new tariff legislation known as the Hawley-Smoot Bill on 17 July 1930, the Canadian stockmen's worst fears were realized. A prohibitive 30 percent levy (three cents per pound) was placed on live cattle entering the United States. It was the bitterest pill yet. In admitting failure, a subdued Dan Riley told the WSGA Annual Convention in 1930 that future judges would deem the association's efforts and expenditures justified, and that now the only hope for the western Canadian cattle industry lay in the domestic market.

It cannot be denied that through this whole period of tariff agitation, the WSGA and western Canadian cattle interests had enjoyed a measure of support in the United States, especially from corn belt farmers. In 1925 Professor James Boyce of Cornell University said that the tariff was costing the American farmer $300 million a year. The Illinois Farm Bureau went on record early as being in favour of free entry for feeders. The Montana Stock Growers' Association supported the Canadians and stated that it "did not believe that the exporters of feeder cattle to the United States would be of great menace to the industry."[60] The Indiana Agricultural Association referred to the Canadian case in 1923 as "absolutely unanswerable."[61] In July 1925, the WSGA claimed to have the support of nine state farm bureaus.[62] Supportive articles appeared in U.S. journals condemning the tariff on Canadian feeder cattle. The Chicago *Daily Drovers' Journal* commented On 7 July 1922 that it "won't hurt us any to be just a little generous in considering the tariff claims of our neighbour to the north."[63] A Fair Tariff League was formed in the United States, and in a subsequent pamphlet the league made mention that the tariff on feeder cattle was of no benefit to the United States but a distinct injury to Canada.[64] Meetings were held in the Midwest and resolutions passed condemning the Fordney-McCumber Tariff. The Chicago Livestock Exchange went on record as supporting the removal of all or part of the tariff.[65] Supportive comments came from influential individuals, including the dean of agriculture at the University of Minnesota and a member of Coolidge's agricultural committee, and Gray Silver, legislative representative for the American Farm Bureau Federation.[66] The American livestock commission agents continued to press for tariff relief. Robinson told Cross in 1924 that he was "keeping up a steady fire in Washington … and doing some missionary work on behalf of our Canadian friends."[67]

In the case of the Hawley-Smoot Tariff, the Canadian stockmen's disquiet was subsumed in the widespread general opposition to the inherent global dangers of mounting protectionism. President Hoover was under intense pressure not to sign the bill that was later described as the "culmination of one of the major mistakes of the Hoover administration."[68] As it was, the Senate narrowly approved the Bill 44–42, and then only by enticing five Democrats to support it. Newspapers like the *Milwaukee Journal*, the *Chicago Tribune* and the *Christian Science Monitor* were loud in their condemnations.[69] John D. Black, a professor of agricultural economics at Harvard University, wrote in 1929 that "it is greatly to be doubted whether what our agriculture would gain from excluding Canadian farm products almost entirely is worth the ill will that would be aroused by it."[70]

Yet the fact remains that the energetic efforts of the Canadian stockmen were doomed from the start. First, the protectionist mentality in the United States was evidenced by powerful lobbies from the range states, and in particular by prominent spokesmen in the U.S. Senate. The American National Livestock

Association's curt dismissal of the Canadian case and its total misinterpretation of the Canadian argument evinced its thoroughgoing opposition and indifference.[71] It was also held in some quarters that Canadians had profited unfairly from the Underwood Bill of 1913 and that the Canadian government had broken good faith by not enacting reciprocal legislation. T. W. Thomlinson, the secretary of the American National Livestock Association, told the Western Canada Livestock Union in 1927 in blunt terms that he believed the tariff should stay until the United States had reached the absolute limit of its production.[72]

Regardless of pockets of support, the fact remained that all three American farm organizations were in favour of the tariff.[73] Some of the corn-belt farm bureaus contacted by the WSGA in 1925 for support were not as enthusiastic as expected and parried the issue with references to a divided membership and a need to examine the matter more thoroughly.[74] In Nebraska, for example, it was pointed out that while farmers in the eastern part of the state might have welcomed Canadian cattle, livestock operators in the western areas had no such inclination. One expert who supported the Canadian cause doubted its chances of success given the overall agricultural mentality in the country.[75] Other references were made to the agricultural community being misled over the implications of the McNary-Haugen Bills and how tariff issues were caught up in a web of misunderstandings.[76]

Finally, the agents responsible for implementing the 50 percent reduction were either unsympathetic or ineffective. The Permanent Tariff Commission had become increasingly notorious for its reluctance to act. In 1926 Knappen said that its only tariff reduction to date had been on hair brush handles, and two months later wrote of the Commission having "lost all credibility."[77] President Coolidge's agricultural commission was described as "a group not likely to come out with radical proposals that would be embarrassing to Coolidge."[78] Coolidge himself had gone on public record as saying that he would never yield on the issue of tariff reductions on cattle.[79] Herbert Hoover was personally committed to tariff increases and had waged his 1928 presidential campaign on that platform. In his inaugural speech he referred to the need for agricultural relief and to tariff revisions which could not be postponed.[80]

## Federal Disinterest

North of the border, the real stumbling block to the WSGA's campaign for tariff relief lay in lack of support from the federal government. A major hurdle to effective dialogue was the absence of a permanent official representative in Washington, and unarguably the Canadian government's diplomatic strategies were limited by its subservient place within the British imperial embassy structure in Washington. A Canadian correspondent in Washington told the Western Canada Livestock Union in 1925 that if Canada had been officially represented during the initial negotiations, the original tariff on cattle would never have been applied.[81] Over the ensuing years the WSGA and other livestock agencies petitioned the government consistently and unsuccessfully to place an official representative in Washington to promote Canadian trade interests.[82] It was only in 1926 that the Canadian government finally broke from the British diplomatic umbrella and appointed Viscount Vincent Massey as its first independent ambassador in Washington. It was not enough, apparently. As late as 1928, the WSGA asked the federal government for a grant of ten thousand dollars so it could deploy its own permanent Canadian representative in Washington.[83]

Throughout the WSGA's campaign, the federal government's attitude wavered between disinterest and resignation. Following the imposition of the Young Emergency Tariff, the *Farm and Ranch Review* commented that "Canadian statesmen did not prove equal to the occasion." Again in 1926, the same journal noted that "no official steps have been taken to put the issue squarely to proper U.S. authorities through the usual channels."[84] Calgary Senator and presumed supporter of the stockmen, James A. Lougheed, told the WSGA bluntly in March 1921 that the subject of the tariff was strictly an American affair.[85] When first confronted in the House of Commons with the impact of the Young Emergency Tariff on the cattle industry, Sir Henry Drayton, the Minister of Finance, said that the discounted Canadian currency prejudiced the American cattlemen, and a day before the tariff became law denied even having heard of it.[86] Then, when matters heated up in 1922, the Liberal Minister of Finance, the Hon. William Fielding, hinted that the fault really lay with Canadians who had turned the Reciprocity Bill down in 1911. He admitted discussing the matter with the U.S. president, but then shrugged off the issue with the comment, "whether anything will come of it remains to be seen."[87] While expressing his willingness to reopen negotiations with the United States, Fielding closed the door to reciprocal arrangements by affirming in the House that any proposed tariff reductions would not apply to the United States.[88] Officially the government refused financial aid to the stockmen in 1926 and 1928, and excused itself on the grounds that it could not interfere in another country's business.[89]

Support from the Department of Agriculture was conspicuously absent. Agriculture Minister, W. R. Motherwell advised the WSGA in 1925 that in his opinion the case was hopeless and that it was best "to face the facts of the situation."[90] A year later, when questioned in the House of Commons, he again dismissed the issue, saying that Canada had forfeited its opportunity for free trade in 1911. He added that an opportunity might come round again but "that it [did] not look like it."[91] In 1925, Livestock Commissioner H. S. Arkell, in congratulating the WSGA for securing some staunch allies in the United States, declined any government involvement on the grounds that "our hands are tied," and that "we think the initiative best lies with you."[92]

The only support in Ottawa for the western Canadian anti-tariff initiatives was both covert and tentative. The most significant example was a six thousand dollar grant to the WSGA to help the latter's campaign in 1922–23, secured through the personal sympathies of Hon. Charles Stewart, Minister of the Interior and former Premier of Alberta, who made his co-operation contingent on the WSGA not revealing that it had ever asked for a grant or that the government had ever issued one.[93] During the WSGA campaign in 1922, the federal government allowed the widely respected Duncan Marshall, its Livestock Commissioner and former Minister of Agriculture for Alberta, to travel through the corn belt and solicit support as long as he did not do so in an official capacity.[94]

Aside from its one-time indirect financial "gift," the federal government's sole policy of support for the stockmen lay in its amenability to American initiative. In his budget speech of 1923, Finance Minister Hon. William Fielding offered to insert a clause in the tariff regulations stating that if the President agreed to utilize his 50 percent reduction option on cattle, the Canadian government would make similar reductions "as may be deemed reasonable by way of compensation."[95] Three years later, in response to a request to define the term "reasonable by way of compensation," an Order in Council was issued promising to reduce duties on cattle in proportion to any American reduction.[96] Both measures assumed American initiative. Then, clearly in response to the Hawley-Smoot Tariff, Finance Minister Charles Dunning introduced into Canadian Customs regulations in 1930 what he termed "countervailing rates" on 495 products including livestock. Under these powers, the government could respond in similar kind to tariff increases by another country.[97] That it essentially meant that the United States could then virtually define the Canadian tariff on 495 items, or that a similar duty on Canadian live cattle was inconsequential to American livestock interests, was conveniently overlooked. The secretary of the American National Livestock Association put the matter squarely if patronizingly in 1927 when he said "The reduction of your duties on cattle or beef would mean absolutely nothing to us except the helping out of a very excellent neighbour."[98]

This "hands off" official approach eroded the stockmen's confidence in Ottawa. The WSGA's final campaign in 1929 to maintain the tariff assumed no government assistance. In May 1929 when Senator Dan Riley was on his way to Washington to lobby on behalf of the WSGA he was dissuaded by Vincent Massey, who informed him that Canada's best chances lay with the resident American opposition to the tariff.[99]

The failure by the Canadian federal government to support the Western stockmen in their campaign transcended apathy, diplomatic lost opportunities, or even fear of American reaction. Put simply, it was simply not worth the effort, particularly given the federal government's overall agricultural agenda. While the cattle industry was of vital importance to Alberta and even to western Canada, it was too small to generate a great deal of political interest at the national level. Furthermore, any opposition to the tariff was regional, not national. The intensive cattle-feeding enterprises in the Eastern provinces were aided by the American tariffs through a more plentiful supply of quality feeders from Western farms and ranches. Not surprisingly, the WSGA could elicit no support from Ontario cattle interests during its campaign.

Canada's trade policy was built around the protection of central Canadian manufacturing interests, with agriculture and related industries being of secondary importance. One has only to note the rhetoric during the elections of 1911 that had pitted free trade and agricultural interests against the protectionism of the national policy. Nothing had really changed by the 1920s. The low tariff on Canadian food imports, for example, showed a federal policy prepared to sacrifice agriculture for lower food prices and protection in other sectors.[100]

Likely, there was another issue involved in the federal government's refusal to help the Western stockmen battle the American tariff. Prime Minister Mackenzie King's bland references to tariff stability and the futility of economic reprisals shrouded his government's real preferences.[101] Trade with Britain was preferable to dealing with the unpredictable Americans. Unlike the stockmen who viewed the British export cattle market as unsuitable and at best a stopgap measure until the Americans came to their senses, the federal government saw it as part of a much wider policy involving a British destination for all Canadian agricultural products. By the end of the decade these products were wheat, pork, and butter in that order, with beef cattle a distant fourth. The result was that, regardless of the American market, the federal government preferred Canadian live cattle to cross the Atlantic. This strong difference of opinion between the Western stockmen and official government policy over export markets was to carry on well into the post-World War II period.

A combination of factors conspired against the western Canadian cattlemen as they unsuccessfully fought to overthrow a threatening tariff. First, they had to deal with the protectionist mentality in the United States knowing that they needed the U.S. market more than the Americans needed them. Second, they faced an intractable federal government whose entrenched trade policies preferred a British market for meat products while favouring central Canadian manufacturing interests over those of agriculture. That they were a minor, regional voice simply rendered a difficult goal virtually unachievable. Their long, futile struggle hammered down another plank in the platform of western Canadian grievances, and evinced a cattlemen's dimension of the also-doomed progressivist movement of the same era. Along with the experience and respect the WSGA had garnered during its tariff campaign, a valuable lesson had been learned. They had seen how much their industry counted in federal priorities. Those with long memories would not easily forget.

The tariff campaign drew the battle lines between the WSGA and the federal government over export priorities. The stockmen knew for certain where their best market lay, a fact vindicated by their frequent success in making money on U.S. export cattle despite the tariff. In fact, it could be argued that the cow-calf operation, later the mainstay of Alberta cattle operations which began in this period, was a reaction to the U.S. tariff and to higher prices south of the border.[102] As one mixed farmer commented in 1928, "we can jump the tariff wall easier with a cow and calf because we can get away with less duty."[103]

## The British Market

The British market for Canadian cattle during this period provided the only export alternative solution. Yet, despite the wholehearted endorsement by the federal government, it remained tenuous between 1923 and 1926, and in the latter year collapsed completely. By the end of the decade it remained a high-risk gamble.

## The Removal of the Embargo

Rumblings over the imposition of the tariff spurred the campaign to remove the British embargo on Canadian store cattle. This renewed interest in the thirty-year-old embargo must be viewed entirely in a reactive sense. Had the American market remained open, the British market would have been inconsequential to western Canadian cattlemen.

Canadian strategy to defeat the embargo took two main forms. The first was to convince the British that lifting the embargo posed no threat to Britain's herds nor to her beef industry. The federal government, not surprisingly, was most co-operative. Canadian Prime Minister Arthur Meighen addressed the British House of Commons in the summer of 1921, stressing the need for fairness and promising reciprocal tariff concessions if the embargo was lifted. When a group of British editorial writers visited Canada in the summer and fall of 1921, the embargo was mentioned in the several boards of trade functions held in their honour. Often delivered by high-ranking political figures, the accompanying speeches bluntly confronted the visitors with the inequity of using animal disease to mask British protectionist policies.[104] The lobbying campaign was also carried on at unofficial levels and involved high-placed British expatriates to North America. Other agricultural organizations became involved. The powerful United Grain Growers, for example, while declining to become a visible participant, informed the Stock Growers' Protective Association that it "had people working behind the scenes."[105]

Other practical efforts were made to convince the British to change their mind. In the summer of 1921 the provincial government of Alberta sold a herd of selected mixed cattle at Birkenhead in an effort to convince British cattlemen of the health and quality of Canadian herds. Like many previous cattlemen testing the British market, the government took a loss on the sale.[106] Measures were taken in late 1920 by Canadian cattlemen together with vested British interests to establish a feeding association in Great Britain using Canadian store cattle.[107] In June 1921, unsuccessful attempts were made to float the Livestock and General Brokerage Company. Capitalized at five hundred thousand dollars, this company intended to erect feeding facilities and abattoirs in Great Britain capable of handling twenty-five thousand head annually.[108] Though its grand motto, Trade Within the Empire, promised more, this proposed Anglo-Canadian feeding association was really designed to show British beef interests that they had nothing to fear and possibly a lot to gain from lifting the embargo.

The second Canadian strategy was blatantly political. Led by W. F. Stevens, secretary of the Stock Growers' Protective Association, a concerted campaign was mounted to incite resentment in Britain towards the embargo. Stevens, formerly Alberta's first Livestock Commissioner, combined a wealth of experience and knowledge with an unswerving commitment to his cause. His policy was simple: "Our proper place to hit is in the large industrial centres and show that the embargo is tending to reduce labour in Great Britain and will place the meat trade in the hands of American meat trusts and so reduce the supply of home killed beef to the British consumer."[109] His British ally was long-time friend, James Lennox, a prominent Scottish farmer and spokesman for the National Farmers' Union of Scotland. Working through Lennox and E. Watson, chairman of the Free Importation of Canadian Cattle Association, Stevens launched an advertising campaign in the fall of 1920 designed to convince the urban British consumer that the embargo was directly linked to high beef prices. With Lennox promising to have something in the press every day, articles began to appear in newspapers in Birmingham, Sheffield, Liverpool, London, Manchester and other major cities inciting resentment among urban residents. Then in March 1921, the English newspapers of Canadian-born peer Lord Beaverbrook infuriated embargo proponents by turning a by-election involving Sir Arthur Griffith Boscawen, president of the Board of Agriculture, into a bitter fight over the looming spectre of "dear meat."[110] Boscawen's unexpected defeat by the Labour candidate was blamed entirely on the embargo issue, and, more importantly, heralded a significant shift in public opinion. A week later, a meeting sponsored by the Corporation of London and attended by hundreds of representatives from local councils and public bodies across the country went on record as opposing the embargo.[111] With Lord Beaverbrook acting as the Government of Alberta's official representative at subsequent meetings in London's Guildhall,[112] these public forums, representing over 75 percent of the British electorate, were unanimous in calling for the embargo's repeal.[113] That Britain was currently scheduling Irish cattle for the sixth time since 1907 because of foot and mouth disease did little to aid the pro-embargo forces.

In response to this mounting public pressure the British government was forced to take action. In May 1921, it appointed a four-man Royal Commission with the mandate:

> To inquire into the admission into the United Kingdom of livestock for purposes other than for the immediate slaughter at the ports; whether such action would cheapen or increase the supply of meat in this country, and if so to what extent, and whether it is advisable having regard to the necessity of protecting livestock bred in this country from the introduction of disease and of restoring their losses to their pre-war number.[114]

Over the subsequent six weeks, the Commission called ninety-two witnesses to its twenty-five sittings in the Moses Room in the House of Lords. Its report, released in August, recommended lifting the embargo, but warned that its removal, while increasing the supply of fresh beef, would not significantly alter the consumer price of meat.[115] The Canadians, it appeared, had won their victory even if their political tactics had been obliquely called into question.

Despite the findings of the Commission, the British continued to delay bringing the matter to a vote in the House of Commons. As late as February 1922 the reinstated Arthur Griffith Boscawen told the House of Commons that "in view of the almost unanimous opinion of all agriculturalists that the removal of the embargo would seriously injure the industry ... and since the commission itself said that it would not affect the price of meat, then we do not propose to introduce legislation to remove it."[116] It was not until July 1922 that the British yielded to the mounting public pressure inspired by the Guildhall meetings and finally agreed to put the embargo issue to a free vote in both Houses of Parliament.

Both debates were long and acrimonious and pitted entrenched agricultural interests in England and Ireland against a mounting swell of popular opinion best represented by the various co-operative societies, Scottish grazing spokesmen and the disenchanted voices of labour. In the House of Lords, W. S. Long, now Lord Wraxall, succeeded in having a motion passed supporting the removal of the embargo, but which imposed restrictions respecting quarantine and eligibility requirements.[117] Despite the outspoken opposition of Boscawen, the House of Commons voted 247 to 171 for "the removal of the embargo all round." Though the Colonial Secretary, Winston Churchill, delivered a brilliant summation urging his fellow MPs to honour the 1917 pledge, it was obvious that the issue had been carried by urban sentiment. The tally of the Yea votes showed a preponderance of MPs representing cost-conscious consumers in the big British cities.[118] Stevens's campaign, masterminded in western Canada, had won the day.[119] The subsequent Importation of Animals Act which came into effect in April 1923 was hailed as a great success for Canada which once again, ostensibly at least, had unrestricted trade in cattle with the mother country.

### The Federal Government and the British Market

Canadian government officials reacted quickly to the lifting of the embargo. The federal government established connections with British firms interested in store cattle by providing a news service to graziers through the British press. A weekly cable service on the British market was also made available through the press to Canadian producers.[120] Political statements were made. Prime Minister Mackenzie King said in 1923 that he hoped to see "ships in Britain laden with cattle from western Canada," a sentiment echoed by his Deputy Minister of Agriculture, J. H. Grisdale, who foresaw Canadian control of the entire cattle export trade to the United Kingdom.[121] In 1923, Grisdale regaled the Special Select Committee of the House of Commons on Agricultural Conditions with the limitless potential of the live cattle trade to Great Britain.[122] These opinions blended well with those of federal Livestock Commissioner H. S. Arkell, who was adamant that the ultimate market for Canadian cattle would now be in Great Britain.[123] It was a message to be preached loud and often over the succeeding years, particularly by Arkell, who used every opportunity to persuade Western stockmen of the virtues of the British market.[124] Blood, loyalty, and the move towards an imperial preference were all touted as reasons to keep Canada's cattle trade within a proper British spectrum. Other promoters included eastern Canadian cattle dealers and shipping agents, who also downgraded the American market, terming it "something that was 'thar' and then wasn't 'thar.'"[125]

The federal government's seriousness of intent was further demonstrated through several experimental shipments to Britain between 1923 and 1926. Cattle of various ages, weights, and states of finish were chosen from six experimental farms across the country in order to determine the type of product best suited for export in terms of type (live or chilled), price and profitability.

In 1926 the results of these experimental shipments were published. Although they could scarcely be regarded as unqualified successes, the federal livestock branch seemed to think they were.[126]

One outcome of these federal experiments was the resolution of the long-standing chilled meat question. Predictably, the issue of a chilled meat trade had again emerged in the early 1920s coincident with the proposed export restrictions on live cattle. During the embargo campaign, an Ontario-based group had lobbied against its removal on the grounds that an open live cattle market would be detrimental to its own promotion of the dressed meat trade.[127] In 1921 the Alberta Government sent a committee to Great Britain to inquire into the possibilities of starting up a chilled meat trade. Despite the latter's optimism, more astute observers such as WSGA secretary W. F. Stevens and the Western Livestock Union believed that a profitable Canadian chilled meat trade was impossible. Between May and December of the same year, the Harris Abattoir Company of Toronto lost twenty-eight thousand dollars on seventeen shipments of chilled beef to Great Britain totalling 1.2 million pounds.[128] The current average selling price in Britain was $12.98 per hundredweight, $1.64 per hundredweight above Toronto prices. Transportation and other expenses, however, were $3.98 per hundredweight. Further unsuccessful trial shipments were conducted by Canadian packing houses in 1923.[129] Only two of a hundred shipments showed a profit. The federal government ran its own experimental programme in the spring of the same year. Fifty steers, including eighteen from Lethbridge, were slaughtered in Montreal, all classified as "fat," averaging 1,252 pounds and dressing out at a respectable 60.4 percent. Yet once in Britain, the chilled beef suffered in comparison with its Argentinean counterpart and netted a paltry $2.96 per hundredweight. Together the federal and private initiatives proved conclusively that Canada could not compete successfully in the chilled beef market. "Practically impossible" was the official summation of this longstanding dream of chilled beef being the best solution to Canada's beef export problems.[130]

The federal experiments with live cattle shipments were far from conclusive. However, it was felt that cattlemen could make a profit by shipping both long- and short-term store cattle providing they were properly finished and of a lighter weight. While the tone of the reports indicated a measure of caution, there was no doubt that, to the federal livestock experts, the experiments had vindicated the viability of the British market.

Yet on examining the reports closely one wonders at the authors' optimism. Fat cattle, particularly those from western Canada where both shrinkage and transportation costs were much higher, were not successful on the British market. This was not surprising, since stockmen knew that finished fat cattle could not stand the journey and return satisfactory profits.[131] The experiments showed that transportation costs might be as high as 27 percent of the sale price. Lethbridge shippers paid over six dollars more per animal than shippers from Ontario to land animals in Britain. Shrinkage ate into producers' profits. In one batch from Lethbridge, shrinkage was 12 percent on the trip to Montreal. Moreover, the through rate to Montreal ($1.145 per hundredweight) did not allow for extended stopovers in feeding areas in Ontario where the animals could be further fattened before the ocean voyage.

The experiments showed that the British did not want heavy cattle or the thin type of feeder wanted in the United States. Consumer demand in Britain was for a lighter but well-finished animal weighing around a thousand pounds. As one expert put it in 1922, "the type of unfinished or off-graded steer is not wanted and cannot be shipped at an advance over local prices at any time." If the task of landing a thousand-pound animal in the proper state of conditioning was difficult even from the more intensive cattle enterprises in eastern Canada, it was impossible from the more distant western Canadian range operations where the economics of extensive leasehold grass called for four-year-old grass-fed steers or lighter unfinished feeder stock. In disagreeing with government officials like Grisdale and Arkell, respected meat packer John S. McLean, then of Harris Abattoir, told the Select Committee on Agricultural Conditions in 1923 that Canadian cattle were too inferior and of the wrong type to compete on the British market.[132] By the late 1920s, the increasing British demand for "baby beef," meat cut from animals less than a year old and as light as seven hundred pounds, made it even more difficult for ranching operations to compete.

Nor did the federal livestock experts seem worried about other threats. First, the British pound was subject to fluctuations. One shipment resulted in greatly reduced returns because of the pound's sudden deterioration. Uncontrollable factors like the coal strike of 1926 and the packing house war of the same year led to diminished prices. Competition was fierce. The Irish Free State was capable of shipping almost a million animals a year. In 1923 she shipped 812,000 head to Britain compared with Canada's 40,000. The

*Spaying heifers on the Willis Ranch in Eastend, Saskatchewan, 1921 (NA 4021-2).*

Argentine threat was even greater. Canadian shippers were warned to time their arrivals in Britain so as not to coincide with Argentinean shipments. Controlled by U.S. packing interests, Argentinean chilled beef undercut Canadian prices in Britain by five to ten cents per pound. Furthermore, Argentina used its volume capacity to transport large numbers of cattle to Belgium, killing them there and then selling the meat as fresh beef in England the following day.[133] Claiming that the lush pampas country could produce a head of beef for a dollar, one WSGA spokesman blamed the ultimate loss of the British market solely on Argentinean competition.[134]

The Canadian government's infatuation with the British market was not reciprocated in Britain. The Select Committee on Agricultural Conditions was told in 1923 that British butchers generally believed that Canadian cattle were inferior meat animals. Canadian cattle were prejudiced by British policy. Following the Importation of Animals Act in 1923, the British changed the rules. Regardless of their Canadian designation as either fat animals or stores, they were reclassified by British veterinarians at the port of entry. The "fats" were slaughtered immediately while the "stores" could be taken inland for finishing. These new regulations showed clearly that British agricultural interests retained their prejudice against Canadian cattle. For example, from 23 April 1923 to 6 March 1924, of the 28,183 head shipped from Canada to Britain as stores, 10,896 were declared fat and slaughtered at the ports of entry.[135]

In one instance, two identical shipments of designated stores were landed in two separate British ports. One lot was declared fat and immediately slaughtered; the other was accepted as stores and sent inland. The best example, however, came in one of the federal experimental shipments. In October 1923, sixty steers of good beef type—short-legged, thick, well-fleshed animals—were selected from the pastures of the Central Experimental Farm in Ottawa. They were classified as stores, and in the opinion of the federal livestock authorities were two hundred pounds under their finishing weight. Yet when they arrived in Britain all were classified as fat by the chief inspector of the British Ministry of Agriculture and immediately slaughtered. The dressed meat compared unfavourably with properly finished British animals and therefore brought less. The message was quite clear. Differing opinions by experts on both sides of the Atlantic as to the quality of beef on the hoof showed how difficult it was for the average producer to predict the disposition and price of his animals in Britain.

The British made it difficult for the Canadian producer in other ways. Their regulations stipulated that only spayed heifers could be imported as stores, thus adding a further financial and temporal burden to the cattlemen. The importation of breeding stock was prohibited. Other criticisms charged that pulmonary conditions continued to exist in Canadian cattle, and that shipping practices out of Canadian ports were inhumane.

Thus it was not surprising that reality conflicted sharply with the official optimism regarding the British market. Comments from local cattle dealers like "English quotations are quite a bit out of line for us," or "there is little encouragement from that source" were more the rule than the exception.[136] Winnipeg cattle dealer James Speer summed it up in 1927 when he said that the British market could change several times during the same shipment and that there were just too many obstacles to trading there.[137] According to W. F. Crawford, secretary of the Canadian Council of Beef Producers in 1930, the British market was useless and gave no price advantage even before transportation costs were deducted.[138] The WSGA maintained in 1922 that it could never be profitable without at least a 50 percent reduction in transportation costs. As the decade progressed, cattlemen became less and less inclined to export to Britain despite assurances that it was the market of the future. It is also likely that the British market in these years acted as a damper on domestic prices since exporters were forced to buy cheap in order to ensure

*Making sunflower silage, Kerfoot Ranch, Cochrane, 1924 (NA 4286-3).*

a profit. According to one exporter in 1923, he could not afford to buy anything locally for more than eight dollars per hundredweight.[139] The fact that this was only about thirty cents more than current Toronto prices meant that the yardstick of export quality as a price determiner was not working in the producer's favour.

Export figures belied the federal government's optimism. Live cattle exports to Britain between 1923 and 1926 averaged about 80,000 annually, well below any year in the period 1891–1906, dramatically less than those during the open American market years, and nowhere near the 150,000–200,000 deemed necessary to clear national surpluses and maintain satisfactory domestic price levels. And it only got worse. In the four years 1927–30, a dismal annual average of four thousand head made their way across the Atlantic. The limited importance of the British market as compared to the American is revealed by figures which show that, even with the tariff, shipments to the United States exceeded exports to Britain by more than 680,000 head between 1923 and 1930.

The continuing popularity of the American market despite the tariff provided the most telling statistic.[140] American prices were proportionately better than Canadian. A. E. Cross was consistently assured by his Chicago livestock agent of far better prices and profits in Chicago even allowing for the tariff.[141] The effect of the tariff was diluted by the 10 percent discounted Canadian dollar which, when translated into actual figures, meant that it cost

*Bailing alfalfa in the Vauxhall area, 1921 (NA 4800-21).*

about $2.20 per hundredweight to ship a 1,300-pound steer from Calgary to Chicago. Equivalent shipping to Montreal was $1.145 per hundredweight, a differential more than balanced by the higher selling price in Chicago.[142] In August 1925, good butcher steers in Toronto were bringing $7.47 per hundredweight. In the same month, A.E. Cross received $13.00 per hundredweight for his best steers in Chicago. In 1927 he shipped nineteen carloads of cattle weighing an average of 1403 pounds, which returned him $43,500 per hundredweight after paying $10,000 in tariff levies.[143] His price in Chicago was $15.50 per hundredweight. Its Calgary equivalent ranged from $7.15 to $9.50 per hundredweight.[144] A group of Saskatchewan ranchers shipped forty-one carloads of cattle to Chicago in 1925, doubling their money even after paying the tariff.[145] The export figures tell their own story. Between 1920 and 1929, almost 1.5 million head were exported from Canada to the United States, including 204,000 feeders in 1927.[146] In 1921, G. Hutton, superintendent of Agriculture and Animal Husbandry with the CPR's Department of Natural Resources, complained about the presence in Alberta of American cattle buyers, and accused producers of "plundering our birthright." Two years later the journal *American Co-Operative Manager* commented on "the steady stream of cattle to us from Canada."[147] The *Farm and Ranch Review* enthused in 1927 that Canadian cattle "were jumping the Fordney tariff with ease."

## The Japanese Market

The search for markets in Japan began during this period. Hitherto Canada had been reluctant to pursue export opportunities outside Great Britain and the United States. In the winter of 1919/20, entrepreneurial western Canadian stockyard operator H. P. Kennedy toured France, Belgium and Switzerland with Toronto's Grand Champion Black Angus and second-place Shorthorn in an unsuccessful effort to convince Europeans to buy Canadian cattle.[148] In 1924, the Alberta government sent a trial shipment of twenty-eight head to Japan. They sold well at over a thousand dollars above their Canadian value, and averaged around eight cents per pound. However, the cost of getting them to Japan, which included $2,407 in transportation alone, was eight hundred dollars over the selling price.[149] Freight rates brokered by the government of Alberta a year later reduced transportation costs by two-thirds. It was not enough, however, and neither the government nor Calgary cattle baron Pat Burns, who had also conducted trial shipments, carried the experimental trials any further. The Japanese market was too uncertain to warrant the large-scale shipments necessary for significant profits. The fourteen-day voyage, the unpredictability of the yen, the small potential for profit, and the lack of market familiarity in a little-understood country were deterrents. The British market was simply more familiar, and the American market better still, even with the tariff.

The tenuous export market led Alberta producers to consider changes in the way they operated. In attempting to meet export demands for a lighter and younger finished animal, some producers began taking the proper feeding of their stock more seriously. Equally significant was an emerging realization, certainly by industry spokesmen, that the domestic market had been taken for granted, and that its cultivation provided the best alternative to the capricious export trade. But while the rationale for these significant shifts in thinking may have been consistent with difficult times, their adoption flew in the face of tradition and hard economic realities.

# Feeding and Finishing

The merits of feeding and of changing livestock practices increased during this period. The use of a cover crop for winter feeding owes its origins to this

*Luxuriant cornfield, Medicine Hat, 1912. This photograph shows that corn growing was possible in southern Alberta in the pre-World War I period (NA 4061-9).*

period, and was a precursor to later feeding programmes in the irrigated districts. Also, the feedlot emerged as a viable avenue for marketing cattle. In 1925 it was estimated that ten thousand head were being finished in Alberta feedlots. The popular stock and feeder shows, which usually featured a large number of entries attracted by the generous prize money, were designed to encourage the production of finished animals at a lighter weight. Co-operative efforts to promote feeding were made through the establishment of corn and hay associations. The formation of the Southern Alberta Co-operative Association in 1924 represented the first serious efforts in the province to market alfalfa hay from the irrigation districts for feeding purposes. With over a hundred members, the association was selling fifteen thousand tons of alfalfa hay annually by the late 1920s.[150] The tentative beginnings of integration occurred during this period when ranchers began contracting farmers to grain-finish their stock. Farms in the Edmonton area became destinations for feeders from southern Alberta. In 1929 the Red Label Feeders Association in the

Lethbridge area fed cattle on contract at six cents per pound of gain. In the same year, Pat Burns paid Pincher Creek farmers two dollars per head per month to feed yearlings "for as long as the feed lasts."[151]

The beginning of the feeding industry during this period was a direct response to changing demands in the export market rather than to a need to develop a better-quality animal generally. It also showed that the industry continued to be dominated by the 10 – 15 percent of its product which left the country. In 1926 the *Farm and Ranch Review* editorialized on the emphasis placed in developing a beef product suitable to the British market.[152] Three years later, the Eastern Canadian Society of Animal Production noted that "the traditional reliance on the export market to provide the primary incentive for the improvement and finishing of our cattle."[153]

Evidence supports these contentions. The first commercial feedlots in Alberta which included the Burns Feedlot, Calgary (est. 1922), the Livestock Producers of Canada, Edmonton (est. 1924), and the Lethbridge Central Feeders Association, an affiliation of six feeder associations (est. late 1920s) all had the British market as their primary focus.[154] Within months of its establishment, the Edmonton feedlot shipped one thousand head to Great Britain.[155] The co-operative venture near Lethbridge was a specific response to the British demand for finished baby beef.[156] The decline in feeding intensity following the American tariff of 1922 and the closure of the British market in 1926 also demonstrated the close association between finishing and the export market. The traditional notion that export equated with quality remained unchallenged as long as international markets existed.

The federal government's serious support for feeding programmes was linked to promoting the British market. Dominion Livestock Commissioner and British market advocate A. H. Arkell admitted as much in 1923 when he told Alberta ranchers that if they would undertake to winter feed their stock to eighteen months to two years of age, he would guarantee a ready market in the East where they would be finished for the British market.[157] The association of finished animals with the export market was made clear in a 1922 Department of Agriculture pamphlet that informed Ontario feeders that feeding Western cattle for export was "the most pronounced movement we have had in recent years."[158] In its 1924 report the Livestock Branch of the federal Department of Agriculture referred to Britain as the world's outlet for surplus livestock and that Canada should feed carefully in order to hold her

*King of the Fairies, prize shorthorn bull. Imported from England in 1923 by the Prince of Wales to his*
*EP Ranch at Pekisko. Grand Champion, Canadian Royal Winter Fair and Chicago International, 1925*
*(NA 2046-3).*

valuable place within it.[159] In an article published in 1925 in the *Farm and
Ranch Review*, C. W. Peterson equated government measures with specific
policies designed to support the British cattle export trade.[160]

This initiative for feeding and finishing was top-ended, not a grassroots
movement. The provincial Department of Agriculture and the University of
Alberta made concerted efforts to convince Alberta stockmen to finish their
own cattle. In introducing its feeding experiments in 1921, the Department of
Animal Husbandry at the University of Alberta commented, "we believe the
business of finishing cattle will become one of the most important sources of
revenue for the many cattle raisers of the province."[161] Two years later the
provincial Department of Agriculture referred to feeding as "an industry which
should receive every encouragement as the profitable end of the cattle
industry."[162] The feeding experiments at the University of Alberta were to
ascertain the feasibility of finishing cattle on locally grown feeds. Consistent
advice to cattle raisers in agricultural publications, government pamphlets,
and academic articles included information on feed rations, nutrient value,
forage crops, and barley as the northern answer to corn. Scarcely an issue of
the *Farm and Ranch Review* went by without some testimony to successful
feeding. The federal government gave financial backing to the annual Stock

*"Climsland Broadhooks," prize shorthorn bull, EP Ranch, Pekisko, 1921. The man in the background is the Duke of Devonshire, the Governor General of Canada (NA 2046-14).*

and Feeder Show which began in 1923. Other measures, which included a bull lending programme, ongoing feeding trials at the various experimental farms, a permanent feeding consultant in Alberta, and the encouragement of feeding and finishing of livestock through loans and freight reductions, testified to the official commitment to the better finishing of cattle.[163]

These measures were inhibited by both economic and attitudinal factors. Taken together, they resulted in a lack of incentive to cultivate the local markets. Between 1916 and 1924, 183,000 steers and heifers were returned to farms under the federal government's Car Lot or Feeder Freight Policy.[164] Yet the number of feeders which went to the United States in 1927 alone was 204,000.[165] Thus, throughout this entire period the bulk of Alberta cattle destined for local and regional markets consisted of unfinished cattle, or to quote one livestock dealer, "horned half fat cattle that have to be sacrificed because no one wants them."[166] Interest in growing barley for feed declined.[167]

The systematic and widespread finishing of cattle in Alberta was contrary to the way the industry had developed, particularly in the purely cattle-raising

*George Lane's mixed farm, Nanaka No. 1, 1922. Note the presence of dairy stock and hogs (ND 8-121).*

areas. The range-based enterprises were equipped to produce either fat mature cattle marketed off grass or feeders destined to be finished elsewhere. The American market was popular because it received both types of cattle. Alberta ranchers consistently topped the Chicago market with their mature grassers. Over the years, the list included John Mitchell, Pat Burns, Billy McIntyre, and A. E. Cross, who managed the feat six times during the 1920s. The persuasiveness of American livestock agents in assuring an ongoing demand added to the belief that Alberta grass and winter hay was sufficient to produce a cost-efficient product for United States buyers, many of whom preferred range-fed animals. One implied to Cross in 1924 that Canadian range animals were needed since American grass-fed beef was a thing of the past due to conversion of grazing land to dryland farming.[168] Another wrote in 1925 that it did not pay to feed cattle for too long as a good price for grassers was still assured in Chicago.[169] A study undertaken by the U.S. Bureau of Animal Industry concluded in 1941 that beef from a three-year-old range-fed steer was as good as that from a grain-fed feedlot animal in terms of fat and desirability.[170] From a purely economic viewpoint, grass-fed cattle presented a lower risk. It was possible to buy light animals in the spring, feed them for six months on grass, and then sell them in the fall for a lower price per pound than they had cost and still make a profit.

The British market, on the other hand, wanted a light, well-finished carcass which dressed out at 450–500 pounds, exactly the type of animal the western

Canadian operator was not accustomed to producing. Medicine Hat area rancher R. Gilchrist maintained in 1928 that he had to keep his cattle for over three years to make a profit and that the production of baby beef was a blueprint for financial ruin. R. A. Wright of the Western Canada Livestock Union put it simply when he said "the steer at three or four years old on our hard short grass makes us money."

On the mixed farm operations, the practice of feeding cattle was hampered by traditional practices that continued to see cattle as a low priority. In a promotional pamphlet released in 1917, the Edmonton Board of Trade wooed prospective farmers by claiming that raising farm cattle ensured high profits since a straw diet met all winter feeding needs.[171] In 1921, former Alberta Livestock Commissioner W. F. Stevens referred to Alberta farmers as "wheat growers unable to feed cattle."[172] Furthermore, the typical Alberta mixed farms of this period, unlike their late-nineteenth-century predecessors, emphasized grain more than livestock. They contained livestock to dispose of surplus grain or the necessary nitrogen-fixing legume-based forage crops. Not all contained beef cattle. Many preferred dairy stock and hogs.

The presence of dairy stock was a major factor retarding the beef cattle industry during this entire period. It did so in two ways. First was the habit of farmers to raise dual-purpose cattle like Shorthorns and to cross them with dairy Holsteins in order to get larger calves. Heavier weight, regardless of quality, brought higher selling prices. According to Grant MacEwan, a student at Guelph Agricultural College during the early 1920s and the son of a Saskatchewan mixed farmer, "a lot of cattle marketed from mixed farms had a shot of Holstein in them."[173]

Second, in sharp contrast to beef cattle, dairy cattle numbers increased during this period. As early as 1923 the trend elicited a warning from meat packers that "the situation demanded earnest consideration." The mixed farms were a contributing factor. The Alberta Department of Agriculture commented in 1922 on the increased presence of dairy cattle in mixed farm operations.[174] One mixed farmer told the National Beef Cattle Conference in 1928 that "the majority of mixed farmers wants the majority of his cows for milk production." Statistics bear out these contentions. Between 1921 and 1926 Alberta's cattle population fell by 194,540, yet the number of cows milked increased by 45,829. In 1921, 29.8 million pounds of milk were sold in Alberta. By 1926 the figure stood at 65.4 million pounds.[175]

Dairy stock were popular on mixed farms because of the security they afforded. They were safer financial risks than beef cattle. Figures show that between 1921 and 1941, the number of dairy animals bore an inverse proportional relationship to the price of beef cattle.[176] This mingling of dairy animals into what essentially were beef cattle marketings endured well into the 1940s, and explained in part the presence of low-quality beef and the vastly disproportionate number of unfinished animals.

Farmers with cattle were interested in breeding and raising their own, rather than finishing superior animals bred on the range, whether they be stockers or feeders bought at regional stockyards or those delivered on contract from the ranches. Despite the pleas from ranchers like Senator Dan Riley, President of the Western Stock Growers' Association, for farmers to finish more cattle, the involvement of farmers in proper feeding practices was haphazard and nowhere near as popular as feeding promoters hoped.[177] Feedlot owner and cattle baron Pat Burns agreed. In 1922 he wondered why farmers continued to pay him and his men to do a job that should be done on farms.[178]

Many stock owners lacked the expertise to finish their animals properly. The finishing process had to take into account differences in breed, age, and the careful incrementation of feeding rations. The tenor of a government pamphlet directed to Saskatchewan farmers in 1922 stressed problems more than the advantages associated with feeding.[179] The incompatibility of grain with the ruminant digestive system dictated careful and expert feed management to ensure optimum weight gain and herd health. The tendency towards marketing lighter animals was a further complicating factor, since it is much more difficult to properly finish animals which are still maturing.[180] The incorporation of fat into lean meat is much easier when the animal has matured than when it has to be marketed as a long yearling. Improper grain feeding practices often resulted in inconsistent fat dispersement, lower market prices, and complaints from consumers. Commenting on a feeding experiment at Lethbridge Agricultural Research Station in 1929, W. F. Fairfield emphasized the care and management necessary to successfully undertake feeding. He was supported by an agricultural agent with the Canadian National Railways who emphasized the special knowledge prerequisite to the successful production of baby beef.[181] These sentiments were reiterated five years later by the expert, who referred to feeding as "a parlous business which must be entered into with care."[182]

Uncertainty and inherent caution were further contributing factors. There were conflicting arguments on when to buy and sell. The consensus favoured buying when grain prices were low to reduce costs. W. F. Stevens warned farmers in 1920 of inevitable losses in converting high grain prices to beef.[183] Yet Duncan Marshall, former Alberta Minister of Agriculture, argued that it was best to buy when grain prices were high to ensure a premium for the subsequent limited quantity of finished animals.[184] Fluctuating beef and grain prices made it difficult to predict profits. Many farmers, faced with rising costs and shortage of cash flow, preferred to market their grains immediately rather than gamble on future and uncertain prices months ahead. During the First World War, the editor of the *Farm and Ranch Review* criticized the tendency to sell everything and anything for instant cash.[185] According to Grant MacEwan, farmers during lean times resisted change or risk.[186]

The practice of marketing unfinished animals was not restricted to Alberta. It was a national phenomenon. At the fourth annual meeting of the Western Canadian Society of Animal Production in 1930, mention was made that "the greatest problem in connection with beef cattle production in Western Canada arises out of the fact that there is no beef cattle finishing tradition in this country."[187] The speaker was referring not only to a reluctance to finish in the West but to the lack of integration within the industry on a national basis. While western Canadian cattle were marketed in the East as fat animals, Ontario and Quebec farmers did not buy enough Western feeders to guarantee the sort of intensity necessary to integrate the industry. Three contributing factors were at work. First were the high transportation costs of $1.145 per hundredweight from Calgary to Montreal. Second was the lure of the closer British Columbia market which took from between 15 and 25 percent of all Alberta's cattle marketings. The third factor involved the ubiquitous American export market. An open American market meant that eastern Canadian buyers could not compete with the prices being paid in the Midwestern states. When the American market was restricted as it was during this period, domestic prices dropped to the level where they did not warrant the purchasing of Western feeders.[188] And in spite of Livestock Commissioner Arkell's comment in 1923, the British market was not reliable enough to encourage Eastern feeders to gamble on finishing western Canadian light cattle. In the early 1920s, alarm was expressed over the propensity of Ontario farmers to move from beef to dairy cattle.[189] Only in the period of higher prices 1927–28, and in the 1930s when the government arranged transportation deductions, did the eastern Canadian market function as a major source for Western feeders.

Marketing and price factors were crucial impediments to a strong feeding and finishing programme in Alberta. The western Canadian market was not large enough to support one. Finished cattle had to be sent out of Alberta and only the export market would pay the prices justified by production costs. According to Alberta cattle producers, the nub of all their marketing problems was that the domestic market would not pay higher prices for finished beef. The Canada Irrigation and Land Company sold cattle off its Kinlock Farm in January rather than feeding through to spring because it was not worth it financially.[190] The CPR agricultural farm at Strathmore could only make money on a baby beef experiment in 1921 by selling it to the company's own hotels.[191] Statistics taken from the Moose Jaw Feeder Show between 1926 and 1931 showed that production costs exceeded the selling price by ninety-eight cents per hundredweight for yearlings and eighty-seven cents per hundredweight for two-year-olds.[192] R. J. Speers, a Winnipeg cattle dealer, told the National Beef Cattle Conference in 1928 that the prime factor discouraging feeding was its low profit margins. As proof he quoted recent Winnipeg prices where good steers sold at only half a cent more per pound than old cows. Speers further compared the spreads for finished cattle in the United States and Canada—two dollars per hundredweight in Canada versus six dollars per hundredweight in the United States—and blamed Canadian cities for not creating the same demand as American cities. Inadvertently, Speers touched on the crucial issue that producers had failed to realize during most of the period under discussion. The question as to whether urban Canada could be persuaded to pay more for quality beef had never really been put to the Canadian consumer.

## The Domestic Market

This lack of profit for finished animals explained the importance of the western Canadian feeder trade with the United States. It also underscored an enduring deficiency in the cattle industry in Alberta and in the country as a whole. Taken together, the reliance on the export market to determine acceptable domestic price levels and the resulting mediocrity of beef prepared for the home market assumed a very inelastic domestic consumer demand for beef. Compounding this was the fact that retail prices were generally higher than demand warranted, due to packer monopolies and the price-setting mechanisms of the export market.[193] The industry's efforts in the late 1920s to upgrade the quality of beef consumed in Canada was not linked to consumer dissatisfaction nor competition from beef producers elsewhere. It grew from a need to increase national consumption in the light of curtailed exports. Other factors included increasing competition from pork, the "vegetarian fad" of the mid-1920s and an anti-red meat campaign in the schools.[194] The consumer was not yet perceived as a discriminating factor. The importance of the domestic market had emerged by default.

The poor quality of domestic beef was recognized in the early 1920s. In 1922 it was estimated that only 10 percent of all marketings, including exports, were top-quality animals. A year later, the meat packers admitted that "we have not taken into consideration the obvious fact that our markets have been handling enormous quantities of inferior beef that certainly could not be expected to popularize it as a food."[195] The frequency of comments attesting to low quality domestic beef are too compelling to ignore. In 1926 S. F. Tolmie told the House of Commons that the trainloads of cattle being sent to Winnipeg for slaughter looked as though they were "built for speed rather than beef."[196] Another Member in 1927 referred to Canadians as "tough jawed people" who turn to chicken or pork after finding their Sunday roasts just too unpalatable to endure.[197] A Winnipeg cattle dealer commented in 1928 that "Montreal which should be our best customer" is "the dumping ground for the poor beef in Canada."[198] It was alleged that CPR restaurant managers only provided Canadian beef for their trains out of patriotism and would prefer to buy American beef.[199] R. S. Hamer, chairman of the Beef Production Committee, blamed unpalatability for beef underconsumption. The Dominion Livestock Commissioner, who had gone on record the same year as saying that beef was the worst meat on the Canadian market, told the Ministry of Agriculture in 1929 that "the system of merchandising has resulted in the sale to consumers of low quality beef and therefore has discouraged the consumption of beef as a whole."[200] In 1928, the annual per capita consumption of beef was at a ten-year ebb of 50.5 pounds, well down from the decade high point of 58.2 pounds in 1922.[201] A leading meat-packing official in the same year said that 63 percent of Canadian beef would not help to increase consumption, while the other 37 percent hardly bore advertising.[202]

Professor J. P. Sackville of the University of Alberta Department of Animal Husbandry commented in 1927 that better-quality beef would double consumption.[203] Like most sweeping statements it was only partly correct. Other factors beside taste were at work discouraging Canadians from eating beef.

Competition from pork intensified during this period. Swine had been the mainstay of eastern Canadian mixed farms for years, and had furnished the foundation of the Canadian meat-packing industry during the First World War.[204] The hog industry in western Canada grew rapidly during the 1920s. By the end of the decade, pork—and later, bacon—had become the most important product of mixed farming. Two related factors were at work. The American tariff diverted export interest to Great Britain where the demand was for a different kind of hog than the big, fatty animal popular in the United States. The development of the "streamlined bacon hog," or more accurately the leaner Wiltshire side, to compete with the cost-efficient Danish competition, was promoted ardently by the federal Department of Agriculture.[205] The results were obvious on the mixed farms of Alberta. Hogs lent themselves more readily to intensive agriculture than did cattle. They were better suited to diversification on the farm since they could be kept indoors and fed a wide range of food not suitable for cattle. The short hog cycle made them much more adaptable to mixed farm practices than were cattle. They farrowed two or three times a year, and produced litters often numbering more twenty piglets. As a food commodity, pork was also cheaper, and rose more slowly in price than beef in response to increased demand.

Statistics show the tremendous growth of hog production in Alberta. There were about sixty-five thousand fewer hogs than cattle in Alberta in 1920. In the same year the value of cattle sold off farms in Alberta was $10.62 million, compared with $3.1 million for hogs. The annual per capita consumption was 57.4 pounds for beef and 42.1 pounds for pork. By 1925 the number of hogs in Alberta being sold off farms had tripled and were approximating cattle in terms of value. In 1930 there were over three times as many hogs sold off farms than cattle. The value of cattle had dropped by almost $4 million. In comparison, the value of hogs had risen to $4.7 million. Canadians were not only eating more pork, but they were eating more pork than beef.[206] After exceeding beef in per-capita consumption for the first time in 1924, pork maintained a seven-pound per capita advantage over beef in 1927–29.[207] These gains signalled the arrival of western Canada as a major pork-producing region and consolidated pork and bacon as the mainstay of Canadian meat production.

Another barrier to beef consumption was the intense vegetarian campaign in the mid-1920s. Described by critics as a sad carry-over from the aftermath of the war when "new ideas were paraded with equal silliness," the dietary criticisms of red meat were regarded by industry experts as a major factor in the under-consumption of beef.[208] Calling vegetarianism "one of the most dangerous and destructive propaganda this side of the Atlantic," the editor of the *Farm and Ranch Review* downplayed any possible dietary deficiencies of beef by referring to the two-hundred-pound per capita consumption of meat in Australia, and describing that country's male residents as "among the most perfect physical specimens the world has ever known."[209]

*Ha Ha!*

A move to increase domestic production was evident in 1924 through a national Eat More Beef programme, an initiative that the WSGA declined to support for financial reasons. By 1925 leading exporters like A. E. Cross were wondering if the domestic market might really be persuaded to absorb all marketable cattle. Yet most producers generally did not begin taking it seriously until 1926 when the British export market collapsed. Late in the year, the livestock associations initiated a national committee representative of government, producers, and packers to investigate ways of improving the domestic market. In its final report, presented in 1927, this committee concluded that the unpalatability of domestic beef was linked to indiscriminate marketing and finishing programmes aimed only at the export market. Its chief recommendation was for a grading system that would enable the consumer to choose good beef with confidence.

In June 1928, industry representatives met at the Royal Alexandria Hotel in Winnipeg to deal with the grading issue and the problems of the domestic marketplace.[210] Ranchers, mixed farmers, packers, cattle dealers, butchers, retailers, government officials, and academics agreed that the average housewife did not know how to recognize good beef, and therefore was not prepared to pay the price for a choice cut. In response to a statement that inferior beef was being sold in Winnipeg as good or choice, J. Guest of Eaton's nervously commented that he would not want such information to get out; a poor assessment, one might think, of the tastebuds of the average Winnipegger. The chief result of the conference was the endorsement of a beef grading system as the best way to build consumer confidence and selectivity.

121

The new voluntary grading system was restricted to two grades only—choice and good—and was intended to be the first step in stabilizing the industry in the domestic marketplace. In reality however its modest scope indicated a lack of consensus and underscored some real difficulties within the industry. First, there were not enough cattle for the grades created. Choice beef comprised only one percent of cattle marketings in Toronto in 1927, with good beef accounting for a further six percent. In November of the same year the corresponding figures were 0.5 percent choice and 3.5 percent good. Industry critics contended that the quality of cattle produced on ranches and farms in Canada made a mockery of the grading system.

Furthermore, the grading system obscured the chief marketing problem. The optimum slaughter weight of cattle remained a contentious issue. It was widely believed that an adequate supply of lighter cattle would negate the need for grading since the current domestic market wanted, but was not getting, smaller cuts in quantity. As J. H. Tapley of Swift Canadian Company put it, "the demand is for one to one a half pound sirloin roasts and you can't cut them properly from heavy animals." Given the costs of feeding, ranchers in southern Alberta could not profitably produce the beef demanded by the new grades. A delegate to the 1928 conference put it another way when he said that, "the great bulk of cattle marketed in the fall are grass finished cattle and are not good enough to be graded." Finally, since graded beef had to come from federally inspected plants, only about 50 percent of all marketed beef was available for grading.

The packers, while accepting the grading principle, were the most skeptical. They considered grading to be both unnecessary and unworkable. They felt that grading was not worth the effort since they had to take whatever producers gave them anyway. They were concerned that the high prices they might have to pay for quality beef would dissuade retailers and consumers.[211] The packers also feared a longer inventory turnover if grading was adopted. Their five-month turnover, compared to a general industrial average of fourteen months, more than made up for their small profit margins and allowed them to borrow up to 25 percent of their requirements instead of the 15 percent normally available to other industries.[212] They also felt that their brand names represented a form of grading, and although reluctantly agreeing to the resolutions at the 1928 conference, they registered their displeasure by refusing to surrender their own labels in favour of the new red (choice) or blue (good) government stamp.

*George Lane cowboys dipping on the Bow slope, 1925 (ND 8-72).*

The delay in adopting a modified system of beef grading was not entirely linked to packer resistance. They had been involved in bringing about a system of hog grading in 1922, mainly to counter Danish competition in the export market. In contrast with the hog and grain industries, most beef producers did not want grading. First, they were uncertain over the effect of grading on retail prices. Furthermore, there was no consumer call for grading—and generally, shopper dissatisfaction was directed at the individual butcher or retailer, not at them.

Grading was irrelevant to most small producers since they were often not involved in the marketing process. Many consigned their cattle to a single buyer, or "drover," and accepted whatever price he was able to secure. Direct-to-packer buying began in this period, and was mainly due to the commissioned drovers who turned higher-volume sales by taking truckloads of cattle direct to the packing houses and avoiding stockyard delays. Cattle dispatched to stockyards might go through several other markets before slaughter. By the mid-1920s it was estimated that 75 percent of cattle sold at western Canadian yards went to other markets before slaughter. Furthermore, the producers' version of grading equated to "sorting" which involved the organizing of stockyard cattle into batches aimed at specific markets. The United Grain Growers organized its cattle selling pool in 1924 on this basis, and encouraged its farmers to take part, arguing that better prices would be obtained with carefully sorted cattle destined for a targeted favourable market.[213]

Moreover, as long as the export market functioned as it should, there was no need for grading. Export quality was the only grade that mattered, and was restricted to live animals. Breeders of high-quality cattle had known for years that quality in the live animal was often not translated into its equivalent as dressed beef, as witness the discontinuance of a short-lived practice of killing and dressing prizewinning steers at stock shows.[214] Apparently it was not uncommon for a prizewinning steer at the Calgary Bull Sale, after being assessed by a judge as "the best fleshed animal I have ever laid my hands on" to display four inches of fat and very little flesh when dressed.[215] Conversely, producers of inferior stock were convinced that they would lose out to those who could afford to grain feed their animals. Neither group trusted the packing houses where the grading took place.[216]

Deficiencies in the fledgling feeding industry demonstrated faults in the grading process. Feeders would take cattle of marketable weight and fatten them further in order to qualify for the Red Label grade. This practice reinforced the belief that fattening was synonymous with finishing. Butchers and retailers, faced with two inches of fat above the meat, could well be excused for any skepticism about the merits of purchasing graded beef.

However, the adoption of a grading system, regardless of its limitations, was the first indication that the domestic market was being perceived in a new light. The need to convince the consumer to eat more beef was linked to improvement in quality, and marked a new approach to beef production in Canada. But since these were essentially reactions to a restricted export market, it now remained to be seen what a rejuvenated export market would do to this new resolve to optimize the potential of the Canadian market.

## Conclusion

The malaise of the cattle industry during this period was due to a poor export market, a continuing lack of a finishing tradition, and consumer resistance to high prices. Combined, they underscored the fundamental problem with Canada's beef cattle industry. Despite the frequent assertions about Canada's unparalleled cattle country, the cost of producing beef was simply out of proportion to the price consumers were willing or able to pay. The domestic demand for beef was always related to disposable income rather than to supply or quality.

Compounding the problem was the fact that beef producers received proportionately less for their product than the other sectors of the industry. This period saw the first realizations among producers that their industry was more complicated than the traditional "produce and sell" attitude. Yet the factors which would create a viable domestic market were not yet really understood. Thus despite the stirrings of change the status quo within the industry remained unchallenged.

# Land Use

Land issues during this period emerged on three fronts. The first was the challenge to leasehold tenure. The second was increasing land degradation. The third was the rising cost of land usage. Like the battles against the U.S. tariff or the British embargo, the reactions of the stockmen to these threats reflected a determination to look after their own interests. With respect to overall land usage in Alberta, beef cattle operations made very little advancement in the 1920s.

## Leasehold Tenure

By 1920, western Canadian stockmen faced a familiar problem. Leasehold tenure was again threatened by the federal government. The ten-year closed leases granted in 1914 had less than five years to run, and it was clear that the government intended to make new regulations more stringent and expensive. In early 1919, the rental had gone up from two to four cents per acre for new leaseholders.[217] More significant was the move towards reinstating a cancellation clause.

Easily the most contentious issue for stockmen holding leaseholds was the cancellation clause. While threatening security of tenure it inhibited long-range planning and herd build-up, and therefore ranchers' credit ratings. The cancellation clause's disappearance in the 1914 regulations was hailed as an industry saviour, and its potential reinstatement in 1920 was considered as damaging as the American tariff.

The federal government's rationale for a cancellation clause in its leasehold regulations concerned the need for flexibility pending the transfer of natural resources to the province. Arguing that closed leases restricted provincial freedom respecting land disposition, especially in areas under or scheduled for irrigation, the Department of the Interior moved to reinstate a two-year cancellation clause in the fall of 1920.[218] It was a devastating threat, one which would have penalized leaseholders even more than 1905–13 since it covered ten-year leaseholds instead of the twenty-one-year leases granted between 1905 and 1912.

The impetus for this change was unexpected since it involved the Minister of the Interior, Sir James A. Lougheed. A Calgary scion whose portrait hangs prominently in the Ranchmen's Club on Thirteenth Avenue, Lougheed was a long-time supporter of the ranchers. He had been their popular choice for the senatorial position in 1888. He was part owner of the *Calgary Herald* in the 1890s when its editorial policy was strongly supportive of the stockmen's interests, and it was he who had carried the ranchers' cause to Ottawa in 1912 during their quest for leasehold revisions. His hostility, therefore, represented a real turnaround, and must have come as a surprise to the old-time cattlemen who had long considered him their ally. W. F. Stevens, then secretary of the Stock Growers' Protective Association, placed Lougheed on the lowest rung of respect when he compared him to the hated Frank Oliver, whose policies as Minister of the Interior after 1905 had put the ranching industry into a rapid state of decline.[219]

Lougheed's motives for abandoning his old allies remain unclear. It is possible that he viewed leaseholds as a threat to Alberta's prosperity because they restricted mixed farming enterprises and curtailed economic and population growth. Given that reasoning, community pastures would serve Alberta's agriculture far more than individual leaseholds did. More likely, however, Lougheed was playing political games. With a new federal election pending, the embattled Conservatives probably were using community pastures as a lever to gain farm support at the polls.

In November 1920, ignoring advice from B. L. York, head and later controller of the Department of the Interior's Timber and Grazing Branch, to leave well enough alone,[220] Lougheed reinstated the hated cancellation clause covering all new leases.[221] He had yielded to York's suggestions only slightly, in that the new cancellation clause gave three years' notice instead of two. The impact was immediate. Denied the security of tenure they had worked so hard to achieve, the stockmen did the only thing they could do. They went to Ottawa to press their case.

In February 1921 a three-man delegation of the Stock Growers' Protective Association sought a meeting with the Minister of the Interior to secure "a definite guarantee of the permanency of the tenure of the grazing lands under lease from the Crown."[222] The subsequent interview with Lougheed was described as "unsatisfactory to the extreme." Lougheed gave the stockmen short shrift, not even hearing them out, and stating unequivocally that a ten-year extension of grazing leases was out of the question. The delegation, however, refused to yield and secured an interview with Prime Minister Arthur Meighen. A more conciliatory Meighen promised the delegation a second meeting with Lougheed, one which was granted, according to the delegates, "only after a very considerable delay which one can only conclude was deliberate." Lougheed's sole concession hinted at a possible commission to inquire into grazing conditions. However, when he decided on its mandate and composition, he underrepresented stock interests by leaving them off the commission and by widening its focus to include the entire agricultural spectrum with no specific mention of leasehold tenure in its five-point mandate.[223]

Intensive lobbying continued through the spring and summer of 1921 by the WSGA and the larger Saskatchewan Stock Growers' Association. Added support came from the Interior Stock Association of British Columbia, the Western Livestock Union, the Shorthorn, Hereford, and sheep associations as well as by boards of trade representing cities in all three provinces. In several meetings with the Minister of the Interior and various members of Parliament, the stockmen pressed for lease permanence and security while giving ground in certain areas. They tempered their conditions by acknowledging the need for a one-year cancellation right in leases wanted for irrigation, and were even prepared to accept a five-year cancellation clause for long-term leases. Partial success was achieved in two areas. In September, through an Order in Council that recognized "the depression now existing in the livestock industry," lease rentals were reduced from four cents to their original two cents per acre. A month later the cancellation clause was extended to four years.[224]

It was not enough for the stockmen, though it was certainly more than Lougheed wanted to give. In a memorandum to B. L York, R. A. Gibson, Acting Deputy Minister for the Department of the Interior, referred to Lougheed's instructions that any lease granted under the new four-year cancellation clause should be inspected very carefully before it was declared non-agricultural, and furthermore that neighbouring farmers be given the opportunity to apply for the lease under community pasture provisions.[225] According to the WSGA, Lougheed later tried to repudiate the rental reduction.[226]

These concessions were not entirely due to the stockmen's influence on federal authorities other than Lougheed. They also reflected the opinions of the two provincial governments of Alberta and Saskatchewan. In July 1921, the Grazing Committee of the WSGA met with Alberta Premier Charles Stewart, who agreed to press the stockmen's views personally in the form of a letter to James Lougheed.[227] In August the Saskatchewan government endorsed the stockmen's modified proposals.

As matters stood at the end of 1921, the existing leasehold system was in a state of chaos. There were five types of leases, all subject to differing regulations respecting size and term.[228] An intransigent Minister of the Interior was exacerbating the situation by refusing to grant security for all leaseholders upon the expiry of their leases. As such, the recurring comments predicting the imminent death of the industry were linked as much with lease uncertainty as with market problems.

Salvation came in the form of the federal election at the end of 1921 which saw the Conservatives, and Lougheed, swept from office. It was not so much that the Liberals were in power that gave the stockmen such cause for hope in early 1922. Rather, it was the fact that the new Minister of the Interior was none other than Charles Stewart, the former Alberta Premier and long-time supporter of the cattle industry. Defeated by the United Farmers of Alberta in the July 1921 provincial elections, Stewart was asked by Mackenzie King to join the federal cabinet as Minister of the Interior, even though he had not sought election. This gesture of confidence by the wily King speaks well of Stewart, whose abilities have gone largely unnoticed by historians. His later policies respecting irrigation, water conservation, and the forest and mining industries stamped him as one of Ottawa's most effective and farsighted ministers.

In the three months between the federal election and Stewart's victory by acclamation in a by-election for the Liberal seat of Argenteuil, Quebec, the WSGA worked to capitalize on its new opportunity. A resolution was forwarded to Ottawa in January calling for action on lease renewals "so as to put the industry on a permanent basis." Stewart promised his early attention and passed the matter on to B. L. York through the Deputy Minister, W. W. Cory. In his detailed report submitted on 8 February York took a much different view of the lease problem than had Lougheed. York recommended closed ten-

*Mixed farming in Sturgeon Valley near Edmonton. The successive dry years ultimately fostered a move towards mixed farming The fact that many Alberta soils dried out quickly necessitated diverse land-use practices to offset lack of soil moisture (ND 8-150).*

year leases similar to those governed by the 1914 regulations. He also advised consolidating all leases under the new regulations. Over the subsequent two months the WSGA kept the pressure on. Several correspondences to Ottawa cleverly set the future of the reeling cattle industry against the absolute necessity of secure leasehold tenure.

Within six weeks of his tenure as Minister of the Interior, Charles Stewart acted. On 3 March 1922, a new set of grazing regulations were approved by the Governor General.[229] Promulgated on 14 April, they mirrored York's earlier recommendations, with few exceptions.[230] The ten-year period and twelve thousand acre limit were maintained, as was the two-cent-per-acre annual rental. Cancellation provisions were identical to the 1914 regulations, and leaseholders were assured priority rights regarding renewals. Consolidation under the new regulations was allowed on existing leases that had less than five years to run. An important addition was the stipulation that any lessee assuming an expired or cancelled lease was obliged to make monetary compensation to the former leaseholder for improvements made.

The WSGA was quick to voice its thanks and appreciation. In a letter to Stewart dated 5 May 1922, the chairman of the Grazing Committee, E. D. Hardwick, thanked the Minister for his prompt action which "would go far to enable stockmen to survive the unprecedented depression which for the past two years had threatened [their] existence." The stockmen had won their battle thanks to a sympathetic Minister. That the president of the WSGA, Dan Riley, was a leading Liberal himself and a personal friend of Stewart further aided the cause. Together they underscored the irony that the cattle industry, founded on the graces and largesse of the federal Conservative party, now had the once-hated Liberals to thank for their newly obtained security of leasehold tenure.

## The Community Pasture Issue

The 1922 grazing regulations contained provision for community pastures, a sure indication that they were still considered a viable alternative to individual leases. However, these provisions for community pastures did not concern the WSGA; they were too vague. When set against more precise stipulations in the 1922 regulations, it was clear that they contained far more bark than bite.

Community pastures were endorsed by the commission promised by Lougheed in 1921. Formed by Order in Council, 14 November 1921, and chaired by Charles A. Magrath, the four-man committee included W. H. Fairfield, the superintendent of the federal government's Lethbridge Research Station, and irrigation proponents A. A. Carpenter and C. R. Marnoch. The Southern Alberta Survey Board, as it became known, was charged with making recommendations on the future of the drought-ridden lands of southern and southeastern Alberta, with a special emphasis on the potential of irrigation. Its report and recommendations submitted in February 1922 to both the federal and Alberta governments had little to say about the cattle industry. Blaming the present abysmal agricultural conditions on greed and the ignorance of proper summer fallowing procedures, the board was convinced that the future prosperity of the area was dependent upon continued population growth, best achieved through cash crop farming and, where possible, irrigation.

It is doubtful if there are any great stretches of land in the world of a character so uniformly rich as to the soil itself and as to potentialities if carefully used for quick convertibility at the hand of man to immediate wealth by the production of grain.[231]

In the Board's report, cattle grazing emerged as a secondary activity, associated with but dependent upon grain farming. Chairman Magrath's letter to A. E. Cross on 15 February 1922 noted that "my view at the time was that a few million dollars would be invested in cattle with practically no addition to the population of the country."[232] The Board felt that any area set for irrigation should pre-empt grazing leaseholds, and that community pastures in marginal agricultural areas might induce a few ruined grain farmers to remain on the land. Thus its only reference to the cattle industry was an approval in principle of converting expired grazing leases in non-agricultural areas into community pastures. The vague wording of its recommendation seemed an exercise in indifference:

> That representation be made by the government of Alberta to the Dominion Government respecting that whenever any opportunity arises whereby any part of the areas within the region held under grazing leases from the Dominion Government become available for leases, the attention of the Government of Alberta should be called to the fact so that inquiry may be made to the feasibility of making use of the land for community pastures.

This sentiment was translated into almost equal vagueness in the new federal regulations of April 1922. While retaining control in the form of ministerial approval, the Department of the Interior authorized the provincial governments to make application for vacant leases on behalf of interested farmers. The provincial government would pay the lease rental of two cents an acre and recover it from the participating farmers. In other words, the provincial government would become the de facto lessee only if it so desired and had obtained federal authorization.

In 1923, the provincial government enacted legislation enabling the creation of grazing associations and Crown grazing areas.[233] Both demanded collective action by farmers, and the wording of each act precluded significant change to existing conditions. The grazing association was in fact a collective leaseholder and subject to the same conditions as individuals, the only difference being that the association received its lease from the province.

*Cowboys in the Milk River area, 1922. This photograph shows the wide grassland vistas that identify the true ranching areas. Over forty years after the leasehold system was introduced, ranching in the dryland area still retained its original character (ND 3914-133).*

"Crown grazing" simply referred to the right of the province to classify existing community grazing land as a specific community grazing area for the exclusive use of surrounding farmers, providing half were in favour.

Only two such community grazing areas were formed by the end of 1925, both in marginal areas in terms of cattle population.[234] It was hardly surprising. The community pasture impetus originated in the earlier period of prosperity when cattle prices were high. Extremely low prices in the early 1920s diminished their appeal. The need to reimburse former lessees for the cost of improvements dissuaded the financially strapped provincial government, which then would have to negotiate with the new lessees for reimbursement. Furthermore, the precise stipulations in the federal grazing regulations precluded a great deal of opportunity. Legally, the present lessee had prior right of renewal if his lease was in good standing. Generous consolidation provisions allowed soon-to-expire leases to come under the new ten-year term. Finally, there was the uncertainty over the timing of the transfer of natural resources to the provinces. The Province of Saskatchewan, although in favour of community pastures given its reliance on a grain-based economy, declined to become involved until the natural resource issue had been resolved.[235]

The failure of community pastures during this period provides another statement about mixed farming in Alberta. Grain farming was still dominant.

*Alfred Ernest Cross, 1861 – 1932. Cross studied veterinary medicine in Montreal before coming to western Canada to work for the Cochrane Ranch in 1884. He started his own ranch, the A7, a year later and over the next forty-seven years became one of Alberta's foremost cattle ranchers and breeders. He was a founding member of the WSGA and the Ranchmen's Club in Calgary and was involved in several business ventures, including the establishment of the Calgary Brewing and Malting Company in 1892. He also invested in Alberta's fledgling oil and gas industry. His diversified activities enabled him to endure the difficult economic times associated with beef cattle raising for much of this period (NA 2787-5).*

133

The Livestock Encouragement Act, hailed in 1917 as marking a major step forward in the progress of mixed farming, had been a dismal failure. Dismantled in 1922 by the newly elected UFA government, the incentive programme had left the government carrying $1.5 million in unpaid loans, the bulk of which had to be eventually written off.[236] Any provision for livestock as a safeguard against the volatile fortunes of grain farming was not worth the effort. The expense of acquiring cattle did not jibe with ongoing depressed beef prices, especially in the more expensive irrigated areas promoted so arduously by the Survey Board. Despite the Board's recommendations, the fate of irrigation seemed anything but rosy after 1921. In the depressed years 1921–26, more than thirty-five thousand irrigated acres reverted to the CPR. A subsequent committee appointed to examine the plight of irrigation on railway lands reported that the company's annual expenditures were five times that of revenues, and that low prices and high equipment costs made it difficult for farmers to pay their annual rentals.[237] Ironically, this poor assessment on the value of irrigation forced the ultimate solution on land users that livestock raising was essential if irrigation was to succeed.

Finally, the provincial government felt little need to promote a non-viable alternative in agriculturally marginal lands. In that sense, the stockmen's success in securing some measure of security of tenure in 1922, and the failure of the community pasture initiatives, indicated that large-scale grazing enterprises were becoming recognized as an important and permanent component of Alberta's economy.

The community pasture issue in the early 1920s brought the provincial government into the issue of grazing rights on Crown land. Even with friends in Ottawa, the stockmen were quick to realize that with the pending transfer of natural resource control to the provinces, their security might last only as long as their ten-year leases. The fear was enough to prompt a WSGA resolution asking Ottawa not to hand over control of natural resources to Alberta.[238] A more practical and effective strategy pursued by the WSGA between 1922 and 1925 tried to thwart any provincial interference by extending the term of leases. Its steady campaign was rewarded in 1925 when revised grazing regulations increased the maximum holding to twenty-five thousand acres, and extended the term of closed leases from ten to twenty-one years. It marked the biggest victory yet for the WSGA, one that deserved celebration. President Dan Riley told his membership, "[it] was a result of several trips to Ottawa by your delegates and could not have been secured except through an agency such as your association, commanding as it does universal respect and confidence."[239]

## Range Degradation

The concept of the range itself as a dependent and fragile variable was much slower to emerge in leasehold considerations before 1925. Ranchers did not feel culpable. Instead, they exercised stewardship over their leases by attacking cash crop intrusions as an inappropriate land use. This attitude repeated itself continually in the interviews by the Southern Alberta Survey Board with drought-stricken farmers in 1921, and was described graphically by A. E. Cross:

> If the old cattlemen were allowed to utilize the country and settlers prevented from settling on dry and arid lands, there would be no need of a survey board today for southern Alberta … a lot of the country more or less destroyed by being ploughed up, the surface earth blown away and bountifully sowed with injurious weeds where the country was originally covered with the finest quality of grasses which cannot be replaced.[240]

Cross was right. By the end of 1926, there were 10,400 vacant or abandoned farms in Alberta, most in the southeast where almost two thousand farming families had abandoned the land.[241] Over two million acres lay broken but uncultivated in a tragic and belated recognition that leasehold grazing was the best land use for most of the shortgrass country.[242]

Range management was not considered in leasehold administration. Through the first quarter of the twentieth century, government officials were woefully ignorant of the principles of effective range management.[243] The federal research stations during this period issued many reports of experiments designed to improve cash crop farming. Livestock experiments, however, concerned themselves with nutritional studies, mostly involving grain finishing and legume forages.[244]

The stipulations on stocking rates in the various grazing regulations showed a profligate attitude towards land use. Under the 1914 regulations, the Minister of the Interior could compel a rancher to stock more cattle if he felt it necessary. In 1925 the new provisions for twenty-one-year leases contained a clause which prevented renewal if the leasehold was not being used to its fullest extent. In

1928 the federal government rejected a request by the Dry Belt Ranchers' Association to set the stocking rate at sixty acres per animal in the shortgrass country. At the dawn of the great depression, leasehold stipulations set thirty acres as the *maximum* stocking rate. This clear indication that land differentiation was not part of official policy had dire consequences in the harrowing times to follow.

For years most ranchers had agreed with the principle of heavily stocked ranges. Accustomed to an extended period of favourable grazing conditions, they accepted the idea of limitless grass.[245] All they wanted was equitable access to it. By the early 1920s, overgrazed ranges and the vegetative degradation that accompanied the reversion of abandoned cropland to its natural state brought stockmen face to face with the fragility of the land. The ensuing ten years marked the beginnings of an understanding of the principles and merits of range management.

Thus it was the stockmen and not the government research stations that first recognized the implications of range degradation (as opposed to agricultural land misuse). In 1924 the WSGA appealed to the federal government for assistance in arresting the erosion of grazing lands.[246] The subsequent establishment in 1927 of a research station at Manyberries on a private lease in the heart of the shortgrass country led to the first studies of range management principles. Located eighteen miles south and nine miles east of Manyberries, and comprising eighteen thousand acres typical of the eighty thousand square miles of shortgrass country, the station was the result of a co-operative effort between the ranchers and the government.[247] Experiments at the station focused on the determination of the yields and carrying capacities of rangelands, and methods of management to secure the best utilization of grazing resources.[248] Further experiments began at other federal research stations in Lethbridge and Swift Current. Studies on rotational and deferred grazing, forage crops, regrassing, and water conservation methods were well underway by the time of the natural resources transfer in 1930.[249]

## Rising Production Costs

The burden of taxes and rentals continued during this period. Tax arrears began to build. The adoption of supplementary revenue tax instead of the former flat levy in 1920 hurt grazing leaseholders, who were now assessed differently.[250] In 1921–22 alone, the Province of Alberta took title to 105 sections of land in forfeiture for unpaid taxes.[251] Uncollected taxes exceeded the actual levy in Alberta's municipal districts every year in the 1920s. In 1930 taxation arrears exceeded the levy in municipal districts by $1.6 million.[252] Cattlemen were hit hard by the tax burden, both on deeded and leased land. For example, A. E. Cross was paying about 8.2 cents per acre on his leased land in 1922. The situation was so bad by 1924 that the WSGA successfully negotiated tax reductions on leased lands, a measure which led Cross to write to the provincial Agriculture Minister, George Hoadley, expressing his thanks on behalf of the shortgrass stock growers who had had "a difficult time these last few years making ends meet."[253] In 1928, the newly formed Dry Belt Ranchers' Association unsuccessfully petitioned the federal government for a 50 percent reduction in rental rates.[254] Even before the full impact of the depression, Alberta ranchers were already in dire straits. One source quoted a rate of return of 0.83 percent on the typical ranch balance sheet between 1926 and 1931.[255] A survey of twenty-seven ranches by Manyberries Research Station concluded that stockmen barely met their operating costs in 1931 and that ten of the twenty-seven had to use reserve capital or borrowed money to keep afloat.[256]

## Overall Land Use

The security of leasehold tenure in 1925 consolidated beef cattle operations, especially in southern Alberta. Elsewhere, it was offset by other factors that limited the appeal of beef cattle. Increasing wheat acreage was a major contributor to this imbalance. While beef cattle numbers dropped by about half a million head during this decade, wheat acreage almost doubled. This increased focus on cereal grain production and the general uncertainty over the long-range profitability of forage crops meant that Alberta was no more a mixed farming province in 1930 than it was in 1920. Moreover, as has been pointed out, beef cattle suffered on the mixed farms at the hands of both dairy stock and hogs in the 1920s. If anything, the diversification of land use and the overall integration of beef cattle took a backward step during this period.

## Conclusion

As the uncertain decade of the 1920s closed, the Alberta cattle industry remained in a state of transition. On the positive side was the hard-fought and -won security of leasehold tenure and the recognition of range management as an important component of cattle raising. Grass—not just *cheap* grass—could no longer be taken for granted. A realization that the domestic market may be an important outlet for non-exportable beef had begun to take hold. On the other hand, the decade was one of mainly depressed prices and rising production costs. The crucial export market was returning vastly diminished profits. Beef cattle were losing ground to dairy stock and hogs in mixed farming practice. The lack of integration meant that quality beef could not be produced profitably by ranching enterprises, or by the bulk of disinterested mixed farmers who regarded beef cattle as a fall-back venture, secondary to their grain operations.

# FIVE

# The Depression Years, 1930 – 39

*We face the probability of Alberta grasslands being*
*completely overgrazed and developing into a desert.*
ALBERTA SUPERVISOR OF GRAZING, 1936

T HE CATTLE INDUSTRY'S PARTIAL RECOVERY IN THE LATE 1920S was not
sustained. Beginning in 1930, a combination of climatic and economic
conditions plunged it into another critical period. The depression era
influenced the Alberta cattle industry in three main ways. First was the
widening of conflicting views between the federal government and the
stockmen over export markets. Second, the increasing importance of the local
market underscored gross inequities in the national marketing system and
raised serious questions about the marketing process. Finally, the economic
miseries of the depression forced new solutions to unendurable problems.
Production costs came under scrutiny, and, for the first time, the concern of
leaseholders devolved on land costs as well as security of tenure. The
accompanying recognition that grass was a production variable and not an
inexhaustible resource led to the first applications of range management
principles. Despite these developments, however, there was no fundamental
change. The dominant place of the export market remained firmly entrenched
after 1935. The uncertainty of the domestic market forestalled confidence in
the emerging feeding industry, which in turn delayed industry integration in
the West. The emphasis on range management did not appreciably change
traditional attitudes towards grazing land, especially among the stockmen,

*Farm at Nevis, June 1932. The impact of the depression can be seen in this farm which was offered for sale for twenty-seven hundred dollars with one hundred acres of wheat. The desperate owner had only eight hundred dollars to pay down his mortgage (NA 1869-5).*

who were more interested in leasehold tenure reform than they were in optimizing their grazing practices.

Aside from growing numbers in the North, the demographics of the cattle industry did not change during this period. By 1939 less than one-third of the province's cattle were located south of Calgary, fewer than in those census divisions from Edmonton north. The heaviest concentration was in the Red Deer, Lacombe, and Stettler districts.[1] Overall numbers rose slowly, increasing by only twenty-four thousand between 1936 and 1940 and stabilizing at around eight hundred thousand by the end of the decade. In 1941, 79,918 farms reported livestock, of which over 62,000 had fewer than twenty head and only 1,821 had more than seventy-five head. Of the 20,306 farms reporting strictly beef cattle, almost 3,800 were less than two hundred acres. Less than 40 percent were greater than a section (640 acres).[2] The depressed conditions led to greater leasehold consolidation. In 1931 there were 3,778 leases covering 3.2 million acres.[3] By 1938, although the number of leases had dropped dramatically to 2,553, the area under lease fell by only 4 percent to 3.07 million acres. In 1940 the aggregate of unimproved land suitable for grazing exceeded one million acres in eight of the province's seventeen census districts. Only three districts, two of which were in the far north, contained less than half a million acres of unimproved grazing land.

*Ruined farmer circa 1933. The dried-out land in southern Alberta is clearly visible (NA 2108-1).*

## The Export Market

The export market continued its woes throughout the first five years of the decade. The American market remained volatile, beginning and closing the decade on different levels. This unpredictability reinforced the federal government's commitment to the unreliable British market as the best outlet for Canadian export cattle. These conflicting views were not resolved by the end of the decade.

With respect to the American market, things could not have been worse in 1930. The Hoover Administration's passage of the Hawley-Smoot Tariff placed a prohibitive 30 percent duty on live cattle entering the United States, virtually closing the door to Canadian exports. According to the president of the Canadian Chamber of Commerce, the new tariff "put an end to fifty years of Canadian effort to trade with the United States."[4] The value of cattle exports to the United States fell from $21.18 million to $617,745. John Cross put it bluntly when he said that the ranching community was pushed to the brink of survival.[5]

The imposition of the U.S. tariff on a host of agricultural products underscored the complexities in Canadian-American relations, and has been described as one of the major mistakes of the Hoover Administration.[6] The fact that the tariff was directed against grain as well as cattle elicited alarm in Ottawa. Given the federal government's mistrust of the American market as a permanent outlet for Canadian surplus beef cattle, there probably would not have been any official ire had the Americans targeted cattle only. Others shared the federal government's misgivings. In 1935 a British co-operative meat wholesaler echoed official policy when he told his Canadian counterpart in Montreal that the American cattle industry viewed Canadian cattle as a temporary convenience to be utilized only as necessary.[7] Similarly, spokesmen in the CPR's Department of Natural Resources voiced their nervousness over the permanence of any American downward tariff revisions.[8] Alberta Livestock Commissioner W. F. Carlyle believed that Canada's reliance on the American market was often detrimental to the industry.[9]

It cannot be disputed that the Canadian cattle industry suffered more than other agricultural sectors from the federal government's perennial mistrust of American farm policies. The British market was always available for Canadian wheat and bacon. The same, however, did not apply to cattle, despite the federal government's arguments to the contrary. The Alberta cattlemen, on the other hand, maintained that an open American market was vital. J. S. MacLean, president of Canada Packers Ltd., summed up the cattlemen's feelings about western Canada's export priorities when he said in 1936 that the U.S. market provided "the permanent solution to Canada's cattle problems."[10] This difference of opinion between the federal government and industry spokesmen over market preference reinforced the political vulnerability of a product not highly ranked in official agricultural export priorities.

The closure of the U.S. market in 1930 threw the Alberta cattle industry into disarray. In September 1930, for example, A. E. Cross complained that he had two to three hundred top-quality home-grown range-fed steers but had no idea of what to do with them.[11] Shipments to the United States from Canada dropped from over 160,000 in 1929 to less than ten thousand in 1931. In Alberta the reductions were even more dramatic. From 27,650 in 1929, the number fell to just forty-eight in 1931 and a year later no cattle left Alberta for the United States. The impact on domestic prices was immediate. Alberta Department of Agriculture figures showed that prices immediately declined after the imposition of the tariff by $1.00–2.50 per hundredweight, followed by another fall a few months later of $2.00–2.50 per hundredweight.[12] According to some ranchers, the effect of the Hawley-Smoot Tariff translated into half the value of the animal when sold locally. The value of cattle in Alberta in 1931 was $34.94 million. Five years later, though numbers had increased by over 400,000, values had slumped to $27.51 million.[13]

The impact of the American tariff and the resulting cattle surpluses were reflected in dramatically falling prices through the first half of the decade. Between 1931 and 1936 the average yearly price paid for good butcher steers in Toronto fell over 34 percent from that paid in the decade 1920–29.[14] The Alberta Livestock Commissioner referred to 1931 as recording the lowest prices for livestock in the past thirty years,[15] a situation exceeded in the following year when good butcher cattle brought $2.90 at the Calgary stockyards.[16] Again, in 1933, the Livestock Commissioner spoke of the lowest levels on record, when steers off the range brought less than $2.00 per hundredweight.[17] A Winnipeg cattle dealer told the federal Minister of Agriculture in January 1933 that more than half the cattle sold at the St. Boniface Stockyards brought less than $1.50 per hundredweight and many went as low as thirty-five cents per hundredweight.[18] In 1936, low-end cattle were bringing one cent per pound in the Lethbridge area, while canner cows were selling at fifty cents per hundredweight. Some cattle shipments actually brought less than the cost of transporting them.[19] Grant MacEwan, then professor of animal husbandry at the University of Saskatchewan, recalled low-quality animals being worth more for their hide than for their meat.[20]

The official Canadian reaction to the American tariff was an intensified commitment to imperial preference. Both Mackenzie King and Richard Bedford Bennett, who succeeded him as Prime Minister in 1930, believed that the best solution to Canada's trade difficulties with the United States lay in closer ties with Great Britain. This was accomplished during an Imperial Conference in Ottawa in August 1932 when Great Britain, then widely recognized as the "centre of the global food system," formally abandoned her century-old commitment to free trade. The Canadian agricultural industry, with those of other Commonwealth countries, received preferential treatment on products hitherto prejudiced by competition from European countries and the United States.[21] Thus did the British market for Canadian cattle become firmly integrated into official agricultural policy, one which also recognized the fact that beef cattle exports were to be minor players in the new grand design. Grain and pork products were the big winners. The five-year agreement gave Canadian wheat a six-cents-per-bushel advantage, and shut out Danish competition for Canadian bacon. Following passage of the agreement, grain and flour exports to Great Britain almost doubled.

A CPR official commented in 1935 that "the Agreement has proven of inestimable value to the swine producers of Canada."[22] Under the agreement, 2.5 million pounds of bacon annually faced unrestricted entry, a fact that resulted in an increase in the number of packing houses in Canada from 76 to 146 by 1940. Hog prices in Calgary jumped from $2.95 per hundredweight in 1933 to $8.75 a year later.[23] In the four years 1933–36, bacon exports to Britain increased fivefold, reaching 159.2 million pounds in 1936. By 1935 Alberta was leading the country in hog production, and the popularity of hogs in the irrigation districts had pushed Alberta's share of national production to 27.5 percent by 1937.[24] The market supremacy of hogs over cattle was encapsulated in a 1938 editorial comment which noted that hogs were the one livestock for which there is an uninterrupted market.[25]

The British market was nowhere near as kind to cattle. An historic prejudice remained. Unlike bacon and ham, beef exports to Britain were specified in the agreement as being subject to change as required by the government of the United Kingdom.[26] Following the export of fifty thousand head in 1933, Canada was asked by the British Board of Agriculture under terms of the agreement to limit future cattle exports to that figure.[27] In the same year The Irish Free State shipped 582,000 head to Britain.[28] Three years later, the British seriously considered a levy on Canadian cattle to subsidize their own producers.[29] In comparing hogs with cattle on the British market, the editor of the *Brooks Bulletin* commented in 1937 that "the Canadian hog raiser is already well-established in Britain but the export of Canadian cattle to Britain has never proved lucrative."[30]

In terms of live cattle, the imperial preference did not discriminate against non-empire beef-exporting countries like Argentina and the Irish Free State. In 1937, for example, the Irish Free State shipped 641,000 live cattle to Great Britain compared with Canada's nine thousand. The low end of the market was dominated by Australia and even more so by Argentina with her large volume of cheaply produced frozen and chilled beef. In 1937 Argentina put 250,000 head into cans to accommodate British demands. George Hoadley made a valid comment in 1934 when he said that "cattle producers cannot be blamed if they feel that the Imperial Conference Agreement did not give them the same consideration as the pork industry."[31]

The low place of cattle within imperial preference was supported in other areas. In a radio address in 1930, Hoadley enthused over the potential of imperial preference for grain, pork and dairy products in that order, omitting beef cattle altogether from his rosy predictions about Canada's food links to Britain.[32] An article on intra-empire trade which appeared in 1933 in the Canadian journal *Scientific Agriculture* focused on the potential for hog and wheat production but made no mention of cattle.[33] Even H. H. Arkell, Dominion Livestock Commissioner and ardent promoter of the British market for Canadian cattle, equated success with a national beef policy that included subsidization for export losses.[34]

There was also the effect of imperial preference on Canada's beef imports. Enjoying a sevenfold tariff advantage over the United States, Canada's Commonwealth cousins, Australia and New Zealand, sent her over 2.6 million pounds of frozen beef between January and September 1930.[35] Australia, it was claimed, could sell beef in Canada at $17.00 a head and still make a profit. In 1930 New Zealand frozen beef retailed in Montreal for 12.75 cents per pound.[36] The equivalent price for Alberta beef in the same city was over 19 cents per pound. Furthermore, the cost-effective advantages wielded by countries like Australia and Argentina virtually cut Canada out of the processed and canned meat trade both in the export and in the domestic market. In this period, Canada was the fourth largest importer of canned meats in the world, averaging over eight million pounds annually.[37]

The federal government promoted the British market in several ways during this period. A prime example was the 50 percent freight rate reduction on Western feeders going to Eastern feedlots, providing the animals were destined for export. In 1933 the federal government actively negotiated ship transportation for forty-five thousand head of export cattle.[38] This official interest in building up the eastern Canadian finishing industry for the British export market was reinforced by the Ontario government when it guaranteed loans at 6 percent to Eastern feeders fattening stock for export.[39]

After 1935, the federal efforts to promote the British market were intensified by the Agricultural Ministry of the forceful and energetic James (Jimmy) Gardiner. A strong imperialist, Gardiner told the 1936 Annual

Convention of the WSGA that it was the government's duty to see that Canadian cattle were marketed abroad successfully.[40] He backed up his words by spending six weeks in Britain helping Canadian efforts to persuade Britons to buy more Canadian beef.[41]

Two years later, and accompanied by the familiar rhetoric about permanent agricultural ties with the mother country, the federal government initiated yet another cattle export experiment. In launching the weekly trial shipments of dressed baby beef, an official with the Department of Agriculture called the British market "a story of neglected opportunities."[42] Predictably, the results were not good. An average loss of 2.5 cents per pound was recorded on forty-one shipments involving eight hundred head. Equally predictable was the Department of Agriculture's recommendation for continuance of the trial shipments.[43] Typically, H. S. Arkell delivered the government line about the ideal Canadian beef export market and who was to blame for its underutilization. His 1939 castigation of Canadian producers for not taking the British market seriously and for using it solely as a convenience clearly showed that neither he nor his government was prepared to waver in their long held conviction that "Canada must cater to the British market."[44] The subsequent years would further solidify this belief.

The appeal of the British market was less in western Canada than in the East. The 50 percent freight reduction applied to the Eastern feeder who bought the cattle in the West. A farmer in Melfort wanting to feed cattle bred in southern Alberta faced freight costs almost double that paid by the Eastern feeder buying cattle from the same area.[45] Furthermore, the stockmen made no progress in their efforts to achieve a flat transportation rate that would allow them to detrain their animals for further finishing en route to Montreal. The freight rate of $1.145 per hundredweight to Montreal did not change to reflect the lower prices, and unlike frozen or processed meats, live cattle were not subject to reduced export rates. The Alberta cattleman interested in exporting in winter faced an additional 6.5 percent in transportation costs to ship from ports other than Montreal.[46]

Transportation costs to Britain cut deeply into profit margins. The cost of getting an animal from Alberta to Britain in 1934 had risen sixfold since 1905, whereas prices were actually lower.[47] A study carried out by the Alberta Department of Agriculture in 1933 estimated that transportation costs amounted to over 60 percent of the value of the animal, and showed that producers netted a niggardly $1.93 per hundredweight for their animals on the British market.[48] To the producers, the best solution to their British export problems would be a 50 percent reduction in freight rates to Liverpool, and even then it would still be well over double the cost of shipping wheat to Britain.[49]

Other factors discouraged the producer. A pound heavily discounted against the Canadian dollar threw the export market into chaos in 1932–33.[50] The difficulty in securing ships to go to the favoured markets in Glasgow, and the unpredictability of price, especially for well-finished animals, further combined to make the British market "a very hazardous gamble." Finally, there was the ongoing problem with the typical Western-produced beef animal. The British market still wanted the lighter, well-finished animal which western Canadian producers could not supply in volume or with regularity.[51]

Yet when confronted by so many diminished options the stockmen still had no choice but to co-operate in trying to make the British market work. Shipments to Great Britain picked up after 1930, particularly baby beef. Over eight thousand head were shipped to Britain from Alberta in 1933 and approximately ten thousand a year later.[52] In 1932 a small, well-finished batch of thirty-five head from the LK Ranch recorded a top price at the Smithfield Auction. The Red Label Feeders' Association sent one thousand baby-beef-quality yearlings in the spring of 1932. One of these loads, averaging 934 pounds, was described as "the favourite cattle on the British market." The quality of the Red Label export cattle was so impressive that a leading British importer financed the placement of one thousand head of cattle in central Alberta feedlots.[53] Producers in Alberta's irrigated areas found the British market attractive. Shipments from the Brooks area were small but steady in 1933–34. In October 1933, the Nanton area reported its best week in seven years when 1,882 head were exported to the old country.[54] The baby beef market was pursued on an experimental basis. In 1932 the University of Saskatchewan sent a variety of live animals and dressed carcasses to Britain from its lease on the old Matador Ranch.[55] Interestingly, the experiment showed that the shipment of live animals was the most profitable.

Following the Hawley-Smoot tariff, cattle producers looked to the British market not so much in terms of profit but rather as a way to clear surpluses and so raise domestic prices. It was held that an increase of twenty-five thousand in export numbers translated into a domestic price increase of 1.25 cents per pound,[56] a belief which was reinforced by the meat packers who complained that when exports were low they had to assume the surplus which resulted in higher volumes and lower prices and profits.[57] Leadership here was supplied by the Council of Western Beef Producers, a federally chartered body that had been formed in 1930 to promote beef sales and exports.[58] In 1932 the Council equated a small improvement in domestic prices with its success in exporting five thousand head.[59] According to Jack Byers, General Manager of the Western Stock Growers' Association, domestic prices would have dropped to one cent per pound without the 1933 exports.[60] In the same year, southern Alberta rancher George Ross asked fellow members in his feeding co-operative to send 30 percent of their grain-fed cattle to the United Kingdom regardless of return, in order to counter the drastic drop in exports and raise domestic prices.[61] One producer told the Price Spreads Commission that though "we went broke anyway," the export trade saved the cattle industry in 1933 by removing the need to feed unmarketed animals over the ensuing winter.[62]

Probably the most outstanding example of the need to clear surplus production through export markets came in the winter of 1932–33 when a group of Winnipeg speculators tried to convince the federal government to help finance a cattle/oil barter deal with the Soviet Union. The proposal involved a swap of a hundred thousand head of grade beef and dairy cattle and ten thousand tons of hides for $7 million worth of coal and petroleum products. It was thought that the deal would have the effect of raising domestic beef cattle prices by up to four cents per pound while putting much-needed money in producers' pockets. The level of endorsement by stock growers' associations and related organizations across the country was a graphic example of how desperate the cattle industry had become. The federal government, however, declined to take any action.

It is true that the proposal was highly speculative and problematic from a practical standpoint. Problems existed with respect to the viability of the Winnipeg syndicate, the intent and extent of involvement of the Soviet government, the transportation of the animals, and the marketing of the bartered products in Canada. However, the proposal did provide an opportunity worth pursuing. The Russians were interested in building up their cattle inventories and there had been a recent precedent in which Canadian aluminium had been bartered for Russian oil. The federal government's disinterest was political, and had had nothing to do with feasibility, nor with cattle for that matter. The real issue was the need to reserve the Canadian market for British coal, and to protect Canadian lumber in the British market against Soviet competition. The failed proposal became just another example of the relatively low status of Canadian beef cattle in the federal grand design for national trade.[63]

The export market took a turn for the better in 1935. The Franklin Roosevelt administration, under the direction of Cordell Hull, responded to the negative effects of the imperial preference on United States trade with Great Britain by unveiling its reciprocity plan, which allowed individual product-specific trading agreements with certain countries including Canada. This American willingness in 1935 to offer concessions in the form of tariff-reduced quotas was described as "a bolt from the blue," and did much to restore the confidence of the debt-ridden Western stockman. Under two trade agreements reached in 1935 and 1938, Canada was allowed to ship a certain number of cattle to the United States at reduced rates of duty.[64] In 1935 the levy on an assigned quota of Canadian cattle over seven hundred pounds was reduced to two cents per pound and later in 1939 to 1.5 cents per pound. In addition Canada was given 86.5 percent of the American annual import quota of 225,000 head, with no more than 51,750 head to be shipped in any one quarter. Surplus cattle shipped over and above the quarterly quota were subject to the regular duty rates.

The impact of these trade agreements was immediate and dramatic. In 1934 Canada exported only 6,341 head to the United States. In 1935 the number had jumped to 102,934 and two years later reached 208,552.[65] In 1939 the winter quarterly quota was filled in one month.[66] Of the 284,463 head that went to the United States in 1939, Alberta sent 130,000, which represented 54 percent of the province's total marketings.[67] Domestic prices rose. The average yearly price for good butcher steers in Winnipeg 1931 – 34 was $4.65 per hundredweight. In 1937 the figure was $6.12 per hundredweight. In 1940 the equivalent price in Toronto was $7.75 per hundredweight, an increase of 50 percent over the 1931 – 36 annual average. A further advantage of the American market was that, unlike its domestic counterpart, it continued to favour the heavy beef animal that was still the staple product of the Alberta ranches.[68] With a natural equilibrium partially restored, Canadian stockmen entered the World War II period on a positive note, confident that the renewed American market would enable them to recoup some of the losses incurred during the 1920s and early 1930s.

The British market was a predictable casualty in this movement of cattle across the border. Only six thousand head were exported to Britain in 1935. In 1937 the *Farm and Ranch Review* editorialized on the failure of the British market in spite of the Anglo-Canada trade agreements, and echoed what every stockmen already knew by adding that "Canada will have to look elsewhere." At the outbreak of the Second World War, cattle exports to Britain were negligible. Figures given for Alberta in the years 1936–40 totalled 246.[69]

The long experience with the British market had hammered home some basic realities. The cattle producer understood them well even if officialdom in Ottawa was loath to draw the same conclusions. Experiments over the years had shown that only live cattle could be shipped to Britain with any degree of profitability. Australia and Argentina controlled the frozen and chilled meat market and there was no way Canada could compete without heavy subsidization or individual preferential arrangements, concessions that neither government was willing to negotiate. Second, the only available niche in the British market was for top-end, well-finished, lighter animals that Canada could not supply in sufficient numbers. Third, the supply needed to be continuous year-round in order to build up the long-term contracts necessary for stability at home and retailer confidence in Britain.[70] Here, western Canada was at a distinct disadvantage because of high production and transportation costs, especially in winter.

The 1930s reaffirmed the belief that the American market was necessary for the survival of the Canadian cattle industry. It absorbed the national surplus and stabilized domestic prices. However, it was the virtual closure of this market between 1930 and 1934 that heightened the importance of the domestic market, and at a wider level opened the volatile debate on cattle marketing generally. This intensified focus after 1930 revealed the institutional immaturity of an industry hitherto governed by the impersonal mechanisms of a distant export market.

## The Domestic Marketing Problem

The cattlemen's main problem with the domestic market lay in its unwillingness to pay top prices for quality meat. The demise of the export market in the early 1930s and the sustained period of low prices re-emphasized the importance of consumer demand in more focused terms than in the late

1920s. For the first time, national marketing practices were questioned and solutions sought. In many ways, these were the exploratory times that signified the beginnings of the industry's coming of age.

The domestic market certainly had plenty of room for expansion. Since the mid-1920s, per capital beef consumption had been falling in Canada, and in 1939 was lower than it had been in 1928.[71] Between 1929 and 1932, per capita beef consumption in Canada dropped by more than ten pounds.[72] After 1927, beef lagged behind pork as the country's favourite meat. The anti-meat sentiments of the early 1920s had found their way into school health and hygiene textbooks across the country, and had begun to undermine the cattlemen's conviction about the appeal of beef in the consumer marketplace.[73] The federal government's national campaign in 1938 calling for Canadians to eat more fish was further source of concern.[74]

The main reason given for this lag in beef consumption was related to quality and the ignorance of the buying public. Better-quality meat, it was reasoned, would mean greater consumer interest, which would in turn drive up the price for the better meat cuts. As Jack Byers, General Manager of the WSGA, said in 1938, the poor quality of meat in the domestic marketplace "was gradually driving the Canadian consumer off the beef diet."[75] Producers, however, were unable to respond to a call to send more quality beef to market for a variety of reasons.

Producers always argued that their production cost bore little relation to the prices they received for their animals. This period threw the issue into sharper focus. Cattle could not be raised, let alone fed, for a profit during the early 1930s. A study involving ten thousand head undertaken between 1928 and 1931 at Manyberries Research Station showed that production costs were more than double stockyard prices for cattle in 1932 – 34.[76] A subsequent study at the same institution undertaken by respected agriculturalist L. B. Thomson showed that land costs alone amounted to $4.65 per calf raised.[77] Another study by Thomson had serious implications for the emerging cow-calf operation. According to Thomson, the expected rate of return on a calf was dismal 1.1 percent.[78] In commenting on its "considerable loss" over the winter of 1931–32, the Red Label Feeders' Association indicated that the prices being offered for finished cattle put every feeder in a loss situation.[79] As late as 1938, a study showed that it cost a rancher $6.42 per pound to produce a thousand-pound animal, or thirty-eight cents per pound more than the average price of good butcher steers in Toronto for the first seven months of that year.[80]

The impact on individuals is even more telling. In 1933 one well-established farmer received $23.00 per head for steers that cost him $35.00 each to raise. Rod McLeay told the Price Spreads Commission in 1934 that he had sent cattle worth 3–3.75 cents per pound to a feedlot only to lose money when they came out 120 days later and sold for 3.5–4 cents per pound. A feedlot near Olds in 1935 sold steer calves for less than two cents per pound after they had been wintered on oats worth eight cents per bushel and barley at five cents per bushel.[81] One High River Rancher fed fifty head for 159 days on grain and hay at a cost of six cents per pound of gain. He lost $257.19.[82] The secretary-treasurer of the Central Alberta Livestock Feeders' Association told the 1936 Western Stock Growers' Annual Convention that his association had a thousand head of the finest finished beef cattle on hand that had to be sold at scrub prices.[83]

Producers' marketing expenses were considerable. These included shrinkage levies, condemnation insurance, brand inspections, weighing and yardage expenses, selling commissions, transportation costs and, later in the decade, a horn tax. The condemnation insurance levy had always been a source of contention. Amounting to 0.5 percent of the value of every animal marketed, it was designed to recompense packers for losses associated with diseased animals.[84] The packers' introduction of the horn levy whereby animals with horns were discounted by one dollar per head depreciated overall returns by as much as three dollars per head.[85] The impact of these various levies is revealed in this typical example involving a farmer from Piers, Alberta. In 1933 he sold three steers in 1933 for a total of $31.30, or one cent per pound. His net return after expenses was $12.55.[86] It was alleged before the Price Spreads Commission that freight and yardage costs from Alberta to the St. Boniface market in Winnipeg amounted to 55.8 cents per hundredweight, more than half the cost of the animal in the early 1930s.[87]

To a certain extent the producers were a contributing factor. The manager of the British Columbia Livestock Exchange blamed producers for the marketing problems, claiming that they "could care less what happened to their animals or who made what after they left their herds."[88] Giving evidence before the Price Spreads Committee, the Minister of Agriculture for Manitoba described a typical pattern. Generally, farmers contracted their animals to the first packer-buyer who visited their farm or ranch. Often, they would consign trucks to transport their animals to market, deferring the matter of price solely to the truck driver. Wanting to maximize the number of trips he could make, the truck driver habitually bypassed the more competitive stockyards and took the cattle to the packing houses where they could be marketed more quickly but at depressed prices.

Producers were bothered by the monopolistic meat packers. Evidence taken at the 1934 Royal Commission on Price Spreads lent substances to these historic grievances. Ranked third nationally in terms of gross value and output and first in order of cost value of materials used, the packing industry was dominated by two companies, Canada Packers and Swift Canada. Together, they controlled about 80 percent of the national industry, and were proportionally stronger in Canada than were the infamous beef trusts in the United States.[89] According to the Royal Commission, this "dominant position of the two large companies with extensive storage facilities and control over a great proportion of the slaughtering equipment in the country has undoubtedly secured for them some measure of control over both livestock prices and selling prices for their products."[90] This centralization led to collusive bargaining practices. It was alleged that the packers colluded to predetermine their prices and furthermore had tacit agreements not to contest each other's price bids. It was also claimed that they withheld bids at public markets until the price had dropped to a prearranged level.

Unlike the producers, who faced ruin and bankruptcy in the wake of falling prices in the early 1930s, the packers maintained respectable profits. Between 1929 and 1933, the producers' share of the consumer dollar fell by 5.4 cents, whereas the packers' share had increased by almost the same amount.[91] In 1941 The *Farm and Ranch Review* quoted figures which showed that between 1923 and 1939, the packers had netted an average net profit of $3.22 per animal.[92] In the five years 1930–34 Canada Packers realized a total profit of $4.78 million, diverting much of it to a depreciation reserve and to a repair account.[93] The company declared a profit of 12.3 percent in 1933, and, between 1927 and 1933, its net income on average invested capital was over 10 percent.[94] Canadian Packers president, A. J. McLean, openly admitted his company's built-in profit structure when he told the Price Spreads Commission that "the total livestock is sold for the total sum, whatever it is; from that sum is deducted the packer's expense and the packer's profit and the farmer gets the balance."[95]

*Joan Oliver feeding cattle on Diamond L Ranch near Millarville in the 1930s (NB 37-28).*

With the elimination of the small packer and wholesale butcher, the packing companies could dominate the retail trade. For example, in order to facilitate the quick inventory turnovers necessary to optimize profits, the packers were sometimes able to lower their selling prices to retailers. This in turn translated into a lower price for the producer. Their system of differentiated prices in various areas worked against the smaller independent merchants. They would also weaken prices by bypassing the stockyards and dealing directly with needy farmers. In 1931 it was estimated that 70 percent of Alberta cattle marketings were direct to packers.[96] Producers were further discouraged by the practice of the meat packers who helped control prices by buying cattle and finishing them in their own feedlots.

Retailers also contributed to the upward price spiral. Despite high production costs and low prices on the ranch or farm, beef prices in Canada, especially for the better cuts, were always higher than the consumer was willing to pay. The depression years brought the issue to the forefront. Retail meat prices remained inordinately high through the early depression years and did not follow the fall in stockyard prices. Meat prices in 1934 were still 7.1 points above the 1926 retail price index.[97] In 1931 the manager of the Alberta Co-operative Livestock Feeders told the Alberta Government Agricultural

Committee that retail beef prices exceeded those paid to producers sixfold, and were inflated at the retail outlet by at least 30 percent.[98] According to William Young, Red Label beef at thirty-five cents per pound retail was at least ten cents overpriced. Rod McLeay informed the Price Spreads Commission that certain beef cuts of cattle he had sold for a maximum of two cents per pound were retailing at more than fifty cents per pound. The disparity was even higher in restaurants. As the *Brooks Bulletin* put it in 1938: "A slice of cow is worth 5¢ in the cow, 14¢ in the hands of the packer, and $2.40 in a restaurant that specializes in atmosphere."[99]

It was also argued that the retail trade contained too many profit-driven operators who were uninterested in quality and consumer satisfaction. In 1938 one expert, in calling for more stringent government regulation, referred to meat retailing as being rife with incompetents who "jumped in and out of the business."[100] Generally, retail beef was sold on a 25 percent mark-up on the price paid to the packers. Butchers employed by Dominion Stores testified that they were instructed to make 32 percent profit on their meat sales, and that by manipulating their scales they could raise that figure to 36 percent.[101] Upscale stores often charged more than their list prices. Poor beef was rolled in with good beef and then sold at a premium. Ungraded beef was sold as Blue Label. The commission was told of cut-rate butchers who bought canner beef at one cent per pound and then sold it as graded beef at an 800 percent markup.[102]

The wide differential between stockyard and retail beef prices evinced a vicious circle in a domestic industry that had always regulated itself solely by the dictates of the export market. Beef prices to the producers were too low to justify production costs, a situation of no real consequence to the packers, who saw to it that their profits were guaranteed. This, in turn, retarded significant development in the feeding and finishing industry. Consumers already paying overly high prices were definitely unwilling to pay more for quality. Producers therefore saw little need to upgrade their herds. The end result was a continuing delay in the industry's development.

## Feeding and Finishing

Low prices, restricted export opportunities, and internal marketing problems affected the feeding industry's growth and sustained the widespread attitude that feeding animals to finish was not profitable or worthwhile. Although the period showed some development in feeding practices, the progress towards an integrated cattle industry in Alberta remained largely unrealized.

Feedlot feeding showed some growth, especially in the second half of the decade. More ranchers supplemented range grass with grain while the rancher-farmer contract system begun in the late 1920s was maintained in the early 1930s. In 1930 it was estimated that there were ten thousand cattle in feedlots in Alberta. In 1932 the Alberta Livestock Commissioner noted with satisfaction that ranchers had put a total of twenty-seven hundred head out to farmers for finishing.[103] The Red Label Feeders' Association fed two thousand head in eight feedlots by 1933.[104] In the same year feeding associations were in operation in Olds, Red Deer and Innisfail.[105] By 1940 the number of feedlot cattle had increased to thirty-five thousand.

The growth in feeding and finishing during this period was not associated with domestic price-for-quality factors, but with the limited export market and government incentives. Mention has already been made of the federal policy that allowed a 50 percent freight rate reduction on export cattle. However, payment to the Eastern feeder did not help the western Canadian feeding industry.

Cattle feeding was also aided by the federal government's feeder freight policy whereby farmers were given reduced rates to move their cattle to feeding areas, or to move feed to their farms and ranches for winter feeding purposes.[106] More than thirty-five thousand head were shipped to feeding areas in 1937.[107] In the early 1930s the provincial government aided drought-stricken ranchers in the South by moving their cattle north to be finished by farmers on coarse grains and hay. The difficulty with this policy was its impermanence, since it was mainly a relief measure and was not applicable when regional range conditions and feed supplies were adequate.

By far the greatest incentive towards developing a feeding industry in Alberta lay with the Alberta government. Eager to capitalize on revitalized irrigation projects in the South, and to encourage livestock development in the agriculturally devastated areas of eastern and southeastern Alberta, the Aberhart government passed the Feeder Associations Guarantee Act in 1937, whereby the province guaranteed up to 25 percent of loans incurred by feeding associations to acquire their stock.[108] This act, by encouraging joint ventures, removed much of the risk factor associated with feeding. The lack of credit had long been a retarding factor to potential feeders. According to the president

*Calgary stockyards, 1937 (NA 2230-1).*

of the Western Livestock Union in 1934, "the feeling is so general among farmers as a result of refusal of credit from the banks that they have come to the conclusion that further credit for livestock feeding is not in existence."[109]

The impact of the new act was immediate, especially in the irrigation districts. The Red Label Feeders' Association formally incorporated itself and secured a government loan of $75,000. Within a year the association had bought 1,500 head of cattle from neighbouring ranches. The Bow Valley Livestock Feeders at Brooks shipped seventeen car lots of finished cattle within three months of incorporation.[110] The Brooks Livestock Feeders' Association turned over $125,000 in 1938.[111] By September of that year, the *Canadian Cattlemen* was carrying a feeder directory that listed forty-eight sources of feeding operations. Between 1938 and 1940 the government advanced $750,000 in credit to twelve livestock feeder associations containing 768 feeders and 16,248 head of cattle.[112] There were so many feeder associations operating in 1939 under government guarantees that insufficient funds were available to pay the supervisors.[113]

Despite these developments, however, the traditional attitudes towards the proper finishing of cattle in Alberta remained largely unchanged. In 1932 the Alberta Livestock Commissioner equated the cattle industry's export future with its ability to breed better cattle and market them in a finished condition.[114] A year later the same official pleaded for farmers to finish their animals, saying that all they were doing was lowering the price. Three years later, the WSGA admitted that 70 percent of Alberta's cattle "were going out in unfinished condition."[115] According to one source in 1936, only 10 percent of baby beef was properly finished.[116] The Alberta Livestock Commissioner noted in 1938 that it was "anything but encouraging to note that over 50 percent of butcher cattle were classified as undesirable," and that "much work must be done in providing more readily available feeding facilities to encourage finishing for market."[117] In 1939 the provincial Minister for Agriculture affirmed that most of Alberta's cattle were being finished outside the province, and that marketings included far too many inferior and half-finished animals.[118] By 1940, the best year yet for feeding, a little over one in ten Alberta cattle were being fed in feedlots.[119] As late as 1942, before wartime beef policies began to change the nature of the industry, only 8 percent of Alberta's 281,278 marketed beef animals had been finished in feedlots.[120] The feeding industry had still to take off.

The marketing problems of the 1930s emphasized the failure of the beef cattle industry to achieve integration on a local or regional basis. In a brief to Mackenzie King in 1929, the WSGA referred to the reluctance of Alberta farmers to finish ranch-bred cattle.[121] L. B. Thomson said much the same thing three years later when he told a special agricultural committee that the northern districts of Saskatchewan and Alberta had an abundance of feed but that generally it was not marketed through livestock.[122] The practice of farmers finishing stock for ranchers was not sustained following the decline in the British market after 1934.[123] Rancher John Cross was one who noted the reluctance of farmers to feed his cattle.[124] Ranchers also felt that they were undermined by the formation of the Regina-based Dominion Agricultural Credit Company, which provided financing for farmers to buy cattle in the early 1930s.[125] Moreover, the difficulties inherent in the proper finishing of animals, and the equation of Red Label beef with purely fat animals carried over from the previous decade. As the *Canadian Cattlemen* noted as late as 1938, "Not everyone can feed. To be in the feeding game one must be a feeder by instinct."[126]

The high cost of transportation within Alberta was a discouraging factor. The Special Committee on Price Spreads was told in 1934 that it was cheaper for ranchers to ship their cattle to be fattened in the East than it was to send them to farms in the fertile grain belt.[127] The lack of a large local market curtailed the growth of an integrated feeding industry. There were simply not enough people in Alberta to provide either the demand or the purchasing power to drive up prices and warrant the added cost associated with intensive feeding. According to rancher Rod McCleay, the Calgary market could be broken by the sudden arrival of two carloads of twenty cattle. In the early 1930s, before the Imperial Preference Agreement, Edmonton's Swift Canadian plant ran at half capacity due to the inability of the local market to absorb its products.[128]

The cattle industry also failed to integrate itself nationally despite the federal policy of freight rate reductions for Western cattle destined for Eastern feedlots and ultimately the export market. Under this policy over two hundred thousand Alberta cattle entered Eastern feedlots between 1935 and 1937.[129] However, the partial reopening of the American market after 1935 reduced this east-west movement of live cattle. Higher prices in the American Midwest, especially after 1938 when tariff rates were further reduced, tended to divert the best animals from the Eastern markets. Furthermore, the Alberta stock grower predicated his decision to ship east on a number of factors, including prospective price, the condition of his summer and fall range, and the potential for his own winter feed supplies.[130] Thus, despite incentives, the direct movement of live cattle to Eastern feedlots was always secondary to the U.S. market.

## Cattle Quality

The low incentive to feed was also related to the quality of stock on the average Alberta farm. A strong finishing programme was linked directly to stock quality. Experts agreed that finishing cattle was a waste of time if the animals did not possess the requisite qualities to produce a good beef carcass. The low-quality stock on Alberta farms during this decade was a graphic reminder of how far the feeding industry had to go. The cattlemen themselves believed that at least 5 percent of all marketed cattle should be directed towards fox farms.[131] One has only to note the federal Optional Marketing Policy in 1937 designed to clear the prairies of surplus low-quality animals without depressing the local market. Under this policy, which guaranteed producers one cent per pound, over a hundred thousand head were processed into cans for shipment to Japan.[132] This policy was a direct response to the persistent claim within the industry that its chief marketing problem was due to a surfeit of inferior stock.[133]

The best cattle herds in Alberta usually belonged to large ranch operations where care had been taken to build up pedigree herds over a long period of time. There were also smaller operations that concentrated on high-quality purebred animals in their herds. Cattlemen like the Crosses, Billy McIntyre, Frank Collicutt, Rod McLeay, Claude Gallinger, J. D. McGregor, Sam Henderson and Bert Sheppard had taken great care over the years to assemble high-quality herds.[134] Cattle from these ranches captured show honours in Canada and the United States. Alberta ranchers consistently topped the Chicago market with their heavy steers. In 1933 Frank Collicutt took eight head to the Toronto Royal Fair where he won one Grand Championship, two Junior Championships and four Reserve Championships. The best Alberta beef cattle herds were the equal of any on the continent. The care and attention devoted to herd quality were tributes to the professional abilities of the specialized Alberta stockmen.

The situation was far different on the average mixed farm as well as on several smaller cattle operations. Generally, bulls on mixed farms were deficient in quality. The *Farm and Ranch Review* announced in 1927 that the purebred industry was in a sorry state, a sentiment echoed by Dan Riley in the same year when he called for breeders to concentrate on quality rather than quantity.[135] The purebred stock breeders were the victims of high elasticity of demand, and were affected severely by falling beef prices. In 1930 Alberta had the lowest proportion of purebred bulls to total cattle population in Canada.[136] Quality bulls were a scarce commodity despite government programmes to upgrade quality through lending breeding stock. Only 232 purebred bulls were distributed to Alberta farmers by the provincial government between 1905 and 1937.[137] The federal government's bull lending programme, instituted in 1913, was not as successful as it might have been since applicants had to form or join an association to become eligible. Furthermore, all males bred from these bulls had to be castrated within six months. To a farmer in dire straits it was just as easy to send a good bull for slaughter in lean economic times than to try and sell him for breeding purposes. A graphic reminder of forced priorities is contained in a 1930s photograph belonging to Grant MacEwan that shows a well-bred herd bull pulling a democrat in tandem with a mule. In 1936 the district agriculturalist in Cardston spoke of large-scale liquidation of breeding stock.[138] In some areas the low number of bulls per cow led to high mortality rates in calves.[139] Commenting in 1936, the district agriculturalist in Lethbridge noted that if nothing else, selling inferior cattle at one cent per pound would have a beneficial effect on herd improvement.[140] Many mixed farmers, in admitting to the inferiority of their stock, attributed the problem to higher prices than they could afford, and to the fact that the big operators were able to dominate the markets for the best bulls.

The mixed farm was heavily criticized for harbouring the scrub sire, once described as "Canada's greatest handicap in the race for markets."[141] An animal of indeterminate breeding, the scrub sire not only diminished the quality of calves bred on the mixed farm but often impregnated better-quality cows when released into open grazing country, especially in newly settled areas. In 1931 the district agriculturalist in Myrum referred to cattle breeding for type and quality as being "sadly neglected," and laid the blame on the continued use of the scrub sire.[142] The CPR's Department of Agriculture and Animal Husbandry referred in 1934 to the improvement of all livestock except cattle and that "the disposal of a considerable number of poor quality offerings had been difficult."[143] Perhaps the most damning general indictment of the lack of quality among stock on the mixed farms of the province came between 1935 and 1937 in the reports of the various district agriculturalists. From Red Deer and Wetaskiwin to Cardston and Lethbridge, from Hanna in the East to Grand Prairie in the North, they were unanimous in decrying the quality of livestock in their districts. Many blamed the scrub sires and the farmers' reluctance to dispose of them.[144] The agriculturalists felt that their efforts to promote better breeding were thwarted by an abiding indifference. The following scathing comment by the district agriculturalist in St. Paul is typical of official frustration: "We still have farmers with scrubs running at large and who will have nothing else but such around their place." A year later, things had not changed: "Scrub sires are in honor throughout the district, the main breed of cattle is mongrel with no definite characteristics of any breed."[145] It was only after 1938 that a more aggressive bull lending programme was initiated, and although it was judged highly successful two years later, it was mainly confined to areas in central and southern Alberta. In 1939 the Alberta Minister of Agriculture, D. B. Mullen, told delegates at the WSGA annual convention that the province had far too many inferior and half-finished stock, and that it was the government's policy to improve quality rather than increase production.[146]

## Solutions to Marketing Problems

The responses to this malaise in the industry were several, and ranged from simplistic short-term measures and radical interventions to some serious and practical modifications to current marketing practices. The latter included the widespread adoption of beef grading, the promotion of beef on a national basis, and the establishment of marketing boards. The stockmen, however, were loath to support these measures designed to place the cattle industry on a more stable marketing basis. To them, the solution was obvious. Their call for marketing reform was based on a belief that the major profits from meat production were going to the packers and retailers and not to them. They felt that if profits were more equitably distributed over the production process, then the quality and demand factors would take care of themselves. Attitudinally, they were opposed to any measure that diminished their independence.

Accustomed to the menaces of climate, the impact of herd disease, the vagaries of price, and to shifts and swings in the cattle cycle, stockmen were mindful of the risks associated with their industry. On the other hand, they guarded their role in the marketing of their product. They firmly believed that simple measures like lower freight rates, a secure export market, and the control of cattle inventories through the diversion of low-grade beef to fox farms and other animal sources of consumption were viable solutions. Thus, the several marketing initiatives in this period were either resisted or ignored by the stockmen. Predictably, none made any real progress.

The movement towards a voluntary system of beef grading lagged even though it was generally believed that it was the best way of ensuring consumer confidence in purchasing quality beef. In 1939 only 4.6 percent of cattle slaughtered in Canada were graded.[147] The packers were averse to government-supervised grading and argued that it was haphazard. The producers did not trust the packers and felt that grading had no affect on prices paid for beef on the hoof. Both doubted the consumer's enthusiasm for the new grades. Many retailers continued to subvert the system by misrepresentation. The solution was seen in a system of compulsory grading of all marketed beef, a measure supported in principle by many stockmen but resisted overall on practical grounds. As George Hoadley, Alberta's Minister of Agriculture, put it, "prices paid for cattle qualified for the red and blue label when hung on the rail, and those not suitable for grading are one and the same."[148] In 1942, the findings of the Beef Committee of the Western Stock Growers' Association included observations that, while grading may improve the consumption of better-quality beef, there was no proof that it influenced overall consumption, or that beef grading had actually resulted in higher prices for better-grade beef.[149]

Despite their mistrust of government-supervised grading, the packers did believe that carcass grading "on the rail" in the packing house reflected a truer assessment of value. They argued that rail grading also spread the risk associated with buying and selling a live product. Naturally this method was strongly opposed by producers on the grounds that it removed them from the marketing process entirely. They could not accept a process in which a mistrusted group not only graded their animals behind closed doors but did so according to arbitrary and little-understood criteria.

The beef industry wanted to counter declining consumer interest in beef through promotional campaigns that extolled its dietary virtues, and by showing the housewife-buyer how to recognize quality in the butchers' shops. However, given the straitened financial times, no national beef promotion programme was inaugurated, certainly not by the producers, who believed that the responsibility lay with other sectors of the industry. One has only to note the fate of the Canadian Council of Beef Producers in the 1930s. Formally incorporated in 1932 by livestock associations from the three Western provinces to promote beef sales, it lapsed into temporary obscurity. This reluctance by producers to promote their industry led to criticism by retailers for not doing their share in the war against the anti-meat groups which included "quack" dieticians, women's home journals, the public school systems and meat-substitute producers.[150]

Neither did the producers respond favourably to a national livestock marketing board as a solution to the industry's marketing woes. In Alberta, this initiative was taken by the Department of Agriculture in the form of a brief to the Price Spreads Commission in 1934.[151] Following a strong and persuasive argument by George Hoadley, the Commission recommended the formation of a national livestock marketing board in its final report to the federal government. The subsequent passage of the Natural Products Marketing Act in 1934 gave the federal government power to appoint a marketing board to regulate the marketing of natural products, and further obliged itself to co-operate with any marketing board established by the provinces.[152] The Alberta government responded by passing an Act to Supplement the Legislation of

Canada Relating to the Marketing of Natural Products and Providing for the Appointment of a Marketing Board.[153] By November, the Alberta government had struck its fifteen-member livestock marketing board and charged it with drafting a marketing scheme for approval.

Alberta stockmen were furious over government intrusion into their marketing preserve. Even though it was well represented on the provincial livestock board, the WSGA refused to endorse the process, arguing that the Association had not been consulted and that the idea of pooling stock from various owners for joint marketing was counter to their right to market their own product.[154]

The issue was stalled temporarily when the newly elected federal Liberal government asked the Supreme Court of Canada for a ruling on the act's legality. The court found the act to be *ultra vires* on the grounds that it infringed on provincial rights.[155] The Province of British Columbia appealed the decision to the House of Lords Judicial Committee of the Privy Council, arguing that while the act may impinge in part on provincial rights, those sections which did not should be allowed to remain. The judicial committee disagreed, ruling that external and local trade cannot both be ruled by the same authority.[156]

In a sense, the ruling was moot since it did not preclude a provincial marketing board. The Alberta Social Credit government, however, let the matter lie until 1939 when it passed An Act Respecting the Marketing of Natural Products and Other Commodities and to Provide for the Regulation Thereof Within the Province (the Alberta Marketing Act).[157] The bill was benign in many ways. While it provided for provincially controlled marketing boards responsible for the "control and regulation in any or all respects of the marketing, transportation, packing, storing and distributing of natural products within the province," it made the process contingent upon a producer-directed proposal subject to plebiscite within the region to which it applied. Leading provincial spokesmen argued that the proposed producer marketing boards would not be under the control of any central marketing body.[158] As was argued by Ernest Manning in his address to the 1939 WSGA annual convention, the intent of the bill was not to make marketing a compulsory government priority, but rather to improve the process through the formation of legally and politically responsible boards.[159]

Yet the stockmen were infuriated by the act. They viewed it as undemocratic and draconian.[160] The WSGA board of directors unanimously rejected the marketing scheme, and under the slogan Co-operation Ever; Compulsion Never, sent strong representations to Edmonton protesting the failure to consult with the association; and the absence of definite provision for producer membership on the various boards. They were also concerned with the unilateral provincial power to operate and shut down marketing venues; and to their lack of legal recourse.[161] It is a tribute to the growing influence of the WSGA in Edmonton that the intent of the new marketing act was delayed. Only parts two and three, which pertained to the provincial marketing authority, and the general applications of the act, were immediately proclaimed into law.[162] The crucial first section, covering the operation of individual boards, was suspended following a WSGA protest to Edmonton.[163]

The adamant stand taken by the Alberta stockmen against government interference or any measures that inhibited their control over the marketing of their animals had been well defined by the outbreak of World War II. The WSGA had proved once again that it was a powerful lobby. In the wake of the subsequent circumstances that plunged them into a much different role in the wartorn 1940s, this trenchant attitude towards marketing remained as consistent as ever.

The debate over marketing reform demonstrated the industry's growing maturity. It also underscored two contemporary misconceptions about the industry. The first concerned the ability of the industry to act concertedly to achieve marketing reform. The second was the sudden conviction that the domestic market could be improved by offering higher-quality beef.

The main problem preventing industry consensus was the fact that the cattlemen sold live animals while the rest of the industry dealt in beef. The two were treated differently with respect to grading, freight rates, tariffs, etc., and this produced differences in perception between the producer and the rest of the industry. Producers resisted grading because it occurred after they sold their animal. They exerted no control and derived no benefit from the grading process. They resisted meat promotion campaigns for the same reason. The packer was wary of paying premium prices for cattle on the hoof because there was not a high correlation between the live animal and the dressed carcass. One expert estimated that there could be as much as a 40 percent difference in quality between the live animal and its dressed equivalent.[164] The stockmen resisted rail grading for similar reasons. This difficulty in equating live and dressed quality led buyers to adopt other, and to a degree discriminatory,

*Poster advertising auction sale in Carsland, March 1938. Community auctions were held at various points for a few days in the fall. They became so enormously popular that by 1950 the public stockyards had to introduce auction selling in order to compete (NA 3546-1).*

priorities. For example, live animals sorted in large batches according to size, colour and conformity commanded a higher premium than mixed car lots, a situation which hurt the farmer with a few head of stock. A quality animal marketed individually might bring less than a mediocre animal among a uniform car lot. Market timing put the cattle producer at a further disadvantage. Wheat stored well and beef could be frozen, whereas live animals needed to be marketed at a specific time. Packers always maintained that the lack of a continuous supply explained their price manipulations. Stockyard operators, who endured long periods of inactivity in winter months, maintained that the marketing problems were largely induced by the lack of year-round marketings.[165]

Furthermore, the freight rates for dressed and processed meats were reduced for export purposes. Live cattle received no such concession. On the other hand, the packers argued that the duty of dressed beef to the United States at a prohibitive six cents per pound was too high to allow them to clear inventories in times of surplus.[166] They did not receive the benefit of the U.S. tariff reductions in 1935 and 1939, which were applied to live cattle but not to dressed meat exports. Finally, the producer, being far less flexible than the packer, wholesaler, or retailer with respect to fixed inventories and capital investment, was more vulnerable to short-term market fluctuations. Therefore, despite statements attesting to communion of interests, the cattlemen's live product gave them little in common with other sections of the industry that dealt in meat.

Thus, finger pointing was more common than reasoned discussions advocating industry integration. The producers' argument was simple: it did not pay to produce quality since the packers were not prepared to pay for quality, and the consumer did not seem to know or care. Moreover, the price of meat in the butcher's shop bore little relation to the prices they had received. The retailers hurt the industry by selling inferior meat which, according to one critic, consisted of "skinny vealers and derelict substitutes for beef."[167] The retailers countered by accusing the producers of falsely labelling them as the villains. The producers, they felt, did not appreciate the middlemen factors which influenced retail prices. Small retail butchers blamed the producers for undercutting them by selling home-slaughtered beef at discounted prices. The packers had their own axes to grind. They blamed producers for not delivering to them the type of beef necessary to command the best prices.

They also maintained that producers were ultimately responsible for the industry's problems since they would not heed advice regarding the type of beef wanted by the consumer.[168] The packers argued further that they were bound entirely by a supply they could not control either in quality or quantity. They felt that their efforts in co-operating with the federal government to clear inferior beef surpluses were not appreciated. Under such conditions, market reform was impossible.

The rationale underlying market reform was flawed. It was widely held that the solution to increased beef consumption in the domestic marketplace lay in upgrading quality. By implication, this assumed that consumers would both buy and pay more for beef if its high quality could be guaranteed. It also presumed that there was nothing wrong with the cost of beef production, only that its profits were inequitably distributed. The truth of the matter was that the demand for beef was related to price, not quality.[169] The common retail practice of ordering a dollar's worth of steak or a two-dollar roast emphasized quantity rather than quality. Generally, and especially during this period, the amount of money in consumers' pockets when combined with the inflated value of meat prices virtually guaranteed lower consumption which in turn resulted in inferior quality. This is essentially what the Dominion Livestock Commissioner meant when he told the 1936 WSGA annual convention that "people have to buy cheap meat." An overall increase in beef consumption and a better demand for quality was only possible with increased consumer spending power. This had never really been possible in Canada, since the export market contributed to inflated domestic prices. As evidence, one could cite the failure of the voluntary beef grading system and the increasing threats from cheaper pork and non-meat products.

Ironically, the most promising improvement for producers in the marketing process began inauspiciously at the grassroots level. In the late 1930s, under the influence of more efficient truck transportation and the new feeding incentives, a group of farmers in southeastern Alberta began decentrallizing the marketing process by selling their animals in locally organized auctions.[170] The idea spread, and by the 1940s community auctions were operating in many towns across southern Alberta. The presence of more animals, uniformly sorted and attracting more buyers, was a vast improvement on the old practice of a single packer-buyer visiting a ranch or farm and offering uncontested prices. Moreover, competitive bidding placed the selling process in a new public

*Abandoned farm in southeastern Alberta, 1937 (NA 2223-7).*

sphere. The success of this new marketing method encouraged the WSGA to suggest that the community auctions had removed the need for the recently enacted marketing legislation.[171] By 1939 Community Auction Sales Ltd., formed under the auspices of the Southern Alberta Co-operative Association, was marketing over twenty thousand head of feeder and stock cattle in six locations.[172] Though it was to take another decade to entrench itself, the auction method of cattle selling represented the best response, from the producers' viewpoint, to the marketing dilemmas that characterized this period.

As in previous years, rising prices did more than anything else to ease producers' concerns over marketing problems. The logistics of the cattle cycle and the gradual rise in beef prices that accompanied the re-emergence of the U.S. export market after 1935 continued through the end of the decade. When a steer that brought $3.68 per hundredweight in Edmonton in 1933 was selling for $6.87 in 1940 with no great increases in production costs, the idea of tinkering with the system lost much of its appeal.[173] In that sense, little had changed.

## Land Issues

It was in this period that several land issues were faced for the first time. The land reforms of the 1930s were the result of the near-collapse of the agricultural industry amid a sustained period of unfavourable climatic conditions and low commodity prices. The combination of personal financial distress, farm abandonments, and range degradation underscored the need for change in the leasehold system and precipitated serious attention to land use practices. Research advances in range management were apparent by the end of the period. In practical terms, however, the new ideas had yet to take hold.

## Financial Miseries

It is difficult to overstate the financial impact of the depression on rural Alberta. In 1929 the annual provincial tax levy for municipal districts, at $3.6 million, was equal to arrears and indicated a slowly improving position since 1924. This changed markedly in the ensuing decade. Between 1933 and 1937, taxation arrears for municipal districts averaged $6.2 million, more than double the tax levy. By 1936 the total arrears on uncollected taxes totalled $18.22 million, or $52.32 per capita, and $262.00 per farm.[174] The trend continued well into the 1940s, the period 1938–42 continuing to average about $6.0 million annually in tax arrears. The situation in the major leasehold municipal districts was proportionately worse. In 1935 the five municipal districts with the largest leasehold acreage were in taxation arrears of more than half a million dollars, roughly five times their annual tax levy.[175] The leasehold arrears themselves showed a significant increase during the period. At the time of transfer of natural resources in 1930, leasehold arrears totalled $39,771.46. Eight years later the figure was $279,873.44.[176] In the same year, 813 leases were cancelled. Small wonder that a provincial government official described the livestock industry in 1936 as "a hazardous occupation which now depends on exceptionally favourable circumstances and good management to save it from financial disaster."[177]

Falling prices were not solely to blame. The provincial government's policies of consolidating municipal and school districts led to higher tax burdens. In 1932 ranchers argued that the government's policy of enlarging municipal jurisdictions to increase taxation revenue could kill the cattle industry.[178] Eight years later, farmers in the Neutral Hills complained that the enlarged school districts had meant a tax increase of between 50 and 120 percent.[179]

The stock growers were hit as hard as the farmers by the depressed financial conditions. By late 1933, the average rancher's operating costs exceeded revenues by 240 percent.[180] Although statistics varied with year and area, during this period a rancher's land costs were as high as 25 percent of the total costs of production, and the value of his cattle represented only 20 percent of his equity.[181] It was estimated in 1937 that land taxes, together with water and fencing costs, were over 50 percent of the cost of production.[182] In 1931 a study covering twenty-seven ranches in Alberta showed that the average rate of return was a dismal 0.83 percent.[183] One expert told the 1935 WSGA convention that the land charges on beef production were double that of grain.[184] Figures released by the federal government during this period showed that ranchers needed a floor price of six dollars per hundredweight to break even, and to justify leasehold rentals and taxes generally set at four cents per acre.[185] With this floor price unattainable for most of the decade, many ranchers simply could not cope. Arrears in rentals and taxes piled up and lease cancellations increased dramatically.[186]

The land was a casualty in this financial catastrophe. First there were the farm abandonments, which saw over two million acres of farmlands and 9,298 farms left to weeds and the eroding winds of drought.[187] The grazing areas suffered too. In 1936 it was estimated that over four million acres of grazing lands had been abandoned by farmers in southern Alberta.[188]

Land degradation was not solely linked to inappropriate agricultural usage. Overgrazing had also devastated vast areas. In the more prosperous second half of the 1920s, the beef cattle population of Alberta had increased by over 124,000. In the early 1930s, many stockmen retained their cattle rather than selling them at basement prices. In 1932 marketings were down eighty thousand head due to herd accumulation.[189] Between 1931 and 1936, cattle numbers in the province increased by 430,000, and in the ranching districts by 138,000. The impact of these increased numbers was reflected in chronic overstocking and heavy marketing losses due to reduced weight.[190] In 1934 the government was forced to take over three overgrazed leases totalling 223,500 acres.[191] Two years later, the provincial Supervisor of Grazing warned of the "probability of Alberta grasslands being completely overgrazed and developing into a desert."[192] The situation was not confined to the semi-arid lands of the South and Southeast. In 1937 the district agriculturalist in more northerly Camrose commented on the chronic overgrazing of pastures in his district.[193]

The search for solutions involved three major thrusts. First, the cattlemen made concerted efforts to consolidate leasehold tenure on a more permanent and financially secure basis. The second involved the impact of land reclamation and irrigation on the industry. Finally, there was the cautious recognition that range management and profit margins meant far more than differentiated carrying capacities and cheap lease rentals. Only the first had achieved any measure of success by 1940.

## Leasehold Tenure

In 1935, the WSGA secured a reduction in rentals and taxes in the more ravaged areas.[194] In January 1937, further success was achieved when leasehold arrears in rentals and taxation were amalgamated, and arrangements made to forego accumulated interest charges while consolidating all debts over a seven-year period at 4 percent.[195] This consolidation of arrears and rentals meant that all future lease payments would be under a single levy instead of one for rent and another for taxation. Under this new arrangement, the costs of maintaining rented land could be more easily measured against the actual productivity of the land itself.[196] Another aiding factor here occurred in 1936 when the Department of Lands and Mines replaced the Department of Municipal Affairs in collecting this new single levy.[197] With leases now consolidated into a single payment under the auspices of a government department more in tune with the problems of the land itself and less interested in fiscal accountability, the ranchers suddenly found themselves with a more sympathetic ear in Edmonton.[198]

It will be recalled that the WSGA was fearful of its hard-won leasehold tenure victory of 1925 in the light of the pending transfer of natural resources to the province. Its fear was partly realized in the new grazing regulations issued by the provincial government following the transfer of natural resources in October 1930.[199] These regulations mirrored the old federal regulations in many respects, often right down to the actual wording. There were, however, two major deviations. First, the twenty-one-year lease was abolished in favour of a ten-year tenure. Secondly, and far more threatening to ranchers, was the insertion of a three-year cancellation clause.[200] Understandably, the ranchers initially saw the new regulations as a major setback. Writing to his board of directors in 1932, the chairman of the WSGA Grazing and Taxation Committee commented that "if grazing is to continue in the shortgrass country, and those in it not go into liquidation, some drastic adjustment must be made by the Province."[201]

As it was, the WSGA's fears were groundless. The provincial government displayed no intention to amend or transform the leasehold system. Indeed, the only immediate negative impact of the transfer concerned the removal of the Department of the Interior from the cattle scene and with it the loss of a valuable pipeline to Ottawa. Although relations between the WSGA and Department officials had had their stormy periods, the two sides were more or less in constant dialogue respecting matters of mutual concern. On the other hand, the presence of a closer level of government that was prepared to act on their behalf with Ottawa lent the stockmen a new strength. In this sense, the depressed conditions of the 1930s and the common concerns they brought forth served to harmonize the interests of the Alberta government and the cattle industry in their dealings with federal authorities. From a local perspective, cattle interests became more effective through MLAs, and their personal contacts, and above all through the influence spelled out by the industry's growing share of the provincial economy.

Through the 1930s the WSGA maintained a well-orchestrated lobby that linked provincial economic strength with a healthy cattle industry. Indicating rising indebtedness as a prelude to widespread ruin, the WSGA pressed Edmonton with the need for leasehold security as a prerequisite for economic recovery. By 1937, amid drought-ridden crops and starving cattle, the provincial government had decided upon more judicious and realistic land use policies. Among these was a new and positive attitude towards the merits of leasehold tenure in marginal agricultural areas.

In 1938 as part of revised regulations to replace the old dominion government homestead system, the Province of Alberta introduced new rules governing leaseholds. Amended in 1940, these grazing regulations met most of the Alberta stockmen's requests. Though not stipulated in the regulations, rental and tax rates were to be fixed at four cents per acre. There was no maximum lease size, and lessees were to be compensated for improvements should their lease be cancelled. Though the three-year cancellation clause remained in effect, its threat was greatly diminished by a provincial soil survey in 1939 which had clearly classified the true agricultural potential of land. Commenting on the new regulations, the *Canadian Cattlemen* enthused that they were "as near as we could come to getting all we asked for."

Finally, the stockmen used their influence with the government to promote a complete change in the way leasehold rentals were assessed. Though most of the dialogue was conducted by the Short Grass Stock Growers' Association (SGSGA), it did so with WSGA support.

The cumulative effects of rising indebtedness, land degradation, and a growing awareness of range management created an attitudinal shift within the cattle industry. For over fifty years the cost of grass was assumed as a constant. Feed, labour and cattle prices were far more volatile than land costs, especially on leased land. In terms of leasehold rentals, grass was grass; its value fixed, and its state of health irrelevant. By the mid-1930s, the more enlightened spokesmen for the industry had realized that grass was a production variable and that the range itself was in many ways as vulnerable as agricultural land.

The issue of changing the entire leasehold structure was first broached by L. B. Thomson in 1932. In a paper entitled "Economics of the Ranching Industry in Alberta and Saskatchewan," Thomson put forward the notion that taxes and rentals on grazing land should be linked to its carrying capacity.[202] Four years later he reiterated his message to the WSGA annual convention, stating that "in the rating capacity of grazing lands, it should be on the basis of production value rather than on acreage alone."[203] Thomson gave ranchers more hope when he referred to a current study designed to compute the value of land for grazing.

Of all the ranchers who listened to Thomson that day, none was more impressed than George Ross of Aden.[204] Ross, who was already recognized as a leader and innovator in the industry through his work in establishing the Red Label Feeders' Association in the late 1920s, was no stranger to the financial difficulties associated with large-scale ranching enterprises.[205] His family had expanded well beyond its original Milk River location before being curtailed by low prices and diminishing returns. And while there is no proof that he had previously entertained the same notion expressed by Thomson, there is every probability that he had been thinking along those lines. He was certainly quick to act. Shortly after Thomson's address, Ross initiated the formation of the Short Grass Stock Growers' Association (SGSGA) in Medicine Hat in July 1936. After dividing the shortgrass country of thirty thousand square miles into twelve zones headed by a spokesman, the meeting passed its first resolution calling for the provincial government to rate grazing lands on their earning capacity in relation to livestock values.[206] By January 1937, the association had organized its forces sufficiently to approach Hon. N. E. Tanner, Minister of Lands and Mines.[207] Implicit in its suggestion to Tanner was a

*Dust storm on Harry Thomson's farm near Okotoks, July 1933 (NA 2199-2).*

pledge to submit to a voluntary experiment of a new tax on production should it be approved. A sympathetic Tanner promised to undertake a survey with a view to classifying leasehold lands in terms of their productive capacity. Four months later, the SGSGA was able to report to its membership that:

> A signed agreement has been made with the Provincial Government to submit the control of grazing land to a board representing the Government and stockmen … to administer this land on a production basis.[208]

By the end of 1937, the notion of rentals being based on production seemed a foregone conclusion. The only problem seemed to be time. Tanner felt that a two-year survey was necessary to provide the required information "so that rentals may be placed on a more permanent basis, comparative with the producing and earning capacity of the land."[209] In May 1938, at its annual meeting in Medicine Hat, a growingly impatient WSGA passed a resolution which noted government inaction. It also prepared a signed proposal requesting immediate consideration from the provincial government. The proposal, which contained fifty-four signatures representing over one million acres of leased land, called for them to enter into an agreement with the government "to

*Dust storm at Carmangay, 1937 (NA 2209-1).*

base the charge for the range on relation of production to the value of the product raised."

By July 1939 the arrangements for the feasibility study were completed. It was decided that the WSGA's special committee would be entrusted to prepare the report under the chairmanship of Graham Anderson, an inspector with the Department of Municipal Affairs at Brooks. Tanner and his deputy minister were routed into the process through their addition as non-active committee members.

Two points deserve some comment here, particularly in the light of events over the ensuing few years. First, the new formula for leasehold rentals had been worked out and approved by 1938.[210] This formula called for the government to take a 10 percent annual royalty in lieu of a flat rental rate on leasehold land. The amount of this royalty was measured against the cost of production and the selling price, and was determined by multiplying the average annual gain of beef on grass (250 pounds) by the average price on the Calgary stockyards between July and December, and dividing that figure by the assessed carrying capacity of the land. As George Ross pointed out, the adoption of this formula would reduce rentals in the shortgrass country measurably.[211] The point is that the stock growers knew what they were getting themselves into before Graham Anderson made his report and recommendations.

Second was the issue of compulsion. It was assumed by many, and later to be argued as such, that any recommendations by this committee would not be binding, and were to be applicable to southern Alberta only. Indeed, the government informed the SGSGA in July that "when the survey is completed a voluntary experiment plan based on a Production Tax will be offered to anyone in the industry."[212] Yet, from the accounts of the WSGA committees and annual conventions, the notion of universality seemed accepted in that total leasehold costs were under review. If it was seen as voluntary, then, the WSGA did not make this fact clear to its members. One has only to note the resolution passed at the 1938 annual convention approving "the assessment of leasehold rentals on their producing and earning capacity." There was no mention of limitations in this resolution.[213] Echoing this feeling were hundreds of southern Alberta ranchers, many of whom held membership in both associations.[214] It seems that with cattle prices still out of line with leasehold rentals, Ross's formula looked like a good deal.

## Land Reclamation and Irrigation

The collapse in grain prices in this period and the prolonged period of drought led to new attitudes about agrarian land use, especially in southeastern Alberta where the ravages of cereal crop agriculture had been the greatest. Government interventions during the second half of the 1930s were aimed partly at reclaiming degraded wheat lands and converting them into grazing or mixed farming units. By 1940 positive statements were being made at the official level about the resurgence of livestock enterprises through sensible range management practices and irrigation adaptations. It is true that intensive cattle raising was eventually incorporated into the irrigated areas. The same could be said for the dryland areas where cattle ultimately supplanted wheat as the primary form of land use. The results in this period, however, while advantageous, were less than might have been expected.

The federal government's most serious response to the dryland disasters of the 1930s lay in its passage of the Prairie Farm Rehabilitation Act in 1935 which provided for a body popularly known as the Prairie Farm Rehabilitation Administration (PFRA) to implement a long-range scheme of land regeneration. The ultimate importance of the PFRA to the cattle industry was undoubtedly significant. Regrassing programmes restored ruined or abandoned agricultural land to pasture. Dugouts, dams, and irrigation projects provided water for cattle and crops. More importantly in the long run, the water conservation initiatives of the PFRA emphasized the interdependence of irrigation and livestock raising, and prefaced the transformation of small-scale cattle feeding operations in Alberta into a nation-leading integrated industry. Finally, the PFRA, by beginning studies and surveys of the cattle industry, supplemented the work of the government research stations by adding to the growing body of knowledge on range management.

Yet there are indications that Alberta and the cattle industry did not receive the full benefit of PFRA programmes during this period. A major factor here concerned the ongoing friction between Alberta's Social Credit government and the Hon. James Gardiner, the federal Minister of Agriculture. It was held in Alberta government circles that Gardiner favoured his home province of Saskatchewan in implementing PFRA programmes.[215] A good example is contained in the strongly worded letter to Gardiner in December 1938, from Alberta's Attorney General, Wallace Cross, in which Cross accused Gardiner of not treating drought-afflicted areas in the two provinces equally.[216] Statistics would appear to bear out the Alberta case. In 1937 the official drought acreage in Saskatchewan was about four times that of Alberta, while affected populations were seven to one in favour of Saskatchewan. Yet federal relief expenditures between 1934 and 1938 favoured Saskatchewan over Alberta by a ratio of twelve to one.[217]

With respect to the cattle industry generally, the benefits of the PFRA were not realized during this period. First, the PFRA's original mandate was concerned with water development and the improvement of cultivation techniques. Pasture improvement only began after 1937, when chronic feed shortages led to the economic land classification studies that eventually manifested themselves in regrassing programmes.[218] It is not surprising, therefore, to find that range improvement programmes paled before the assistance given to agriculture in the form of crop insurance, rail subsidies for export grain, and income supplements for grain producers. According to C. M. Williams, "The obvious need for a return to ranching in many of the southwestern areas may have made environmental sense but could not match the short term economic benefits to individual farmers from cropping."[219] The Alberta statistics lend credence to Williams. Acreage under field crops in the province increased by 1.7 million acres between 1931 and 1941. About 60 percent of this increase was devoted to wheat. In all, Alberta's wheat acreage increased by 14 percent in the period 1930–40 and by 17 percent in the dryland districts. Provincial cattle numbers, however, declined by about 210,000, of which about 45,000 were in those districts served by the PFRA.[220] In 1934–35, for instance, revenue from livestock sales amounted to about 5 percent of that from grain products.[221] This would appear to indicate that changes in land use to accommodate beef cattle in the province did not occur outside the Special Areas and, to a degree, the irrigation districts.

This friction between the Alberta government and Gardiner was also partly responsible for Alberta not sharing in the benefits of the federal government's community pasture programme. Unwilling to transfer any degree of land control to Ottawa, the Alberta government did not follow Saskatchewan in developing federally operated community pastures.[222] The provincial government established community grazing areas under the Special Areas Act, which applied to over eight million acres of land in southeastern Alberta.[223] Under this act, degraded agricultural land was turned back to grazing and re-grassed where necessary, but only within the limiting confines of the Special Areas. The Alberta government, and Alberta ranchers, were also mindful of Gardiner's dim view of ranching as a permanent economic activity. As he told the Premier of Saskatchewan, W. J. Patterson, in 1937, "A check on the development of the Central Plains of America to the Gulf of Mexico will indicate that the reason for the change from ranching to cultivation of the soil is the fact that more people can live in an area where the soil is systematically cultivated than can live in an area where only ranching is carried on."[224]

The growth of irrigation in southern Alberta during this period was enhanced by the popularity of diversified agriculture involving livestock. In 1939 an official belief that "the future of irrigation lay with livestock" led the provincial government to place high-class stock on the Brooks Experimental Farm.[225] By the early 1940s, a dozen companies and several owner-projects were supplying irrigated water from five Alberta rivers to over 570,000 acres in southern Alberta. The largest of these projects was the Eastern Irrigation District (EID), which was turned over to surrounding farmers by the CPR. The result, according to the *Brooks Bulletin,* was an exodus of farmers to the irrigated lands.[226]

It is undeniable that irrigation aided the cattle feeding industry during this period, especially in the Lethbridge region, where by-products of the

*Ruined field, south-eastern Alberta, 1937 (NA 2223-4).*

sugar beet industry had given a great impetus to the Red Label Feeders'
Association. Yet cattle were not the initial winners in this integration of livestock
into irrigation farming operations. Given the current depressed cattle prices,
and the length of time necessary to establish viable cattle operations, it is not
surprising to find far more lambs and hogs in the EID. In 1934 the twenty
thousand lambs being fed in the EID returned a profit of two dollars per
lamb to their owners.[227] These profit margins and the heavy shipments out of
the Brooks area in 1934–35 led the superintendent of the Lethbridge Agricultural
Research Station, W. H. Fairfield, to comment in 1936 that lamb feeding in
irrigated districts was much more profitable than cattle.[228] In 1935–36, the
Brooks Livestock Feeders' handled over twelve thousand lambs, but only two
hundred head of cattle.[229]

The availability of diverse feeds under irrigation and the attractiveness of
the British market resulted in heavy hog concentrations. In 1937, in a
commentary on Alberta's 27.5 percent share of national hog production, the
editor of the *Brooks Bulletin* noted that hogs and irrigation were an ideal
match.[230] Alberta's Director of Water Services in 1942 gave clear preference to
the potential of hog raising in the irrigated districts. Like lambs, hogs were
well adapted to the intensive operations in the irrigated districts in that they
demanded far less land per acre than did cattle.

*Lethbridge Federal Research Station (ND 8-139).*

## Range Management

In 1936, the provincial Grazing Supervisor, in recommending the adoption of range management principles, referred to the alternative being a sinister one: the probability of the Alberta grasslands becoming completely overgrazed and developing into a desert.[231] Though the science of range management has become more sophisticated with time, its basic principles are unchanged. Range management in the cattle industry attempts to integrate factors of land usage with beef production so that both are optimized. The key variables in the range management equation are carrying capacity—the number of animals that can graze the land without damaging it—and the productive value of the forage they consume. In this period, due to government initiative, land management factors were addressed seriously for the first time.

Agricultural scientists had been carrying the messages of range management principles to the livestock community since the late 1920s. Foremost among these spokesmen for more enlightened grazing practices were L. B. Thomson, superintendent of Manyberries and later Swift Current Dominion Research Stations,[232] and his on-site colleague, S. E. Clarke, an agricultural scientist specializing in forage crops and pasture studies. Throughout the 1930s both men were regular speakers at the WSGA conventions.[233] Between them, they hammered home the concept of differentiated ranching practices necessitated by variable topography, climate and grass cover. By using visual references and statistics based on ongoing research at their own facilities, Clarke and Thomson stressed the need for drastic change if the floundering ranching industry was to survive.

Research efforts to save the cattle industry were well on the way in these years. Field studies focused on new grasses and forage yields, and the problem of developing a species or mixture which would allow continuous pasture from late spring to early fall.[234] Experiments at the Scott Federal Research Station in Saskatchewan showed that introduced grasses like brome, when planted in appropriate areas, had a greater carrying capacity than native grasses.[235] In a series of experiments at Manyberries research station, crested wheatgrass showed its superiority over native grasses in semi-arid areas.[236] According to James Bryant of Boyle, the Canadian "Clover King" and winner of sixty-three prizes in exhibiting grasses, one "can plant crested wheat grass and forget about rainfall."[237] In 1936, experiments began with Russian wild rye as a late-summer and fall grazing forage, especially in the loam and clay soils of the open prairie.[238] In what was the oldest irrigated crop rotation experiment in North America, the Lethbridge Research Station had conclusively shown that alfalfa enhanced soil fertility levels.[239] Similarly, the dominion experimental station at Lacombe had begun demonstrating the value of cultivated pastures in the more intensely settled mixed farming areas of central Alberta.

The translation of the new range management principles into practice was slower in coming. A good example was the concept of carrying capacity that formed the basis of all range management programmes. While it was recognized that semi-arid rangelands could support fewer animals than practice had dictated, numerous farmers and ranchers were still overgrazing extensively at the end of the decade. However, unlike other range management tenets, it could at least be mandated on leasehold lands. George Spence, the Director of the PFRA, was adamant that effective range management principles would be adopted: "if the farmer won't do it himself we will have to do it for him."[240]

The provincial government showed its intent to regulate the pressing matter of range management principles in the 1940 leasehold regulations, whereby the minister was empowered to "require any lessee to adopt such methods … of grazing as may be deemed necessary to prevent soil drifting and overgrazing to provide efficient range management."[241] The regulations also contained provisions respecting stocking rates and compensation for conservation measures conducted by the lessee. The proposed division of the province into carrying capacity zones, and the provisions of the 1940 leasehold regulations, were official indications that the rudiments of range management were no longer an option for producers.

Other range management issues were harder to implement. Outside the PFRA areas, adequate water provision was very expensive. Moreover, the seemingly limitless leasehold grasslands discouraged attention to cultivated hay or forage crops. In 1932 hay and pasture crops comprised less than 5 percent of the land in the shortgrass area, leading one agriculturalist to remark on the tendency to plant hay and forage crops only in areas where wheat could not grow, or as a rudimentary response to soil drifting.[242] While Alberta's cultivated hay acreage showed an almost 100 percent increase between 1930 and 1940, the figures for the dryland belt of southern Alberta were actually down from the 1930 aggregates. Similarly, alfalfa acreage in the shortgrass country remained virtually the same between 1931 and 1941, even though provincial figures increased significantly.

The idea of the forage crop was also slow to take hold. The fixation with wheat and the reliance on a cereal grain cover crop for feeding purposes tended to discourage producers from seeding their land with new and potentially higher-producing perennial forage grasses. The fruits of a reseeding programme were years in coming. For example, though the value of western ryegrass as a fall pasture had been recognized by the mid-1930s, only fourteen thousand acres had been seeded in Alberta by 1936.

In the shortgrass country the need for pasture alternatives was more acute, since only 27 percent of the area contained edible grass with forage value. Here, the problem was exacerbated by aridity and the difficulty of finding a nutrient forage crop that could withstand the dry conditions. Less than a thousand acres were under western ryegrass in 1936. The growth in popularity of the brome grasses during these years was not extended to the South for climatic reasons. While crested wheatgrass was perceived as the answer in the shortgrass country, its implementation was much slower. Though ultimately a million pounds of crested wheatgrass seed found its way to producers in Alberta and Saskatchewan, the fruits were not apparent before 1940. In that year only 1,468 acres of crested wheatgrass had been seeded. Establishment would take several more years.

There can be little doubt, however, that attitudes towards land usage were changing. By 1938 different methods of seeding had been established and sufficient seed of superior strains given to farmers. Between 1937 and 1941, over a million pounds of forage seed were distributed in Alberta. Advice was available on when, where, and how to seed new grasses. For instance, farmers were advised to seed their crested wheatgrass among a cover crop like dormant Russian thistle which shaded the seedlings and conserved moisture, or to plant grass seedlings in the stubble left by spring rye and other cereal crops. These changes had begun to have effect by the end of the decade. In 1940 the Alberta Department of Agriculture announced that "the most important cultural development in recent years in Alberta is the growing of forage crops both legumes and grasses for feed, soil builders and for weed control."[243] The Alberta cattle industry entered World War II in a relatively buoyant state. The American market was open, taxes had been reduced, new and favourable lease regulations were in place, and there was promise of new and more equitable leasehold rental arrangements. Prices were rising in response to the restoration of natural equilibrium. Yet the value of cattle sold off farms in 1940 was the same as it had been in 1921, a year remembered by many as the worst in the history of the cattle industry. Wholesale prices received for livestock based on an index of 100 in 1926 were 153.5 in 1919; in 1940, they were 85.2. The search for stability was far from over.

SIX

# Extraordinary Times, 1939 – 48

*Hogs not cattle are the keystone of Canada's livestock industry.*
J. S. McLean, 1946

THE PERIOD COVERED BY THE SECOND WORLD WAR and the immediate post-war years had enormous implications for the stabilization of the beef cattle industry both nationally and regionally. First, the contentious issue as to which export market was best suited to Canada's beef cattle industry was finally decided. Second, the maelstrom of change that accompanied Canada's war effort propelled the long-delayed feeding and finishing industry into a crucial component of domestic beef cattle operations. Third, the longstanding debate between Alberta stockmen and the government over leasehold reform was resolved, and leasehold tenure paced on permanent and sensible foundations. By the end of 1948, these and other related developments had pushed the Alberta cattle industry to the edge of the modern era.

The demands associated with wartime production resulted in significant growth for the national and regional beef cattle industries. In 1940 Canada produced 717,467,000 pounds of beef. By 1947 the number had risen to 1,601,848,000 pounds, a figure that was reflected in an overall increase in cattle numbers from 8.45 million in 1939 to over eleven million head in 1946. Equally significant was the shift in production dominance to western Canada. In 1939 Alberta, Saskatchewan, British Columbia and Manitoba contributed 45.5 percent of total marketings. By 1945 the corresponding figure was 61 percent.[1] In Alberta, beef cattle numbers rose from fewer than 900,000 in

1939 to a record 1.8 million head in 1945. Values also rose steadily throughout the entire period, marking a change from the 1930s when cattle values lagged behind the rest of Canadian industry. Statistics show that the livestock sector of Canadian industry in the decade 1939–49 advanced 119 points, compared with the national industrial average of 91 points. The value of beef cattle production in Alberta rose from $23.7 million in 1942 to over $82 million six years later. Although all areas of the province grew in beef cattle numbers, the highest upward aggregates occurred in central Alberta, and doubtless reflected the federal government's wartime feeding incentives to the mixed farmer. The most significant change in agricultural practices was a new emphasis on feed grains, and a corresponding reduction in wheat acreage.

## Marketing

The war period necessitated major changes in the way beef cattle were marketed. Government intervention meant a temporary end to the free-market system both domestically and at the export level. These adaptations manifested themselves in three main areas. The imposition of ceilings, and later floors, on meat prices meant a sustained period of price control that affected the industry both positively and negatively. Second, the export market was transformed by the need to supply Great Britain with heavy volumes of frozen beef, a situation that ended the long-established practice of shipping live animals across the Atlantic. Third, the United States export market, as the chief casualty in this production shift, resumed its familiar role as catalyst in the cattlemen's battle with Ottawa over the right to export.

In the fall of 1941 the newly formed Wartime Prices and Trade Board (WPTB) imposed price ceilings on all goods, a figure set at the highest price obtained during a base period 15 September to 11 October 1941.[2] At this point the government was not interested in establishing floor prices, believing instead that it could intervene as necessary and buy beef to maintain the ceilings.[3] Designed to curb inflation, the new wholesale beef ceilings set maximum prices for commercial beef, and were ultimately applied to five different classes of beef in fifteen zones across the country.[4] With this move, national marketing options were removed from producers. The American market, however, remained open. Although subject to periodic changes and revisions, the system of price controls on beef remained in effect until October 1947.

## The Closure of the American Market

The early war years continued the prosperity promised by rising prices and the partial reopening of the United States market. Through 1940–41 and into 1942, this quota-regulated market remained open. American Lend-Lease commitments and her armament priorities resulted in a steady demand and rising prices for Canadian cattle. Exports to the United States totalled 194,000 in 1941 and 175,000 in 1942.[5] Even though home demand for beef escalated in response to Canada's commitment of huge amounts of bacon under the Bacon to Britain programme, Canadian cattlemen were convinced that they could satisfy both the home and export markets through increased production as part of their contribution to the war effort.[6] In 1940 the Western Stock Growers' Association passed a resolution assuring the government of "our earnest desire to assist and co-operate by every means in our power to prosecute to a successful conclusion of the war."[7]

Circumstances, however, dictated otherwise. Higher prices in the United States induced cattlemen to fill their quarterly export quotas with the best grassers and feeders. Furthermore, the original ceilings did not allow for seasonal adjustment. This essentially meant that the more expensive grain-fed cattle came to market under the same domestic price ceiling as grass-fed range beef. One predicable reaction for producers facing heavy losses on feeders was to take advantage of the higher U.S. prices and export as many grain-finished animals as possible within the allowed quota.[8] Not surprisingly, when the first hint of a shortage of supply hit the major eastern Canadian cities, the finger pointing began.

In the spring of 1942, with a dramatic suddenness, the cry of a meat shortage was raised in eastern Canada.[9] Headlines in the eastern Canadian press condemned cattle producers for creating this shortage by holding back supplies in favour of the more lucrative American market.[10] An immediate offshoot of this declared shortage was the suggestion that all cattle exports to the United States should be stopped in order to protect Canadian supplies.[11] The criticism seemed unjustified. The Department of Agriculture was sufficiently upset over the matter to issue a public statement on 17 April acknowledging the increase in beef production, and stating that "strong exception is taken … to widely publicized implications that farmers have created a shortage of beef by withholding cattle from the market in order to obtain higher prices in the

United States."[12] The Department had a point, for while shipments to the United States in the January–May period 1942 had increased by 59,442 over the same period in 1941, the number of head sold to Canadian stockyards and packing plants in the same period was up by 47,222.[13] At the time the shortage cry was raised the American export quota had not been filled.[14]

It was likely that other factors unrelated to live cattle marketings were more responsible for the proclaimed shortage. Frozen meat supplies had been reduced through a substantial and largely unexplained increase in the amount of dressed meat shipped to the United States in the first three months of 1942.[15] Second, short-term pressure had been placed on beef supplies by the increased restriction on pork consumption. Another factor concerned the packing industry and its response to the recently enacted government price controls. When a WPTB ruling in March 1942 compelled the packers to sell to their individual customers at the same price as they had sold to that customer during the base period, many refused to sell, especially to the big retailers who had a low ceiling.[16]

The WSGA first heard of the proposed embargo on 31 March 1942. At a special meeting called the same date, a dispatch was sent to Ottawa requesting clarification. In the ensuing discussion, it became clear that the WSGA preferred an adjustable ceiling that would reward the feeder while maintaining the export trade, even if had to be on a more flexible basis.[17] Less than a month later, producers across western Canada were invited to a discussion in Winnipeg by F. S. Grisdale, Deputy Food Administrator under the WPTB. At this meeting the producers rejected Grisdale's suggestion that the government buy all surplus beef and divert it to export as necessary.[18] Despite these sentiments, an Order in Council was passed on 20 May conferring on the WPTB the power to control the export of cattle whenever shortages in the domestic supply occurred.[19] Then on 29 May, the Board announced a new comprehensive plan of action. The Wartime Food Corporation was to be formed to regulate the export trade through the issuance of export licences covering individual shipments, and to exercise that control by diverting cattle from export as deemed necessary to maintain satisfactory price levels. However, any diverted export shipments would receive the prevailing U.S. price, and would be resold to packers at a loss to maintain prices below the ceiling.[20] This new corporation was to begin operations on 1 July.

The WSGA announced its official response during its annual convention in June. The right to the U.S. export market was not only affirmed but was expressed as an obligation more than a privilege, given that country's enormous commitments under Lend-Lease.[21] In expressing a desire to work closely with government and to increase production to meet expanding demands, president George L. Stringham left no doubt as to where the association stood on the export question: "Let no one delude themselves; should our export market to the States be lost ... Mexico will gain it and at the conclusion of the war it would be most difficult and probably impossible for us again to enter it on the same favourable basis."[22] Clearly, the sentiments were meant to caution the Food Corporation not to abandon the export trade in exercising its mandate. The warning, however, fell on deaf—or more accurately, incompetent—ears.

It did not take long for the Food Corporation to be condemned by the WSGA as hopelessly inefficient. Calls for disbandment met with flat refusals from Donald Gordon, chairman of the WPTB.[23] Time was to vindicate the WSGA's position. The diversion of exports up to the quarterly quota of fifty-one thousand head proved to be chaotically mismanaged. The WSGA held that the U.S. price for diverted export cattle was compromised by the Food Corporation's practice of moving carloads of animals from point to point to obtain lower appraisals.[24] Some stockmen violated the intent of the new policy by declaring cattle fit for export that would never under normal circumstances have gone to the United States.[25] Then in the middle of August, when the Food Corporation announced that the export quota had been filled and that the Canadian ceiling would replace the higher export price, many producers simply withdrew their animals from the market in anticipation of the new quarterly quota commencing in October when again the U.S. export price would be paid.[26]

Faced with this chaotic situation and in light of Gordon's refusal to abolish the Food Corporation or at least amend its mandate, the WSGA called a special meeting on August 25.[27] After an all-day discussion a committee of five was struck to frame resolutions to be forwarded to the federal government. Two motions were brought forward. The motion to have the Food Corporation pay the export price for all the cattle it needed and to sell the rest on the open market was defeated. The second resolution, calling for the Food Corporation to export surplus cattle to maintain a ceiling flexible enough to reflect real production costs, was passed unanimously. The defeat of the first motion and the unanimous acceptance of the second clearly indicated that the WSGA was prepared to give up the export price but not the export market.

In later debates with the government, The WSGA consistently argued that the intent of this unanimous motion showed its willingness to temporarily abrogate its members' hard-earned right to export and to accept the much lower Canadian ceiling price for their cattle.[28] The WSGA prefaced its unanimous motion by mentioning the WPTB's mandate to maintain the export market. The defeat of the first motion mentioned earlier, together with the tenor of the discussions at the various directors and general meetings, reaffirmed the WSGA's priorities. The stockmen genuinely believed that some sacrifice was necessary on their part in order to maintain satisfactory domestic beef supplies and prices. They felt that price ceilings in line with production costs afforded them adequate protection. Most importantly, they were of the opinion that the export market to the United States was not going to be abandoned, that it would continue to be utilized by the Food Corporation when increased supply put downward pressure on prices.

It could also be argued that the stockmen were worried by the alarming trend in the black market trade, a practice already viewed as threatening the industry's stability by jeopardizing price controls and driving up the price of beef to a level where consumers would not or could not buy.[29] One report estimated that at least 20 percent of beef slaughtered in the United States went to black marketeers. In January 1943, the *Montreal Star* quoted representatives of two packing houses who maintained that most Montrealers were eating black market beef. During a debate on the subject in the House of Commons, one MP quoted figures which showed that the number of inspected killings in eastern Canada actually fell in 1942 in spite of the large increase in western Canadian shipments to Eastern points.[30]

Almost immediately following the WSGA meeting of 25 August, the Food Corporation announced in a press release "a complete change in the governmental policy of handling the beef cattle industry." All cattle exports to the United States, except by the Food Corporation, were terminated. Conditions under which it would now operate mirrored closely the WSGA resolution of 25 August.[31] The WSGA responded to the press release with one of its own in which it affirmed the new policy, terming it "the only action to have taken under the circumstances."[32] It was clear that both the stockmen and the federal government had agreed to the closure of the U.S. market. The WSGA could be excused for believing that the new government policy, both in its intent and timing, was a tacit acceptance of the position the WSGA had adopted at its 25 August meeting. Subsequent events would demonstrate how wrong they were.

The Food Corporation did not honour the intent of the new policy. Instead of exporting surplus cattle, it retained them as beef in cold storage pending future needs. From a promise to buy and export any surplus, the policy changed to one of buying when a surplus developed, processing and storing it, and only exporting in the unlikely event of this reserve being oversupplied. By the time the activities of the Food Corporation were curtailed in early 1943, not a single head had been exported. Furthermore, the producers continued to expand production, acceding to the government's request that cattle be kept longer to increase overall tonnage.[33] In 1942, for example, in spite of fewer slaughterings, the annual beef yield was up seventeen million pounds over 1941. In the first three months of 1943, the average dressed carcass weight was 521 pounds. In 1941 it had been 401 pounds.[34]

The stockmen always maintained that they voluntarily suspended their option to export to the United States as an emergency measure, and expected that the U.S. market would be utilized when beef surpluses developed in Canada. The failure of the federal government to honour the intent of their gesture became a major issue when subsequent problems developed with the national beef price controls, and ultimately provided the emotional driving force behind the cattlemen's bitter battles with the government to have the American market reopened.

## The Impact of Price Controls

Wartime price controls helped to stabilize an industry accustomed to market volatility. For the first time, producers had a guaranteed price for their product and thus could confidently plan for herd buildup and consolidation. The rapid increase in production capacity during this period spelled out, for the first time, the real potential of cattle raising in western Canada. In that sense it cannot be denied that price controls were a benefit to the industry. Also, in spite of attendant problems, it must be remembered that the stockmen, a group long recognized for their opposition to interference, retained their faith in price controls beyond the war period. At its annual convention in July 1946, the WSGA overwhelmingly defeated a motion that called for the removal of price ceilings and floors.

What is not so obvious is the fact that the price controls had significant negative impacts on the producer. Doubtless most were inherent in the problems associated with implementing a wide-ranging and complex national policy on such short notice. The fact remains, however, that the establishment of price ceilings and the closure of the American market really meant the end of the free-market system for Canadian cattlemen. Aside from the exigencies associated with the war effort, their tolerance for this situation was based on the belief that their interests would be protected through government intervention, either through careful monitoring of domestic prices or by exporting cattle to the United States when surpluses developed. They also assumed that the U.S. market would be available upon cessation of hostilities. They were wrong on all counts.

In May 1943, seasonal floor prices were placed under the beef ceilings, ostensibly as a response to the absence of the price-setting mechanisms associated with the American market.[35] More likely, however, it was a cautious reaction to the introduction of meat rationing in the same month, an action criticized by producers, who viewed rationing as an unnecessary, negative influence on both prices and production.[36] At the same time the government, mindful of the pending British exports and the need to keep production levels high, and fearful of the possibility of a meat surplus and a collapse in prices, made its strongest move to protect producers. The variable ceilings that had been introduced in October 1942 were abolished in favour of a flat year-round ceiling set at the level reached in May 1943. In Alberta the original flat ceiling was nineteen cents per pound. Though the introduction of floor prices were welcomed by the cattlemen, three problems emerged.[37]

First, in response to ongoing differences between the Wartime Prices and Trade Board and the Department of Agriculture over food administration policies, the federal government re-shuffled its food marketing organization. Responsibility for the marketing of cattle passed to the Department of Agriculture, which immediately gave the Meat Board a mandate to buy dressed beef at scheduled variable floor prices. This move, combined with the abolition of the Food Corporation that hitherto had the authority to buy in competition with the packers under the ceiling, essentially meant that producers now replaced the government as the main agents in subsidizing retail beef prices. Furthermore, the responsibility for the export of live cattle, or in other words the U.S. market, continued to devolve on the WPTB. This division of authority over national beef prices and the export market prejudiced the stockmen's ability to deal with the government over what they believed were complementary issues. One reaction was the revival of the Council of Western Beef Producers in 1943 to protect the stockmen's interest at the national level.

Another problem associated with the floors and ceiling was the price spread. Rising labour costs often made it impossible for feeders to feed for profit within the spread, a situation that was compounded by the uncertainty of supply. For example, in the winter of 1942–43 the 2.5-cents-per-pound spread, plus the highest labour rates in the country, deterred Alberta's commercial feeders from accepting animals. It was always argued that the ceilings, which were set in the fall, were based on grass-fed cattle and were generally lower than warranted by year-round production costs. In calling for higher ceilings in 1945, C. O. Asplund, supervisor of Lethbridge Central Feeders, maintained that the spread for grassers needed to be 2.5–3 cents, and should be as high as five to six cents for grain-fed animals.[38] The unpredictability of feed supplies was a further militating factor. Below-average yields in both 1943 and 1944 drove feed costs up. In the spring of 1944, it was estimated that feeders in Alberta were losing ten to fifteen cents daily on their two-year-old steers in spite of the fact that consumers were paying more for beef.[39]

Even worse was the winter of 1946–47. Its heavy stock losses were compared to the horrendous winter of 1906–07. As early as September, feeders were arguing that a steer bought for eleven cents per pound could not be fed profitably through the winter under the thirteen-cent ceilings.[40] By the following spring, feeders, facing even higher feed prices, were discouraged from feeding altogether.[41] Feed costs continued to rise after the war, especially after the removal of ceilings on coarse grains and meats. By the end of 1947, feed costs were up 57 percent over the previous year.[42]

A third major concern was the lack of direction as to when the Meat Board would step in and buy cattle. The Canadian Federation of Agriculture asked in June 1943, "At what point will the government step in?"[43] The stockmen believed that they should be able to sell their cattle to the Meat Board at any time in line with the current floor.[44] This did not happen. Moreover, the Meat Board announced that it would only purchase certain qualities of beef. In the face of this breach of promise, and denied the export market, producers had to take what they could get for their cattle regardless of the floor. George Ross's rhetorical question in January 1944, "Where is the floor?" was reinforced three months later by the editor of the *Canadian Cattlemen*, who wrote: "The floor policy on beef has been tested and found wanting."[45] The editor was referring to the packers' flat refusal to buy cows at the floor price, and of the Meat Board's failure to take remedial action. When the Meat Board later agreed to buy all classes of cattle, the price of good steers fell well below the ceiling price. The point is that the Meat Board could not regulate supplies and provide the producer with consistent returns. For example, in July 1945 the markets in St. Boniface and points west had to be closed temporarily due to oversupply. A year later, the meat ceilings had to be temporarily lifted due to oversupply.[46] The resulting curtailment of marketings then resulted in a shortage and higher retail prices in 1947. The problem appeared not to worry Agriculture Minister Gardiner, who with pragmatic indifference advised producers in times of oversupply to take their animals back to the farm or ranch, or take the lower price. Either way they did not lose anything. After all, grass and home-grown feed grain was cheap.

It could be argued that the Meat Board was hamstrung by the crucial role played by the packers in the price-control process. Regardless of ceilings and floors they were governed by supply and demand factors. The war had little effect on traditional marketing practices. Frank testimonies by the Canadian head of Swifts and John McLean of Canada Packers to the House of Commons Agriculture Committee in 1948 attested that during the war they had bought as low as possible and sold at the highest profit. Usually when supply was limited the packers buy near the ceiling and sell for whatever profit they could.[47] When supplies were plentiful, they were supposed to buy at the floor price and turn over anything they could not sell to the Meat Board at the price they had originally paid. Naturally, they were disinclined to buy at floors when the possibilities of disposal or profit were slim, or whenever they had large inventories. Thus on many occasions they refused to buy at floor prices.[48] Consequently, the prices paid for live cattle often bore little relation to the floor.

Producers were furious at what they felt was typical packer behaviour in a game that was supposed to have new rules. A member of the Alberta legislature accused the packing plants in 1944 of making exorbitant profits at the producers' expense.[49] In 1945, the editor of the *Lethbridge Herald* criticized the packers for seizing every opportunity to hold cattle prices down at the floor level, and argued that the extremely low prices they paid in the fall more than offset the higher prices they were forced to offer in the spring.[50] George Ross agreed, blaming the packers for misleading producers by encouraging winter feeding but then refusing to pay the commensurate price in the spring. It was also contended that year-round ceilings "wrecked the feeding industry." As for Meat Board officials, they argued that they had no control over fluctuations in supply and demand and possessed neither the manpower nor the capability to redress short-term market gluts. This argument found little sympathy with disgruntled producers, who wondered why surplus animals could not be diverted to the United States as necessary—and as originally promised.

The producers' main problem with the price controls was that they were applied to dressed beef, or the price at which the packers sold to wholesalers. Proponents of the price control system argued that it was impossible to apply ceilings and floors to live animals given the wide range of class and age. Producers did not agree, maintaining that it would not be difficult to arrive at live cattle prices that approximated an average of dressed meat percentages. The editor of the *Farm and Ranch Review* wrote in May 1944: "Since controls were first applied to cattle marketing, the relating of the fair cattle prices under ceilings established for dressed beef has baffled producers. One of the great needs is an established price schedule, even though it be approximate, for live cattle."[51] Increases in ceilings did not translate into proportionate gains to producers. Regardless of production costs or the type, quality, and finish of animals, the packer was not compelled to pay ceiling prices for them. In August 1945, for example, baby beef brought the same price as grassers. This failure to protect the prices of live animals in the beef price control system put producers at the mercy of the packers. It was pointed out in 1947 that when ceilings were raised, the producers' share amounted to less than one-tenth.[52] As *Canadian Cattlemen* editor Ken Coppock put it in 1944, "There is nothing to compel packers to buy in line for the live product."[53] In this sense, the growing popularity of the auction method of selling represented producer leverage to secure near-ceiling prices for their cattle.

The beef price controls were designed to ensure equitability of supply, demand, and price in extraordinary times. From the producers' viewpoint, government intervention was necessary. However, they realized better than Ottawa officialdom the wide marketing fluctuations characteristic of their industry. Always mistrustful of packer monopoly, cattle producers wanted profits and production costs protected by a safety valve. Here, they saw the nearby American market as the best solution to problems of oversupply. Originally, they could not understand the government's intransigence. By 1944 they realized that the federal government was bent on using wartime needs to resurrect an old nemesis: The British market.

## The British and American Markets

The resurrection of the British market as the chief outlet for Canadian surplus beef was a direct result of wartime commitments. The increase in production, the closure of the American market, and the wartime price controls and subsidies were all linked to a need to supply wartorn Britain with meat. The introduction of meat rationing was designed to take 15 percent of beef off the Canadian market for export to Britain. Canada's subsequent measures to supply Britain with beef were quite remarkable, especially given the fact that the industry had just come through a sustained period of depression. Between 1944 and 1948, in three separate contracts, Canada supplied Britain with over 4.7 million hundredweight of fresh frozen beef, the equivalent of a million head.[54] In the peak year, 1945, the beef equivalent of 573,000 head worth over $24 million crossed the Atlantic.

The problem arose when the federal government incorporated its emergency wartime powers into a post-war policy that involved Britain as a permanent export market for Canadian cattle. The possibility was raised in June 1943 when Meat Board chairman, John. G. Taggart, said that "we will in effect be providing a beef market in the United Kingdom as a substitute for the live beef cattle market in the U.S." The comment made by the manager of the Meat Board, L. W. Pearsall, in the same month to the House of Commons Agricultural Committee was more ominous. According to Pearsall, the export arrangements with Britain would last "*at least* for the duration of the war."[55]

It took another nine months before Agriculture Minister James Gardiner delivered official sanction. In January 1944 he announced a pending contract with Britain to supply a minimum of 100 million pounds of beef in 1944–45.[56] He made his intentions clearer in March when he told the House of Commons that "Canada has a double opportunity in supplying surplus beef to the United Kingdom at present to meet urgent needs and to build a market there for the post-war years."[57] Six months later, in announcing his post-war beef price policy, Gardiner proposed that ongoing British beef contracts would serve as a fixed floor price for domestic dressed beef.[58]

The heavy fall marketings in 1944 showed that cattlemen were not fully protected by British beef contracts. Canadian processing facilities could not handle the volume of livestock being moved through them. In the first forty-five weeks of 1944, cattle marketings were up by two hundred thousand over the same period a year earlier.[59] The congestion was so great that some central markets placed embargoes on cattle from Western and country points. Those stockmen with short feed supplies could not hold their animals over for sale at a later date.[60] The results were diminished sales, a general trend towards lower prices and a futile plea from stockmen to add floor and ceiling prices to live cattle. More significantly, the chaotic state of the market set the stage for the final three-year battle between the stockmen and the federal government over the best export market for Canadian beef cattle.

Falling prices and the growing awareness that the federal government was serious about a post-war British market led to the first signs of organized producer discontent. In March 1944, a large gathering of cattle producers at Lethbridge reaffirmed the right to the U.S. market, and referred to the September 1942 policy statement by the Wartime Prices and Trade Board that it would export surplus live cattle to support domestic price levels.[61] The Canadian Federation of Agriculture followed up with a resolution calling for the removal of the American embargo, and a month later the WSGA asked the government to "take steps to move surplus cattle to the U.S. immediately."[62] The *Farm and Ranch Review* later called for a token number of cattle to be bought at Canadian prices and shipped to the United States as a way of reasserting claim to a market "given up with great trepidation."[63] Soon after the surrender of Germany, the Alberta Federation of Agriculture recalled the federal government's 1942 commitment when it passed a motion to its parent body, the Canadian Federation of Agriculture, which called for the resumption of cattle exports to the United States.[64]

While the cattlemen did not dispute Canada's patriotic duty in diverting surplus beef to wartorn Britain, the notion of tying post-war domestic prices to a cheaper and inhospitable market was incomprehensible. In their efforts to convince the federal government not to go ahead with its plans for a post-war British market for Canadian beef, the various lobbies from livestock groups and individuals across the country put forward some old and new arguments.

A livestock expert told the Western Section of the Canadian Society of Animal Production in June 1945 that Canada would never be able to compete with cheap beef nations like Argentina, Australia and Uruguay once peacetime trade relations had been re-established.[65] The sentiment was echoed four months later by J. S. McLean, president of Canada Packers Ltd., when he said that "with stabilization the British market will again discriminate against higher Canadian prices."[66] McLean was more explicit a year later when he said that pork and wheat were the only two food products with which Canada could compete in the world market.[67] In February 1946 J. P. Sackville, a prominent agriculturalist with the University of Alberta, warned that the British market in the long term was "a cause of concern."[68] Ken Coppock referred to the historic role of the British market as a salvage option only, while to James Meeks, a respected cattle dealer, a British outlet for Canadian beef "was and always had been "bunk."

Critics were also quick to point out that the present profitability of the British market was misleading since the wartime purchases of Canadian meat were supported partly by the Canadian taxpayer through extensive Mutual Aid loans to Britain. In effect, the Canadian treasury made up the difference between what Great Britain could afford to pay and the Canadian floor price.[69] They also indicated the fact that Britain was buying Canadian beef in the 1946–47 contract out of the $1.2 billion loan granted by Canada in 1946. It was also pointed out to government officials that Britain would revert to a cheaper market, one favourable to sterling, when the Canadian loan ran out. Another issue concerned the floor prices at which Britain bought Canadian beef. Producers maintained that they were always lower than that warranted by the ceilings.[70] Time was to prove them correct. By 1946 the British contract beef price was lower than Canadian domestic prices and significantly below U.S. price levels. Furthermore, the floor price determined by the British contract was too low to allow feeders to finish profitably for the export market.[71]

The above arguments seemed to matter not a whit to James Gardiner. As the editor of the *Canadian Cattlemen* pointed out in June 1945, "As long as Britain demands all of Canada's exportable meat supply, it will be difficult to convince Ottawa that beef cattle should be allowed to cross the line."[72] Yet Gardiner was no political novice and his notion of tying the post-war Canadian cattle industry to an unpopular and unprofitable export market, at first glance, appears uncharacteristically naïve. Even his most logical argument, which stressed the advantages of long-term security over profit seemed misplaced, for although Canada would be offering lower-priced beef to Britain, Argentina could supply more beef, much more cheaply.[73]

It would appear that Gardiner's aspirations went beyond cattle. There can be little doubt that he was sincere in his belief that stability and security were more important than short-term profits. His address to the Food and Agriculture Organization in Geneva in August 1947 was a reasoned argument for global co-operation in ensuring adequate food supplies at bearable prices.[74] In this sense his decision to base Canada's post-war agricultural stability in blanket trade arrangements with Great Britain for wheat, hogs, dairy products, and cattle was consistent with his philosophy.[75] That beef cattle could not be competitive in Britain seemed to be irrelevant. Gardiner, it appears, was quite prepared to sacrifice the beef cattle industry on his altar of imperial preference. As he told the WSGA in January 1948, "I am not prepared at this time as Minister of Agriculture to advocate that the agricultural industry *or any part of it* should break away from the line of policy which has established this country in the soundest position in relation to industry, the soundest position in relation to agriculture that she has ever occupied."[76] He was even more blunt a month later when he told the Canadian Federation of Agriculture that it would be unfair to allow the cattle industry to enjoy good profits from U.S. trade when other agricultural sectors could not.[77]

It was against this background that the final battle between producers and the government unfolded in 1946–47. The customary political games were played. With the rancher-dominated WSGA, Gardiner tried to employ scare tactics, arguing that the United States was not receptive to Canadian cattle imports and that efforts to reopen the market there would only infuriate a dangerous and powerful neighbour.[78] In speaking to the mixed farmers in the United Farmers of Alberta, he stressed export numbers and quoted the bumper export year of 1945 as proving that the British market would more than clear the Canadian market, leaving them with higher domestic prices for their animals. The government's intentions became clear in 1946, when Meat Board chairman, John. G. Taggart, told the annual convention of the WSGA that he believed that Britain would take all of Canada's export cattle through to the end of 1948, and that the American market was secondary to these more urgent post-war needs. In October, without consulting producers, Gardiner announced the signing of a new beef contract to supply a minimum of 120 million pounds of beef to Britain through 1947 and 1948. Prices for the new British contract were in line with the Canadian floor price for beef, but were $1.25 per hundredweight below domestic ceilings for commercial beef, and about $6.50 per hundredweight below their American counterparts in 1946.[79] By January 1947, the differential between Canadian and U.S. prices was $11.00 per hundredweight, whereas the British prices by early 1948 had virtually become the domestic ceilings.[80] Furthermore, the British contracts were concluded even though it was well known that Britain was also negotiating with Argentina for huge amounts of beef at less than half the Canadian price.[81]

Producers, already facing rising production costs and increasingly marginal ceilings, retaliated by intensifying their pressure throughout 1947 to have the American market reopened. Fearful over the implications of the 1944 U.S.–Mexico cattle agreement which removed the quota and reduced the duty on Mexican cattle exports to the United States, they even offered to accept Canadian ceiling prices for their export beef with any surplus going into a government-managed reserve fund to cover future shortfalls.[82] The National Council of Beef Producers succeeded in having a recommendation for the embargo's removal placed on the Canadian Federation of Agriculture's brief to the federal cabinet. The WSGA and the Northern Alberta Livestock Breeders also passed motions favouring the resumption of trade with the United States.[83]

The government, however, remained unmoved. In fact, its determination to pursue the British solution was crystallized following the announcement of the international Geneva Trade Agreement in November 1947. Under the agreement the United States agreed to increase the annual quota on live cattle imports from 225,000 to 400,000 head, and maintain the duty on cattle over seven hundred pounds at 1.5 cents per pound.[84] Described as "a great boon to prairie agriculture," the Geneva Agreement inspired great hopes for the cattlemen who presumed that the federal government would now be compelled to reopen the American market when the agreement took effect on 1 January 1948.[85] They were wrong. James Gardiner, who had been recently appointed to the elite Imperial Privy Council, responded by trying to convince the stockmen once and for all of the error their ways and of the wisdom of placing their industry at the benevolent feet of Mother England.

On 15 January 1948, in one of the most amazing addresses ever given before the Western Stock Growers' Association, Gardiner laid everything on the line.[86] His session, which lasted more than four hours, was delivered to an overcrowded and standing room-only banquet hall in Lethbridge. Gardiner argued forcefully that a reopening of the American export market was not in the nation's or the cattlemen's best interests. He cautioned cattle producers against tying themselves to the vagaries of U.S. prices and becoming hostages to another country's production-cost cycles. He also emphasized the current U.S. focus on cereal production at the expense of livestock as indicating an American disinterest in Canadian cattle. Gardiner warned of disastrous effects on domestic prices should the U.S. market be open. His solution was to tie Canadian floor prices to a stable and permanent British market, which he referred to as "the freest and most satisfactory market in the world." He emphasized that the British market would not only take greater numbers than the American but far more quantities of inferior beef. Gardiner concluded his speech with imperialist rhetoric reminiscent of a bygone era: "Our economy, our political institutions, our place in the world is going to be established alongside of the mother of nations, a land which has led us all and which can still lead us all … a nation which has led the world in the establishment of democratic institutions … freedom … and sound finance based on sterling."

It was an astounding speech, and while Gardiner's political judgement was clearly deficient, his forthrightness was admirable. Following his delivery, he was subjected to heated and angry questions from the floor. And while he parried them with extensive statistical data from his ubiquitous bulging briefcase, his words fell on deaf ears, or, to quote one observer, "were like seeds sown on stony ground." The audience that had "sat in grim silence" throughout Gardiner's speech could not understand the Minister's naivete. To them, the British market would doom them to extinction. A unanimous resolution was passed the next day calling for the opening of the American market. During the debate on the motion, George Ross, then Chairman of the National Council of Beef Producers, called for Western Canada's secession from Canada should the American market be kept from producers.[87] A Pincher Creek rancher summed the sentiments up with a more thoughtful reminder that cattlemen were not about to admit that government should run their affairs or that agriculture should be used to stabilize the country's whole economy."[88] The *Macleod Gazette* encapsulated the seemingly irreconcilable rift between Gardiner and the cattlemen when it commented that the Agricultural Minister's failure to change anyone's mind was matched by his own intransigence.

Over the ensuing months the WSGA, supported by the National Council of Beef Producers and the Canadian Federation of Agriculture pressured the government to change its position. Other potential allies were wooed. For instance, it was well-recognized that the Minister of Finance, Hon. Douglas Abbott, had long been in favour of removal of export restrictions to the United States. On 27 March, WSGA President, Charles McKinnon sent a long letter to the Prime Minister, the Cabinet, and all members of the House of Commons and the Senate in which he pressed for the embargo's removal. He argued that the cattle industry was being forced to operate under the price controls inherent in the government-negotiated British contract. McKinnon was also openly critical of Gardiner. "Our men cannot understand your Minister of Agriculture's appraisal of our future markets when he insists on binding our country to the unnatural United Kingdom market with contracts against which cattlemen have unequivocally taken their stand."[89] The letter which was read aloud and discussed at length in the House of Commons was a major factor in influencing an official change in attitude by early summer.

Another probable factor concerned the failure of secret talks between Canada and the United States on a free-trade deal.[90] Canada's wartime policy of allowing credit on exports, combined with her purchase of U.S. goods in dollars had created a significant balance of payment deficit of over a billion dollars by the end of 1947. This spiralling dollar deficit induced Canadian officials to approach the Americans in the fall of 1947 for a $750 million loan and a comprehensive trade agreement, hinting at long-range import restrictions otherwise. Realizing the importance of trade between the two countries and possibly wanting to disrupt the present system of imperial tariffs, the Americans responded favourably. By mid-March 1948, the basis for a general agreement had been settled upon. The overall plan included among other things the immediate removal of all duties by both countries for five years and joint consultation on agricultural marketing. Opposition to the proposed agreement included Gardiner of course, and Louis St. Laurent, Secretary of State for External Affairs and Prime Minister King's heir apparent. On 6 May 1948, a vacillating Mackenzie King finally scuttled the whole deal ostensibly on the grounds that he could not conceive of the Liberal Party placing Canada at the mercy of powerful financial influences in the United States. In the light of this failure to achieve a sweeping trade agreement, it could be argued that the eventual resumption of live cattle exports was a recognition that Canada should not completely close the door to the multilateral trade arrangements so favoured by the United States.

In May 1948 Gardiner was still parrying the issue, maintaining that he had no idea when the embargo was going to be lifted. It was clear however that his resolve was weakening. Aside from the failure of the free-trade initiatives several other factors were at work. First, the wide gap between Canadian and American cattle prices was closing, and with the Canadian dollar now on par with the American,[91] the fear of inflation was lessened. Second, a reopened American market for Canadian cattle was seen as a way to reduce the dollar deficit. Third, and most significant was the unravelling of Gardiner's grand scheme for a wide British market for Canadian agricultural products. The British had made it known that they did not want to pay precious U.S. dollars for products like beef and dairy items which they could buy elsewhere and as cheaply with sterling.[92] Thus it came as no surprise when Britain cancelled her beef contract with Canada in early August. The resulting surplus on the Canadian market left the government with no choice. On 13 August, Gardiner announced the reopening of the American market effective three days later. The news was greeted in the industry with as much relief as jubilation. Manitoba Agriculture Minister, D. L. Campbell echoed the opinions of stockmen across the West when he called Gardiner's announcement "the best news Manitoba farmers have had for a long time", while referring to the market itself as "the lifeblood of the cattle industry in Canada,"[93] An article which appeared in the December, 1948 issue of the *Canadian Cattlemen* captured the general reaction:

> Within a week of the lifting of the embargo on August 16 there was a united demand for railway stock cars all the way from the Peace River country to the U.S. border, as Herman Linder used to say, "the panic was on." Every available cattle car was rushed to Alberta and although record numbers were loaded out and headed for Chicago, south St. Paul, and as far west as Seattle and as far south as Los Angeles, the demand for cattle cars continued. The goose was hanging high and Alberta cattlemen were cashing in for the first time in many years.[94]

In the four and a half month period following the reopening of the U.S. market, three hundred thousand head went south, realizing a total of $60 million in American funds.[95] The *Lethbridge Herald's* prediction that Canadian and U.S. prices were close enough to minimize increases in retail prices proved correct.[96] Though beef prices rose immediately following the lifting of the embargo, they soon firmed at less than inflationary levels. In August, the price of good butcher steers in Calgary was $20–22 per hundredweight. After the lifting of the embargo, they jumped to $22–23.50 per hundredweight. By November they were back to the July levels. The mood was buoyant at the fifty-third annual convention of the Western Stock Growers' Association at the Palliser Hotel in Calgary in January 1949. Before receiving a white hat whose high crown was jokingly described as "the embargo lift," the Minister of Finance, Douglas Abbott, had proffered an official olive branch when he told the delegates that their "efforts in presenting the point of view of the cattle growers to the Dominion Government and to the country in general has contributed to a better understanding of one another's problems."[97] In his report, President Charles McKinnon referred to the lifting of the embargo, calling 1948 one of the most important years in the history of the association.[98] WSGA Secretary Ken Coppock probably best summed up the general opinion of western Canadian cattlemen when he told a radio audience in October, 1949 that "the industry has now returned to logic and fact…. The future outlook has changed; the fundamentals of the industry are now sound."[99]

Aside from its arbitrariness and negative financial impact on producers, the maintenance of the embargo after 1945 had two major impacts on the Alberta cattle industry. First, the closed American market, and the lower British price had combined to discourage the production of top-quality beef in the immediate post-war years. Red Brand Label beef could not be produced consistently at a price to turn feeders a profit.[100] This led to a decline in cattle numbers  By 1948, the national beef cattle numbers had dropped over 1.5 million from their wartime peak of eleven million, and had reached, to quote Ken Coppock, "a point no higher than thirty years ago when Canada's human population was 25% smaller."[101] The Alberta Department of Agriculture commented that before the lifting of the embargo, the year 1948 had been characterized by "consternation among producers and a swing to grain farming."[102] Second, from the producers' viewpoint, the embargo and the associated price controls by transferring the pricing mechanism solely to dressed beef robbed them of marketing choices. The loss of the American market made them captives to the packers and the Meat Board. The closure of the

American market also impacted negatively on breeding quality in that it gave American buyers an economic advantage at Canadian bull sales.[103] In 1945, for example, the top ten percent of bulls sold at the Calgary Bull Sale went to American buyers.[104]

To practical men in changing times, it was simply good to return to "business as usual." That their industry had not figured prominently on Gardiner's wider stage of agricultural trade policy, or that the government itself had failed to follow through on its commitment to resume normal operations in peace time did not seem to matter in the new euphoria that accompanied the lifting of the embargo. In terms of the export market, nothing had changed in the Alberta cattle industry by the end of 1948. The United States remained the main venue for quality feeders and finished animals primarily from the ranches of western Canada. From the ranchers' viewpoint, the domestic market remained secondary. In discussing the implications of resumed cattle exports to the United States, the *Farmers' Advocate* in London, Ontario made an accurate prediction when it commented that eastern Canadian feeders would have to resign themselves to a supply that would be both uncertain and of low quality.[105] A spokesman for the federal Department of Agriculture made the same point when he predicted dire straits for the eastern Canadian feedlot industry beef should the U.S. market be made available to western Canadian feeders. Moreover, with the British market no longer a factor after 1948, all of Canada's inferior beef had to be absorbed by the local market.

## The Domestic Market

The domestic market for beef increased considerably during the war. The shortage of pork, the psychological effects of meat rationing, the impact of the black market and the absence of alternative spending options all contributed to a higher demand for beef. Equally significant were the price controls that held meat prices lower than advances in real wages. More surprising was the continued demand for beef in the inflationary post-war period. Evidence suggests however that increased purchasing power and not overall rise in beef quality was the most important influencing factor in the increased beef consumption figures.

Dramatic increases in per capita beef consumption after 1939 were maintained into the post-war period. In 1939 Canadians ate 39.0 pounds of beef per capita. In 1945 the figure was 64.6 pounds, and in 1946 and 1947 per capita beef consumption in Canada reached an all-time high of 67.2 pounds.[106] Although prices also rose after 1939, they were more than offset by wage increases. By 1945 wages were 41 percentage points over pre-war levels, and were another 62.8 percent higher by 1949.[107] Real wage increases give a more accurate measure of purchasing power. They had advanced 24.4 percentage points in 1945 over 1939, and a further 12.9 points over the ensuing two years.[108] The advance in consumer purchasing power manifested itself in increased personal savings in the 1940s, and led to a rise in inflation by 1947–48.

Post-war beef prices rose faster than purchasing power. Evidence given before the Royal Commission on Prices in 1948 indicates that retail beef prices were comparatively higher than other food products like bread and dairy products. Using 1939 figures as a base, it was shown that one hour's of labour in 1947 actually bought less beef than it did in 1939, but far more bread and the same amount of eggs.[109] The same figures showed that the index increase for beef was higher than for other food products over the same period. By 1948 the high meat prices precipitated a significant decline in beef consumption, and, as has been discussed, were used by the federal government as reason for maintaining the embargo on American exports.

The willingness to pay more for beef under these circumstances in the post-war years was not linked to supply or quality. In 1948 for example, beef prices reached an all-time high in spite of marketings that were 37 percent over the long-term average.[110] It was estimated that the parity price or that justified by cost of living indexes and wages was about one-third below that being paid by consumers.[111] In 1948, E. C. Hope, an economist with the Canadian Federation of Agriculture, blamed the high prices on "an abnormally high demand."[112]

It appears that meat quality was not a factor in maintaining a strong demand for beef, either during or after the war. During the war, the need to feed Britain warranted volume production in which quality was sacrificed for quantity. After the war, the low prices in the ongoing British contracts tended to discourage feeding for quality. In 1944 for example only 16.3 percent of steers and 6.7 percent of heifers were graded Choice.[113] In 1947, the first year of compulsory grading, only 12.3 percent of beef carcasses were grade Choice, while a disturbing 43 percent was graded below commercial.[114] The secretary of the Canadian Aberdeen Angus Association commented in 1946 that " the marketings of Canadian cattle during the war were of poor quality."[115] In giving evidence before the 1948 Royal Commission on Prices in 1948, the spokeswoman for the Alberta Branch of the National Council of Women commented on the prevalence of vastly inferior beef at retail outlets throughout the province.[116] In reference to eastern Canadian finished beef, one livestock expert said it was no interest at all to American buyers who said it was fit only for "fox meat."[117] In commenting on priorities for Alberta's post-war beef production, R. D. Sinclair, Dean of the Faculty of Agriculture at the University of Alberta warned that "if Canadian consumers are to be encouraged to increase their purchase of beef or if we hope to enlarge our markets … the general use of good sires … is necessary."[118]

Yet the fact remains that despite indifferent quality and adequacy of supply, Canadian consumers continued to deploy more of their disposable income on beef between 1946 and 1948. While increased purchasing power was the main reason, other factors were at work. First, the lower wartime prices had greatly enhanced the popularity of beef, and created a strong demand especially for the more expensive cuts, or those hitherto available only to more affluent consumers. Aided by advertising that exalted the lusty appeal of thick juicy grilled T-bone steaks over more conservative stews and roasts, the mystique of beef began in this period. The enduring appeal of the urban barbecue dates to these years. The trend was not unnoticed by the National Council of Beef Producers which abandoned its original role as an exporter, becoming instead a powerful voice of beef promotion. Though it was to take several more years, the exalted place of Alberta beef in the national consciousness had its genesis in the war years when average Canadians were able to buy the beef of their choice, a practice they were loath to surrender in peacetime. In this respect, It should be noted that the only references to beef shortages in Canadian cities in 1948 applied to the more expensive cuts.

# Feeding and Finishing

The war had a major impact on the livestock feeding industry both nationally and regionally. Given emergency needs, the higher beef yields commensurate with wartime food demands could only be achieved with enhanced feeding programmes. It took the exigencies of war to introduce legitimacy to Canada's laggard feeding industry, something all the arguments and exhortations of the previous thirty years had never managed to achieve. On the other hand, the wartime conditions delayed advancements in crucial areas of the feeding industry. Questions of uniformity in beef quality, and the merits of grading were put on hold. The belief that fattening was the same as finishing was more entrenched than challenged during this period. Finally, the maintenance of price controls tended to delay the industry's development in the immediate post-war years.

The most significant impact on the feeding industry came in the form of government intervention and was encapsulated in James Gardiner's message to farmers over CBC radio in November 1942: "Feed every beef animal you have the labour for, and feed to finish until it has eaten the last pound of grain." In practical terms this really meant that the only way to increase production in the short term was to encourage gross weight gain through abundant feeding. Government incentives to promote the feeding of livestock were threefold. In 1942 the growing of coarse feeding grains was encouraged through a bonus applied to every marketed bushel of barley and oats. A year later, in order to reward farmers for keeping their feed grains in Canada as opposed to seeking the higher U.S. export price, a system of equalization payments was introduced. Third, livestock feeding was assisted by a fifty percent freight rate concession on feed grains going to eastern Canada. The government also encouraged feeding by giving Special or grain-fed beef a higher ceiling.

These concessions were of significant importance since feed costs comprised over 85 percent of the cost of finishing an animal in a feedlot. The results were large scale conversion to coarse grain acreage, and the heavy movement of cattle to feeding areas.[119] Furthermore, the incentives by stabilizing feed costs fostered the development of a strong feeding industry in Ontario and Quebec.[120] The increased beef tonnage from feedlots across the country was reflected in rising domestic consumption. In spite of rationing and the British export commitments, annual beef consumption in Canada rose 8.5 pounds per capita between 1939 and 1944, an increase of more than sixteen percent. The dramatic increase in feedlot numbers was reflected in Alberta. In 1940 about fifteen thousand head were fed annually in the province's feedlots, and by 1946 over twenty thousand head were in feedlots operated by the Lethbridge Central Feeders' Association alone.

The Government interventions however, enhanced eastern Canadian feedlot operations more than Alberta's. The fifty percent freight rate reduction was applied only to animals going to Ontario and Quebec, and then only if they were fed for ninety days.[121] The discrepancy was not lost on Alberta producers, many of whom could not understand a policy that encouraged shipping young animals half way across the country when ample feeding facilities existed in Alberta. These concessions by the federal government went a significant step beyond its similar freight reduction policies in the 1930s. Then they applied only to animals ultimately bound for export. The wartime feeder freight policies demonstrated the first federal interest in rationalizing the beef cattle industry on a national basis.

While the feed bonuses helped the farmer, the feedlot operators, and the industry in general, there were negative aspects. The WSGA was opposed to subsidies on the grounds that they upset the industry's natural balance between feedlot operator and farmer/feeder. The federal government's feed bonus policy did not help the prairie mixed farmers who were not eligible for the subsidies if they fed their own animals. For the average mixed farmer, this put the price of grain out of line with cattle prices.[122] The impact of this restriction is reflected by the fact that only about thirty percent of coarse grain ever left the farm.[123] The result was a retardation of feeding on western Canadian mixed farms, and a wealth of western commentary on political favouritism. Indeed, the low place of cattle in the federal agenda was later evinced by a proposal to apply the feed bonuses to acreage rather than marketed grain in order to encourage hog feeding, and by implication, James Gardiner's concept of mixed farming. As far as Alberta was concerned, the wartime feeding subsidies and their continuation after the war militated against the development of the industry. In criticizing the subsidized movement of coarse grains out of Alberta, John Cross, President of the Western Section of the National Council of Beef Producers made the following comment in early 1950: "Would it not be better to process this barley through livestock and then ship the livestock to various markets ourselves? It would save Canadian taxpayers about a million dollars a week and encourage the Cattle Feeding Industry in Western Canada."[124]

Rising grain prices after the war and the increasing incompatibility between beef ceilings and feed and labour costs also hurt the feedlot industry. It was argued that the increasing popularity of cattle after 1944 as compared with hogs was linked to the fact that the grazing independence of cattle and their lower feeding costs made them less labour-intensive than hogs.[125] As long as government controls governed the industry, feedlot operators were afforded a measure of protection. The inflationary spiral that began in 1947 pushed operating costs up to a point to where the wartime rate of progress in the feedlot industry was difficult to maintain. This was especially so in 1948 following the removal of ceilings and export restrictions on coarse grains. Moreover, the prevalence of inferior beef in the British contracts, and the related price-setting mechanisms depressed prices and discouraged feedlot production of quality beef, its staple product. By 1948 only about ten percent of Canadian beef came out of feedlots.

One of the most positive wartime developments in the cattle industry was the emergence of barley as a quality feed grain. Often viewed with skepticism because of its low profitability compared with wheat, its acidity, feed value and even resistance to harvesting, barley had never been widely accepted as a premier feed grain. As the *Farm and Ranch Review* commented in 1942, "The lack of appreciation for barley has affected the wide fluctuations in acreages."[126] The release of twenty-one year feeding trials at the University of Alberta in 1941 showed conclusively that barley marketed through cattle was consistently more profitable to the farmer than selling it as grain. The trials showed that the average return on barley was seventy-three cents per bushel if marketed through cattle, but only forty-three cents per bushel if sold as grain.[127] The development of tougher varieties with higher feed value by the Dominion Experimental Farms also increased the popularity of barley. By 1945 the *Farm and Ranch Review* was arguing that "farmers must recognize that the safest market for grain is through livestock and that the feed most generally suited to this purpose is barley."[128] Heavier than oats, and less close in texture than wheat when ground, barley was seen by many experts as the most suitable feed grain.[129] Grant MacEwan, then Dean of Agriculture at the University of Manitoba and recognized expert in livestock feeding, praised barley at the time for its high fibre and feeding value and predicted that it would continue to be the main ration in feeding steers.[130]

# Other Marketing Issues

## Breeding Implications

The prosperity associated with the war period and tax advantages associated with the introduction of the basic herd principle in 1947 encouraged producers to improve their breeding stock. The ongoing efforts by the WSGA to have the entire province declared a TB-free zone also had enormous implications for exports and breeding. Records were set at the Calgary Bull sale during these years. The 1945 sale was announced by the *Farm and Ranch Review* as "the greatest sale ever staged in Canada" at which "all records went by the boards."[131] Furthermore, experiments in the United States were showing the distinct advantages of hybrid vigour through cross breeding. Although Alberta had counted over thirty cattle breeds in 1930, the three major breeds (Hereford, Shorthorn, and Angus) accounted for over 90 percent of Canadian pure bred cattle. However, the use of the Hereford, and to a lesser degree the Shorthorn, to produce crossbred commercial cattle was becoming increasingly popular among producers. In 1946 Harry Hargrave, superintendent of the Manyberries Range Experiment Station, called for breeders and commercial cattle producers to co-operate in producing a superior range animal, one which incorporated the best qualities of the three dominant breeds.[132]

## "Dwarfism"

Probably the most significant development in cattle breeding during this period was a serious attempt to breed quality into smaller animals. For years, the packers had been arguing that the road to quality beef lay in marketing smaller, finer animals. The trend towards "dwarfism" that began in this decade should be seen in the above light. The propensity to favour smaller animals was first reflected by judges in the show ring. Compounding the problem further was the popular concept of the perfect show animals. According to Dr Roy Berg, Professor of Agriculture at the University of Alberta,

> ... everybody believed that production was determined by shape. Beef animals had to be very square and blocky; if you had the right shape you had "quality," by which was meant the right kind of beef and the right kind of roast... University professors (like me a few years later) were often proud to be asked to judge- so we were partly responsible for that show ring mentality. 4-H kids were told that the "comprest" or pony type was exactly what the industry wanted... Anyway, the idea developed that big was bad and all through World War Two cattle got smaller and more compact...[133]

The equation of quality, and therefore finish, with smaller animals was a by-product of a trend evident as early as the 1920s. According to one operator, cattle which "would not grow, would put on fat and didn't have much muscle ... sure killed a lot of business"[134] Larger animals or those which did not conform to the pure bred concept of excellence were frowned upon.

Although the later presence of a hard-to-eradicate dwarf gene was a legacy of this period, it could be argued that the overall effects of the "dwarfism" fad were more positive than negative. It convinced the cattle industry that show-ring standards were not the last word in selecting breeding stock, and that the pure-bred animal might not necessarily be "the ultimate food animal."[135] As a result, crossbreeding, formerly frowned upon by pure breeders, emerged as a legitimate breeding alternative. The later trend towards commercial or unregistered cattle had its genesis in the "comprest" cattle phenomenon of the 1930–50 period. Also, the advent of performance testing whereby beef production qualities were factored into genetic or inherited traits in breeding programmes was partly a response to the inequities produced by the inferior beef quantity and quality associated with "dwarfism."[136]

## Grading

The confusion over grading practices continued throughout this period. Though the WSGA wanted to suspend all activities on grading until after the war, the federal government inadvertently reinforced a longstanding negative aspect of the grading process when it rewarded Special or Red Brand Label carcasses over 375 pounds with a higher ceiling.[137] During the voluntary phase of grading in the 1930s, it had become standard practice by both the packers and the government inspectors to equate Grade A or Red Label with fat animals. The longstanding practice of feeding for fat only, was thus legitimised into grading procedures. Moreover, between 1943 and 1945 domestic price ceilings did not distinguish between Blue Brand Label and Commercial Grade, with the result that all such beef received Blue Label grading regardless of differences in quality. Work on a standard set of grades was begun in 1945. In January 1947, the grading of all beef slaughtered at inspected plants became compulsory. Yet, despite specific instructions on how to evaluate fat dispersal into accurate grading assessments, the process remained sufficiently subjective to result in wide differentials. Many retailers seized upon these vagaries and labelled all their beef "Red Label." These inconsistencies had not been redressed by 1949.

# Land Use

Land use in this period underwent some dramatic transformations that had significant implications for livestock. Most changes resulted from direct government interventions. The conversion to coarse grains, the presence of irrigation, and the development of the legume mix forage crop began to change the rural face of Alberta. Range management became more of an obligation than an option. Moreover, the long-contentious leasehold tenure issue was resolved. The integration of production costs into leasehold tenure provisions contributed markedly to the overall stabilization of the cattle industry.

The most significant development in land use practices in Alberta during this period was the conversion of crop acreage from wheat to barley and to a lesser extent oats. While the increased production of these grains had immediate positive results for the livestock industry, the long-range implications were far more significant. Alberta's soil types, combined with factors of geography and climate precluded wheat as the staple crop of the province. The movement towards hardier crops such as barley and oats during the war represented the clearest practical expression to date of Alberta's optimum agricultural land use. One observer has noted that the 1940s marked an important phase in Western Canadian agriculture. Saskatchewan's heavier concentration on grain and Alberta's movement towards mixed farming changed the parallel course the two prairie provinces had been on for a half century.[138]

Barley acreage in Alberta virtually doubled during this period. By 1951, land sown to barley reached over three million acres. In 1941 the combined acreage devoted to oats and barley was about two-thirds that planted to wheat. By 1951 the two figures were virtually equal with wheat showing acreage reductions for the first time, This trend towards feed grains was accompanied by a greater concentration on mixed forage crops. By 1946, over forty-five percent of Alberta farms contained one or more of alfalfa, clover, and brome grass. Successful American experiments on legume forage mixes were also having their effect. More Alberta farmers were becoming aware of their value especially in the province's extensive nitrogen-deficient luvisolic soil areas. Irrigation was another important development in land use. Ongoing construction had put over half a million acres under irrigation in southern Alberta by 1946. The belated realization that wheat was not the ideal crop for irrigated lands was evidencing itself in changing land use. One example was the growing potential of the Picture Butte area for premier cattle feeding operations.

In the drier areas, land use was enhanced in other ways. The popularity of the cover crop was given the seal of official approval through a three-year experiment at the University of Alberta.[139] Developed in the early 1920s partly to arrest soil drifting, the cover crop was usually planted in summer fallow in late July, and was ready for grazing in about forty-three days when at a height of twelve to twenty inches. Grazed at the rate of about an acre a head for around sixty days, the cover crop was a viable fall feeding alternative. In the university tests it was shown that the cover crop was also profitable, giving an average return per acre of $19.40 while recording an average gain of 2.5 pounds per day. The test also showed that the average cost per acre was $3.08 as compared with $5.00 per acre on a cash crop.

Ranchers were aided by ongoing experiments by the PFRA and the Dominion Experimental Stations on perennial grasses. By 1942, in 153,000 cross-pollinations involving twenty-four perennial grasses and nine species and forty varieties of wheat, a total of 140 fertile hybrid grasses had been developed and were in the testing stage.[140] The regrassing of abandoned croplands with crested wheatgrass was continued during the war years. Its value as a weight-maintaining hay crop and as an early spring and late fall pasture and its ability to crowd out weeds was proven in tests at Lethbridge Research Station.[141] Referring to a community pasture in Saskatchewan seeded to crested wheatgrass, one enthusiastic farmer deemed it "the best darned thing ever to hit Saskatchewan."[142]

However, it would be a mistake to read too much into these advances. The dominance of feed grains in provincial farm acreages was still years away. The use of legume-grass forage mixes was in its infancy. Disease in alfalfa had yet to be controlled. For instance, by the end of the period under discussion, bacterial wilt in alfalfa had resulted in a significant decrease in acreage. The crop share rental provisions in the new government homestead leases militated against feed grains, livestock enterprises or legume crops.[143] Cattle feeding in irrigated districts represented only about six percent of total marketings in 1946. Even by the mid-1950s only about ten percent of all marketed cattle came from the province's major commercial feedlots.[144]

Range management for all practical purposes was still in its early stages. The main advances in range management was the gathering of information. The release in 1942 of the Grasslands Investigations in Alberta, Saskatchewan and Manitoba conducted by the Dominion Experimental Station at Swift Current as well as other government studies added to knowledge of grass varieties and the effects of overgrazing, and reinforced the importance of carrying capacity.[145] However, the growing knowledge base was not yet balanced by a general awareness that took the entire range into account, or which considered the holistic interactions between grass, soil, and water management. In spite of carrying-capacity provisions, overgrazing still occurred. Indeed, in the light of wide variations, one wonders at the criteria used to establish the three provincial carrying capacity zones in 1943. H. E. Clements, Grazing Supervisor for Saskatchewan noted in 1945, "After all, one may estimate the carrying capacity of a quarter section or tract this year, but the weather is the main factor, and there is only one person who knows what that is going to be like and I doubt if He cares."[146] No studies were done specifically on Rough Fescue, a superb pasture grass but one easily damaged by heavy summer grazing.[147] Crested wheatgrass, in spite of its positive qualities, was essentially an invader, and its ultimate impact on the range families into which it had been introduced was certainly not realized at the time. The role of plant litter on grass heights, the implications of water runoff, the long-range effects of introduced grasses on prairie biomass, and the relationship of grazing to plant "increasers" and "decreasers" were little understood.[148] In launching a new series of experiments in 1948 designed to correlate range utilization with beef yields, Harry Hargraves, superintendent of Manyberries Research Station, commented that "we need to get away from guesswork which is all we've had to go on." In referring to grass storage techniques, another expert remarked that "we haven't yet started to make use of better hay and grass silage in the winter. We've just started to put up hay in the green state to preserve the carotene." In 1951, an official with the U.S. Bureau of Land Management felt that the United States had a better record than Alberta in supervising livestock owners on public lands.[149]

The Provincial Government was an active participant in land-use improvements. Provisions in the revised Grazing Regulations of 1940 mandated range management provisions including the regrassing of leased lands when required. The new agricultural homestead policy introduced in 1939 further consolidated government control. Farmers were encouraged to take out grazing leases next to homesteads that had been increased from 160 to 320 acres. The government surveys during this period gave greater priority to land usage. For example, in the 31 percent of land in the Athabasca River and Rimbey areas assessed as suitable for cultivation, provision was made that certain quarter sections were to be sown to legumes only.[150] While refusing to yield to PFRA control over community pastures, the government continued to monitor range management through the establishment of grazing reserves under permanent caretakers and through leases to associations. In 1943 there were eight grazing reserves, the biggest at Vauxhall where farmers ran 3,245 cattle on 165,000 acres. By 1948 there were sixteen grazing leases covering two hundred thousand acres under the control of Associations whose members paid an annual rental sufficient to cover lease rentals and expenses. Despite these interventions, the most significant government influence on the cattle industry during this period came in the form of security and equitability of leasehold tenure.

## Leasehold Tenure

It will be remembered that producers had initiated a strong lobby to the Provincial government in the late 1930s to have leasehold rentals changed from a flat rate to one based on production. Under the auspices of the SGSGA, a group working within the WSGA a pricing formula had been worked out. In 1939 the government agreed to conduct a feasibility study that took into account differing soil types, grazing conditions, carrying capacities and production costs. It was further decided that the WSGA's special committee would be entrusted to prepare the report under the chairmanship of Graham Anderson, an inspector with the Department of Municipal Affairs. Anderson was well-qualified. He had been the Dominion Department of the Interior's Assistant Supervisor of Grazing and in 1924 had written a thesis on range management as part of his graduate work at the University of Saskatchewan.

At the time Anderson began his study, the WSGA both knew and approved of its possible implications. It also approved of Anderson himself who was described by the *Canadian Cattlemen* "as the best man for the job." Though the WSGA was aware that any change to a production tax in the light of the pending Anderson Report would likely be on a voluntary experimental basis, there is every evidence to indicate that it approved of the process and fully expected that any advantages occasioned by any new production tax would apply to the entire membership.

The Grazing Rates Study took two years. It was extensive and wide-ranging, and though it focused mainly on the shortgrass country its findings were advertised in advance as being of general significance. When released in 1941, the "Grazing Rates Report" presented itself as a well-researched, insightful document with important implications for both the government and the livestock industry. The Report covered 237 pages and was based on over a hundred interviews and seventy written briefs. During its investigation, the committee had studied grazing regulations in several American States as well as in Argentina, Australia, New Zealand and South Africa. It had also worked in close co-operation with the Manyberries Research Station. Included in its several recommendations were long-range security of leasehold tenure, the establishment of a Grass Conservation Commission, and an affirmation of the need to shift leasehold rentals from a flat rate to one based on production and market price.

Given the thoroughness of the Report and the ranchers' initiative and co-operation in producing it, the industry reaction to it must have astounded government officials. For the "Grazing Rates Report" received scant attention from either the WSGA or the SGSGA upon its release and was subsequently ignored altogether. The *Canadian Cattlemen*, the official voice of the WSGA, after giving the Report a brief mention of the back page of its September, 1941 issue[151] proceeded to ignore it completely, opting instead to publish in four parts the findings of the federal government's "Grassland Investigations in Alberta, Saskatchewan and Manitoba"[152] which discussed many of the issues contained in the "Grazing Rates Report" but which did not deal with leasehold rentals. It should be added that "The Investigations" seemed to buttress the short grass growers' argument for differentiated rentals, noting that up to ninety-six acres per animal was necessary in some areas, and that overgrazing over a four-year cycle increased weed cover by 250 percent and reduced grass cover by 25 percent and forage yield by 45 percent. The Report's lack of mention in subsequent issues of the *Canadian Cattlemen* was an indication that it had been conveniently forgotten.

The actions of the SGSGA seemed inexplicable and contradictory to its mandate. After claiming that it had achieved that which it had set out to do, it merged with the WSGA Yet, when the provincial government called on its members to honour their agreement to try out the new production-based leasehold rentals on an experimental basis, it was met with indifference and non-compliance. Fifty-four ranchers representing 1,045,000 acres of leased land had indicated that they would be part of the production tax experiment. Yet, only two actually volunteered, and one of those was likely George Ross.[153]

The reasons for this sudden loss of interest in the new leasehold formula had nothing to do with the formula itself, it being public knowledge before the investigation had begun.[154] The new proposal called for the government to take an annual royalty of ten percent[155] of the cost of production to be measured by multiplying the average annual gain of beef on grass (250 pounds) by the average market price of cattle at the Calgary Stockyards between July and December, and dividing that figure by the assessed carrying capacity of the land. As George Ross had pointed out in the late 1930s, adoption of this new formula would reduce rentals in the shortgrass country measurably.[156]

The WSGA's reluctance to accept the Grazing Rates Report had some validity. First, it worried about the implications of the recommended Grass Conservation Commission.[157] Second, it feared that the government really wanted to impose a tax on all production *in lieu* of a general land tax.[158] A third and most important point concerned its recent success in 1939–40 when new lease regulations were negotiated. Under these regulations, the provincial government guaranteed twenty-year security of tenure and reinforced the maximum flat rental rate of four cents per acre.[159] In the light of the *Canadian Cattlemen*'s description of the regulations as being "as near as we could come to getting all we asked for,"[160] any question of a shift to a production tax was of marginal interest. Finally, it could be argued that WSGA members in the higher carrying-capacity areas of the Foothills were sincere in their opinion that the new tax was to be limited to the semi-arid zone delineated by the SGSGA's focus of attention.

The reasons why the SGSGA lost interest in a proposal that it had promoted for so energetically were rooted solely in pragmatic concerns, and were guided by financial motives rather than by the principles of effective long-range grass management. When George Ross devised his formula in the late 1930s, he based it on an average market price of two cents per pound for range cattle at the Calgary Stockyards. He was exaggerating but not by much. Figures given in the Grazing Rates Report quoted an average market price for all cattle at the Calgary Stockyards at about $3.30 per hundredweight.[161] This price translated into a much lower rental rate under the new formula of 1.65 cents per acre in the shortgrass country. However, the rising cattle prices after 1939 changed the situation completely. By the time the "Grazing Rates Report" was released in late 1941, cattle prices were over $7.00 per hundredweight. Suddenly, George Ross' new formula for setting rental rates became an unattractive alternative. At $7.00 per hundredweight, lease rates in the shortgrass country would have been 3.5 cents an acre, significantly more than the ranchers' flat rate in the dryland-zoned areas. Conveniently overlooked was the low cattle price issue, the motivation behind the proposal in the first place. It was also likely that the stockmen had decided to play the waiting game. Realizing that they essentially had given their approval for the government to change the lease formula from acreage to production, they probably knew it was just a matter of time before the issue was forced.

By the end of 1943, the Hon. N. E. Tanner, the Provincial Minister of Lands and Mines, was prepared to do exactly that. He had already gone ahead with his plans of dividing the province into carrying capacity zones as recommended in the *Grazing Rates Report*.[162] Three such zones had been demarcated. A ratio of fifty acres to one animal delineated the shortgrass country of southern Alberta and the drier areas of the east. Along the heavily grassed foothills twenty-four to one was considered a fair allocation, while most of Central Alberta and a narrow trough extending south through High River and opening up in the Milk River country south of Lethbridge was designated at thirty-two to one.[163] By the beginning of 1944, Tanner was ready. On 14 January 1944, he wrote to the WSGA asking for its recommendations on government grazing policies in the post-war period.[164] Tanner followed up his request with a critical article that appeared in the March 1944 issue of the *Canadian Cattlemen*. He referred to the government's commitment to the ranching industry through its recently enacted regulations providing for security of tenure, and to the co-operation between his Ministry and the ranchers in devising the new production tax on leaseholds. He then castigated the short grass ranchers saying that "this plan has been submitted to the members of the Short Grass Stock Growers' Association but to date it is regretted that the plan has not received more favourable consideration."[165] Tanner left no illusions about his perception of the situation:

> It is well remembered by all that during the 1930s the present flat rental rate
> was high in comparison to the price of beef and drought conditions that

prevailed at that time. It was during this period that many of the ranchers got in arrears in their rental which made it very difficult to carry on both from the standpoint of ranchers, as lessee, and the Department, as lessor. Today the same flat rate of rental is charged as in the late nineteen thirties, yet the price of livestock has increased considerably during the same period. The ranching industry will never become stabilized as long as the rental costs are fixed and the selling price of livestock and the quantity of grass vary from year to year.[166]

The WSGA was not impressed. Confronted by rising cattle prices, it attempted to counter Tanner by suggesting a post-war policy that would allow ranchers to gradually become owners of their leases. The present flat rate on acreage was endorsed as the best alternative to the above. As for the new Production Tax, a warning was issued that it "should be thoroughly tested by experienced operators before being considered as a general policy."[167] Bolstered by the support of its membership at the WSGA Annual Convention of 1944, the Grazing Committee responded to a government request, and journeyed to Edmonton in October, 1944 to present the stockmen's views.

The Grazing Committee met on 12 October with a government that had clearly made up its mind with respect to adopt the Production Tax.[168] After flatly rejecting the Committee's recommendation for outright lease purchases, Department of Lands and Mines officials were equally unreceptive to other suggestions which included a universal experimentation period, and the isolation of the southeastern area of the province for a longer trial period. When the Grazing Committee continued to hedge on accepting a tax based on production, the Deputy Minister responded by hinting strongly at substantial increases in the flat rate. Only then did the Grazing Committee bow to the inevitable. The Production Tax on leaseholds was accepted for a period of ten years commencing in 1945 and subject to review at the end of a five-year period.

The WSGA was not surprised by the outcome. President Thomas Usher told the membership that the decision came as no surprise, and that "it was apparent that the Department favoured basing grazing charges on the production method."[169] Usher's conciliatory words indicated that he had accepted the inevitable. "This may seem a pretty drastic change for some, but I would ask all our members to give the plan a fair trial before passing judgement on it."[170] He also indicated the fact that carrying rates had been conservatively appraised, and ultimately would be established on an individual lease basis. He also referred to the appeal process as protecting ranchers from inaccurate carrying capacity appraisals.[171] Interestingly, Usher was more candid in a Director's Meeting a few months later. In responding to a comment that there was considerable criticism among the membership of the new grazing rates policy, Usher noted that the stockmen themselves were to blame not the government.[172] Still, it was a bitter pill to swallow, particularly given the market price of $8.87 per hundredweight that was used to establish the initial three levies. From a maximum flat rate of four cents per acre between 1940 and 1944, ranchers in the twenty-four to one carrying capacity zone were levied 9.25 cents per acre in 1945; those in the thirty-two to one zone paid seven cents per acre while even those in the fifty to one zone accepted a rate of 4.5 cents per acre, a figure higher than the previous maximum.

Following the first year of the new arrangement, the Department of Lands and Mines reported on its satisfactory implementation noting that very few ranchers had resorted to the appeal process. The Department was correct up to a point in that objections were expressed mainly in terms of carrying capacity appraisals. The real issue at stake was not so much the objections but the fact that ranchers realized that the era of flat rates was gone forever and that the production tax was a *fait accompli*. Over the next seven years, the levies continued to rise until, by 1951, the three rates were 25.25 cents, 19 cents, and 12 cents an acre, based on a market price of $25.24 per hundredweight.

With some modifications this process of assessing lease rentals remained in place for the next fifty years. Its flexibility protected both the rancher and the grasslands, and ended the long-prevailing notion that land was an inviolate product to be differentiated productively solely in terms of gross acreage. It took debt, land degradation and low prices to impel producers to seek this new solution. The credit for same, however, belonged to the provincial government which, operating on high moral ground, could easily claim long-range vision as its guiding principle. That these lofty ideals derived immediate fiscal benefit to the province through rising prices was an irony that few ranchers would appreciate.

# Conclusion

What was the situation at the end of 1948? It is undeniable that progress had been made, especially in terms of leasehold tenure, institutional stability, and the final resolution of the export market issue. Range management was seen as increasingly important, and livestock were being recognized as being integral to effective land use. Population increases in the western half of the continent were beginning to affect local prices by reducing differentials between East and West, and promising a viable permanent regional market for Alberta cattle. Higher domestic prices for beef had at last been realized, and seemingly accepted by the average consumer. The industry was further protected and stabilized by the basic herd principle, income tax averaging and professional promotional programmes.

In many ways, though, little had changed. The accumulation of the knowledge necessary for the scientific application of long-term range management principles was barely underway. Traditional marketing practices remained largely unchanged. While the contentious British market for live cattle had gone the way of the dinosaur, the U.S. export market still wielded disproportionate influence in relation to the domestic demand for beef. All in all, it had been an uphill battle for Alberta cattlemen as they strove to achieve stability for themselves and their industry. While some solid gains had been made, much more needed to be done. The road to "good Alberta beef," the proper place of cattle in a province-wide rationalization of land-use, a viable regional market, and the expectation of reasonable profits over a reasonable length of time, had to wait until the next era.

The impetus behind this significant growth after 1950 is partly reflected in the emergence of the commercial feedlot and the upgrading of beef production and quality by the importation of exotic breeds. The general conditions of prosperity that characterized the second half of the twentieth century influenced a consumer market that could and would pay for quality beef. The density of this market was related to changes in population demographics in both western Canada and in the Pacific West and Northwest in the United States. Thus, the second half of the twentieth century did what the preceding eighty years could not do. Increasing purchasing power in the hands of a greater number of people more than offset the higher production costs associated with beef cattle raising in high northern latitudes.

...

# Conclusion

THE FOREGOING DISCUSSION HAS FOCUSSED ON THE IMPORTANCE of market factors and land issues in explaining the development of Alberta's beef cattle industry up to 1949. The most significant market-related factors were the primary role of exports, the relative unimportance of the domestic market, and the retardation of a feeding industry in the province. The success of the ranchers in ensuring security of leasehold tenure solidified their importance while enabling the type of operations that favoured the export market. By 1949 the industry stood on the threshold of change. Increased consumer purchasing power, the availability of the prized American export market, the integration of feed grains into provincial land-use patterns, and the arrival of the mystique of beef combined to usher the Alberta beef cattle industry into a new age.

Other broad patterns may be discerned. Despite its romantic ranching background, beef cattle operations paled before wheat growing in terms of both profitability and popular sentiments. Beef cattle were always in direct competition with wheat in farming priorities, and for most of the period wheat won out. The intrusion of wheat acreage into sub-marginal ranching areas after 1906 speaks for itself. Yet the argument that the beef cattle industry was a simply an economic casualty to the appeal of "King Wheat" can be misleading. Habit and custom played important roles in that many farmers were loath to change their established practices even in the face of trying circumstances. Some ranchers hastened their own downfall by refusing to liquidate after telling winters or other catastrophes. Similarly, many wheat farmers in eastern Alberta continued to labour in "next year country" rather than seriously consider livestock alternatives. The attitude towards barley growing provides another case in point. Its failure to take hold as a feed grain was associated with more than just profitability or hardness of kernels. Barley was mistrusted and associated with diminished alternatives; it was not the "done thing" to sow much barley, even though its benefits as a feed grain had been established by the early 1920s. Mindset as well as economics meant that the travail of the beef cattle industry during this period was also about a preference for wheat as well as markets, the packers, or competition. Though this attitude had begun to change during the Second World War in response to federal support policies that de-emphasized wheat in favour of barley, the premier place of wheat in the thinking of Alberta's farmers was to continue well into the modern era.

Mindset played another important role in defining producers' practices during this period. The unswerving belief that exports determined prices on the hoof was not entirely accurate. First, most studies have shown that consumer demand during this period was linked to disposable income more than to price changes. Figures issued by the Department of Labour in 1949 show that the relative price of beef did not change appreciably during this period. The amount of beef that could be bought from one hour's wages was 2.5 pounds in 1901, 2.4 pounds in 1920 and 2.3 pounds in 1948. Second, the assumption also ignores the add-on value of beef. High retail prices did not translate into commensurate returns to producers. Retail meat prices were also influenced by competition from other meats, the tendency to substitute cheaper beef imports in times of high exports, variability in market weights, the fluctuations associated with the long cattle cycle, and American supply and demand trends. The point is that the export market did not influence inelastic retail prices to the extent that cattlemen believed. Their mindset justified practices that defined the way the industry operated. Yet were other options feasible? Probably not. Like all businessmen, cattle producers went to where they could obtain the best prices for their animals. The export market met the needs of producers. However, its ultimate impact on retail prices was very conjectural.

The continuing importance of ranching during this period allowed the survival of a unique culture. Each of the three western provinces had (and have) a strong ranching industry. Only Alberta, however, has managed to incorporate the ideals of the rancher—through the image of the cowboy—into a wider mythology. The Calgary Stampede of 1912 and the successive premier rodeos in the city drew heavily in these years from the ranks of the working cowboy, and in so doing established Alberta as the earliest and best example of an Old West revisited. More significant, however, was the role played by Alberta's ranching fraternity. Their fight over leasehold security allowed them to maintain what had always been a privileged, even elitist, position. Their individual contacts and their collective strength in the Western Stock Growers' Association gave them strong leverage in government and business circles. Their influence reached into many facets of public, business, institutional, and social life. Economic uncertainty led many of them to explore business options that ultimately forged a mutual affinity with the rising oil and gas entrepreneurs, with whom they were ideologically compatible. Through their divergent roles and outspoken presence in urban-based conventions and through media coverage, they comprised a powerful force that has lasted to the present time.[1] Though the cowboy has given popular identification to romanticized ideals, it was the ranchers on which the Alberta ideological mantle first fell.

In his excellent study of North American cattle ranching, *North American Cattle Ranching Frontiers: Origins, Diffusion and Differentiation* Terry Jordan discusses the "Midwest" ranching system as one of three distinct forms of ranching established in North America.[2] In his address to the Cowboy Conference in Calgary in 1997, Jordan suggested that the western Canadian ranching industry was a variant of this Midwest system.[3] This assessment, when applied to Alberta, needs some qualification. While Jordan's comments on the British influence, winter feeding, the formation and goals of ranching associations, and the versatility of ranching practices are applicable to the Alberta experience, some other aspects did not apply as readily. The extensive leaseholds resulted in some divergence. The presence of non-docile cattle, the absence of fencing in certain areas, and the difficulty in optimizing breeding practices are examples that come to mind. Finally, the lack of complementary feeding districts in Alberta for most of this period is inconsistent with Jordan's criteria for his Midwest ranching system.

Though Jordan may have been expansive in incorporating Alberta into his Midwest ranching system, there can be no doubt that this period affirmed the industry's north/south focus in western Canada. The continental influences described by Evans and Elofson were extended after 1914 mainly through the primacy of the American market. The dialogue between ranchers and their American agents, the cross-border movement of buyers and breeders, and the exchange of information between livestock associations cemented this interrelationship at both the business and social levels. Thrown into conflict with a federal government whose interests lay in furthering more desirable imperial agricultural agendas, the Alberta stockmen demonstrated, for the first time, the value of an integrated continental trade in a single product. Despite some uncertainties and antagonisms, this north-south trade orientation remains as strong as ever.

The stockmen's confrontation with Ottawa over the best export market for Canadian live cattle has wider ramifications than mere differences of opinion. Western grain farmers and their grievances have provided the basis for most discussion on the causes of western Canadian alienation during this period. The stockmen's differences with the federal government over the merits of the British and American markets provides another dimension to this debate. The Conservative bent of the Alberta cattle industry contrasts sharply with the Liberal and CCF orientation of the farmers and completes a regional political spectrum opposed to the national policy of central Canada.

What of the post-1949 period? The export market and the system of leasehold tenure defined in 1944 remained constant factors in the industry's subsequent development. The chief changes after 1950 were due to increased consumer purchasing power that resulted in better beef cuts on middle- and lower-income family tables. The emergence of the commercial feedlot and the arrival of exotic breeds changed the way the industry operated. Cow-calf herds consolidated their importance in both ranching and mixed farming enterprises. The introduction of new, or "tame," grasses, the growing use of the legume/grass pasturage mix, and the adoption of carefully planned range principles further differentiated the post-1949 producers from their counterparts of the 1900–49 era. As compared with the era under discussion, however, the following of different trails did not mean fewer trials.

## Table 1: Beef Cattle Numbers in Canada and Alberta

| YEAR | CANADA | ALBERTA |
|------|--------|---------|
| 1881 | 1,796,596 | 5,690 |
| 1891 | 2,139,911 | 134,493 |
| 1901 | 3,080,384 | 281,127 |
| 1906 | | 849,387 |
| 1911 | 3,930,828 | 592,076 |
| 1916 | | 893,886 |
| 1921 | 5,140,856 | 1,001,718 |
| 1926 | | 775,565 |
| 1931 | 4,450,030 | 685,661 |
| 1936 | | 1,111,685 |
| 1941 | 4,890,912 | 978,504 |
| 1946 | | 1,767,025 |
| 1951 | 5,463,152 | 1,285,421 |
| 1956 | 7,126,428 | 2,237,932 |

Sources: Census of Canada, Census of the Prairie Provinces

## Table 2: Field Crop Acreage in Alberta 1900 – 50

| YEAR | WHEAT | OATS | BARLEY |
|------|-------|------|--------|
| 1900 | 48,062 | 117,765 | 11,055 |
| 1910 | 879,786 | 783,074 | 121,425 |
| 1920 | 4,079,481 | 2,270,149 | 364,696 |
| 1930 | 7,943,014 | 2,163,364 | 698,051 |
| 1940 | 8,871,554 | 2,325,808 | 1,168,776 |
| 1950 | 6,771,522 | 2,242,616 | 2,221,522 |

Source: Census of Canada

## Table 3: Per Capita Meat Consumption in Canada, 1920 – 48

| Year | Beef (Pounds) | Pork/Bacon (Pounds) |
|------|------|------|
| 1920 | 57.4 | 42.1 |
| 1921 | 51.2 | |
| 1922 | 58.2 | |
| 1923 | 57.2 | |
| 1924 | 53.0 | 54.8 |
| 1925 | 56.0 | |
| 1926 | 55.2 | |
| 1927 | 54.8 | |
| 1928 | 50.5 | 58.3 |
| 1929 | 51.2 | |
| 1930 | 49.1 | |
| 1931 | 48.5 | |
| 1932 | 48.5 | 55.3 |
| 1933 | 45.8 | |
| 1934 | 50.6 | 47.4 |
| 1935 | 52.7 | |
| 1936 | 56.2 | |
| 1937 | 54.7 | |
| 1938 | 51.6 | |
| 1939 | 49.0 | 52.0 |
| 1943 | 69.3 | |
| 1944 | 61.7 | 61.4 |
| 1945 | 64.6 | |
| 1946 | 64.5 | |
| 1947 | 67.2 | |
| 1948 | 58.0 | |

Sources: *Canadian Cattlemen*, December 1940,
Annual Reports of *Canadian Packers Ltd.*, 1943–48

## Table 4: Alberta Beef Cattle Population by Census Districts 1921 – 51

| Census District | 1921 | 1931 | 1941 | 1951 |
|---|---|---|---|---|
| 1 | 59,673 | 88,267 | 80,500 | 83,051 |
| 2 | 83,298 | 109,343 | 112,361 | 150,230 |
| 3 | 45,626 | 53,898 | 57,716 | 81,340 |
| 4 | 109,444 | 90,462 | 97,952 | 118,119 |
| 5 | 80,164 | 58,461 | 62,742 | 83,588 |
| 6 | 163,943 | 123,704 | 154,761 | 199,860 |
| 7 | 144,694 | 89,050 | 110,607 | 127,942 |
| 8 | 194,675 | 142,878 | 184,973 | 200,931 |
| 9 | 52,914 | 47,860 | 67,915 | 74,244 |
| 10 | 183,968 | 105,018 | 123,861 | 132,240 |
| 11 | 98,730 | 78,842 | 99,293 | 110,897 |
| 12 | 11,758 | 9,583 | 16,702 | 19,031 |
| 13 | 43,436 | 35,292 | 50,224 | 49,701 |
| 14 | 61,812 | 47,332 | 70,092 | 77,075 |
| 15 | 10,218 | 11,564 | 16,648 | 14,442 |
| 16 | 39,675 | 28,731 | 40,522 | 38,202 |
| 17 | 1,529 | 1,917 | 4,119 | 1,976 |

Source: *Census of Canada*

## Table 5: Prices of Good Butcher Steers (Live) Per Cwt, 1890–1948

| Year | Price | Year | Price |
|------|-------|------|-------|
| 1890 | $3.75 | 1920 | $10.46 |
| 1891 | $3.63 | 1921 | $5.78 |
| 1892 | $5.35 | 1922 | $5.46 |
| 1893 | $3.90 | 1923 | $5.57 |
| 1894 | $2.69 | 1924 | $5.27 |
| 1895 | $3.19 | 1925 | $5.88 |
| 1896 | $3.17 | 1926 | $5.99 |
| 1897 | $3.46 | 1927 | $7.28 |
| 1898 | $3.77 | 1928 | $9.30 |
| 1899 | $3.90 | 1929 | $8.95 |
| 1900 | $3.52 | 1930 | $7.63 |
| 1901 | $3.85 | 1931 | $5.40 |
| 1902 | $4.02 | 1932 | $4.82 |
| 1903 | $3.73 | 1933 | $3.87 |
| 1904 | $3.71 | 1934 | $4.40 |
| 1905 | $3.54 | 1935 | $5.45 |
| 1906 | $3.83 | 1936 | $4.49 |
| 1907 | $4.42 | 1937 | $6.12 |
| 1908 | $4.00 | 1938 | $5.50 |
| 1909 | $4.14 | 1939 | $6.65 |
| 1910 | $4.96 | 1940 | $8.45 |
| 1911 | $5.10 | 1941 | $8.62 |
| 1912 | $5.85 | 1942 | $10.63 |
| 1913 | $6.69 | 1943 | $11.77 |
| 1914 | $7.08 | 1944 | $11.66 |
| 1915 | $7.24 | 1945 | $11.54 |
| 1916 | $7.46 | 1946 | $12.25 |
| 1917 | $9.36 | 1947 | $14.47 |
| 1918 | $12.43 | 1948 | $15.25 |
| 1918 | $12.17 | | |

Sources: WSGA Papers; *Canadian Cattlemen*.
The figures are based on yearly averages in western Canada, mainly Winnipeg.

## Table 6: Canadian Live Cattle Exports to Britain and the USA, 1881–1948

| YEAR | GREAT BRITAIN | UNITED STATES |
|------|---------------|---------------|
| 1881 | 49,409 | 7,323 |
| 1882 | 41,519 | 15,914 |
| 1883 | 37,894 | 23,280 |
| 1884 | 53,962 | 30,593 |
| 1885 | 69,446 | 67,758 |
| 1886 | 60,549 | 25,338 |
| 1887 | 63,622 | 45,765 |
| 1888 | 54,248 | 40,047 |
| 1889 | 60,000 | 37,360 |
| 1890 | 66,965 | 7,840 |
| 1891 | 107,689 | 2,763 |
| 1892 | 101,426 | 551 |
| 1893 | 99,904 | 402 |
| 1894 | 80,531 | 256 |
| 1895 | 85,863 | 882 |
| 1896 | 97,042 | 1,646 |
| 1897 | 120,063 | 35,998 |
| 1898 | 122,106 | 87,905 |
| 1899 | 115,476 | 92,834 |
| 1900 | 115,056 | 86,989 |
| 1901 | 119,050 | 46,244 |
| 1902 | 148,927 | 31,743 |
| 1903 | 161,170 | 10,432 |
| 1904 | 148,301 | 3,517 |
| 1905 | 159,078 | 3,696 |
| 1906 | 163,994 | 4,726 |
| 1907 | 149,340 | 8,184 |
| 1908 | 124,015 | 23,612 |
| 1909 | 143,661 | 16,130 |
| 1910 | 140,424 | 12,210 |
| 1911 | 113,475 | 7,576 |
| 1912 | 47,868 | 9,807 |
| 1913 | 9,878 | 180,383 |

231

| Year | Great Britain | United States |
|---|---|---|
| 1914 | — | 145,722 |
| 1915 | 1,762 | 179,016 |
| 1916 | — | 104,277 |
| 1917 | — | 148,077 |
| 1918 | — | 200,666 |
| 1919 | 159 | 453,606 |
| 1920 | 320 | 236,642 |
| 1921 | 33,053 | 135,257 |
| 1922 | 18,475 | 189,760 |
| 1923 | 57,672 | 96,873 |
| 1924 | 79,435 | 97,847 |
| 1925 | 110,868 | 86,748 |
| 1926 | 79,895 | 92,962 |
| 1927 | 8,263 | 204,336 |
| 1928 | 405 | 166,469 |
| 1929 | — | 160,103 |
| 1930 | 5,400 | 19,483 |
| 1931 | 27,149 | 9,159 |
| 1932 | 16,568 | 9,010 |
| 1933 | 50,317 | 5,686 |
| 1934 | 53,852 | 6,341 |
| 1935 | 6,704 | 102,934 |
| 1936 | 38,495 | 191,149 |
| 1937 | 9,610 | 208,552 |
| 1938 | 26,928 | 146,745 |
| 1939 | 8,692 | 284,463 |
| 1940 | — | 229,514 |
| 1941 | — | 250,573 |
| 1942 | — | 114.078 |
| 1943–47 | — | — |
| 1948 | — | 300,000 |

Source: *Canadian Cattlemen*, December 1938 – September 1948

## Table 7: Leasehold Acreage in Western Canada 1884–1905

| YEAR | NUMBER OF LEASES | LEASEHOLD ACREAGE |
| --- | --- | --- |
| 1884 | 47 | 1,785,690 |
| 1885 | 57 | 2,098,670 |
| 1886 | 100 | 3,793,792 |
| 1887 | 135 | 4,666,844 |
| 1888 | 111 | 3,252,378 |
| 1889 | 116 | 3,113,878 |
| 1890 | 128 | 2,288,347 |
| 1891 | 139 | 2,213,677 |
| 1892 | 142 | 1,801,209 |
| 1894 | 156 | 1,298,871 |
| 1895 | 185 | 904,185 |
| 1896 | 236 | 257,983 |
| 1897 | 375 | 248,219 |
| 1898 | 448 | 333,469 |
| 1899 | 567 | 510,226 |
| 1900 | 641 | 557,454 |
| 1901 | 715 | 605,794 |
| 1902 | 908 | 1,272,847 |
| 1903 | 978 | 2,147,567 |
| 1904 | 889 | 2,229,504 |
| 1905 | 745 | 2,328,113 |

Source: Proskie, "Trends in Security," *Canadian Cattlemen*, June 1939.

## Table 8: Leasehold Acreage in Alberta, 1905 – 48

| Year | Leasehold Acreage | Number of Leases |
|---|---|---|
| 1905 | 996,838 | |
| 1906 | 1,551,372 | |
| 1907 | 1,651,397 | |
| 1908 | 2,132,718 | |
| 1909 | 2,088,736 | |
| 1910 | 1,737,874 | |
| 1911 | 2,023,162 | |
| 1912 | 2,001,234 | 1,424 |
| 1913 | 2,009,912 | |
| 1914 | 2,402,662 | |
| 1915 | 2,330,110 | |
| 1916 | 2,724,500 | |
| 1917 | 2,509,527 | |
| 1918 | 2,563,145 | |
| 1919 | 2,850,002 | |
| 1920 | 3,095,955 | |
| 1921 | 2,908,215 | |
| 1922 | 2,879,504 | |
| 1923 | 2,925,582 | |
| 1924 | 2,870,957 | |
| | | |
| 1931 | 3,220,161 | 3,778 |
| 1932 | 3,367,150 | 3,948 |
| 1933 | 3,172,839 | 3,708 |
| 1934 | 3,078,446 | 3,380 |
| 1935 | 3,081,660 | 3,230 |
| 1936 | 2,403,639 | 2,734 |
| 1937 | 3,152,126 | 2,782 |
| 1938 | 3,068,811 | 2,553 |
| 1939 | 1,812,280 | 1,396 |
| 1940 | 1,856,216 | 1,415 |
| 1941 | 1,996,034 | 1,433 |
| 1942 | 2,358,287 | 1,645 |

## Table 8: Leasehold Acreage in Alberta, 1905 – 48 – continued:

| YEAR | LEASEHOLD ACREAGE | NUMBER OF LEASES |
|------|------|------|
| 1943 | 3,629,731 | 2,459 |
| 1944 | 3,850,412 | 2,627 |
| 1945 | 4,028,895 | 2,724 |
| 1946 | 4,400,610 | 3,146 |
| 1947 | 4,528,482 | 3,250 |
| 1948 | 4,829,496 | 3,438 |

Sources: Canada, Sessional Papers; Alberta,
Department of Lands and Mines Annual Reports

## Table 9: Value of Wheat and Cattle Sold Off Farms in Alberta 1920 – 45

| | WHEAT ($ MILLIONS) | BEEF CATTLE ($ MILLIONS) |
|------|------|------|
| 1920 | 92.69 | 10.6 |
| 1925 | 116.73 | 8.1 |
| 1930 | 42.66 | 6.1 |
| 1935 | 49.14 | 6.6 |
| 1940 | 79.29 | 12.2 |
| 1945 | 72.78 | 40.1 |

Source: *Census of Canada*, 1951.

## Map 1: General Map of Alberta

Fort McMurray ●

● Berwyn

● Grand Prairie

● Athabasca

● Westlock    ● Smoky Lake

● Edson    St. Albert ●● EDMONTON

● Jasper                           Lloydminster ●

Wetaskiwin ●    ● Camrose

● Rocky Mountain House
● Red Deer

● Olds

● Drumheller

● Banff    ● CALGARY

**Province of Alberta**    ● Brooks

● Vulcan

Medicine Hat ●

● Lethbridge

● Cardston

## Map 2: Province of Alberta Soil Divisions

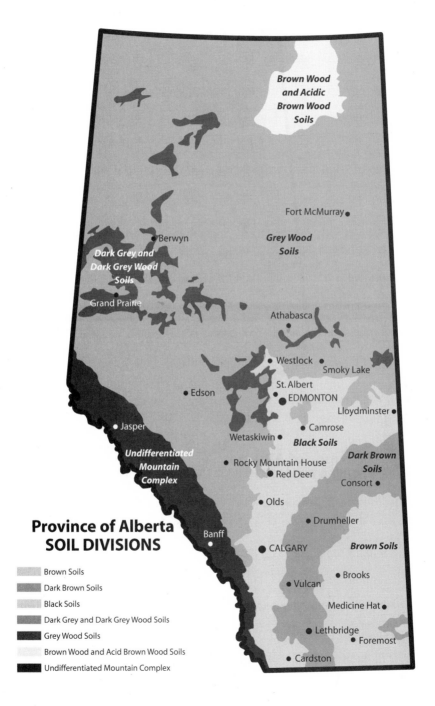

**Brown Wood and Acidic Brown Wood Soils**

Fort McMurray ●

**Grey Wood Soils**

● Berwyn

**Dark Grey and Dark Grey Wood Soils**

Grand Prairie

Athabasca ●

● Westlock

Smoky Lake

St. Albert ●
● EDMONTON

Lloydminster ●

● Edson

● Jasper

● Camrose

Wetaskiwin ●   **Black Soils**

**Undifferentiated Mountain Complex**

● Rocky Mountain House
● Red Deer

**Dark Brown Soils**

Consort ●

● Olds

● Drumheller

Banff ●

● CALGARY   **Brown Soils**

● Brooks

● Vulcan

Medicine Hat ●

● Lethbridge
● Foremost

● Cardston

### Province of Alberta
### SOIL DIVISIONS

Brown Soils
Dark Brown Soils
Black Soils
Dark Grey and Dark Grey Wood Soils
Grey Wood Soils
Brown Wood and Acid Brown Wood Soils
Undifferentiated Mountain Complex

## Map 3: Province of Alberta Vegetation Zones

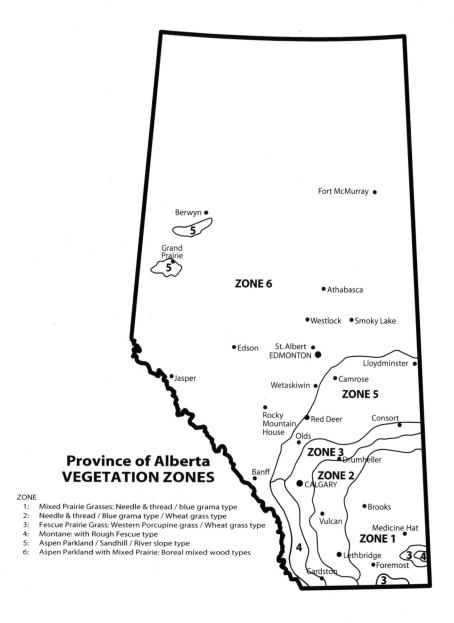

Fort McMurray ●

Berwyn ●

5

Grand
Prairie
5

**ZONE 6**

● Athabasca

● Westlock   ● Smoky Lake

● Edson        St. Albert ●
              EDMONTON ●

● Jasper                          Lloydminster ●

Wetaskiwin ●     ● Camrose

                 **ZONE 5**

Rocky          ● Red Deer        Consort ●
Mountain
House      Olds ●

**Province of Alberta**                    **ZONE 3**
**VEGETATION ZONES**                              ● Drumheller

                              Banff        **ZONE 2**
                                         ● CALGARY

ZONE
  1:    Mixed Prairie Grasses: Needle & thread / blue grama type
  2:    Needle & thread / Blue grama type / Wheat grass type        ● Brooks
  3:    Fescue Prairie Grass: Western Porcupine grass / Wheat grass type
  4:    Montane: with Rough Fescue type                         Vulcan
  5:    Aspen Parkland / Sandhill / River slope type                  Medicine Hat
  6:    Aspen Parkland with Mixed Prairie: Boreal mixed wood types    **ZONE 1**

                                                    4      ● Lethbridge    3  4
                                                        ● Foremost
                                          Cardston            3

## Map 4: Province of Alberta Beef Cattle Numbers by Census Divisions, 1941

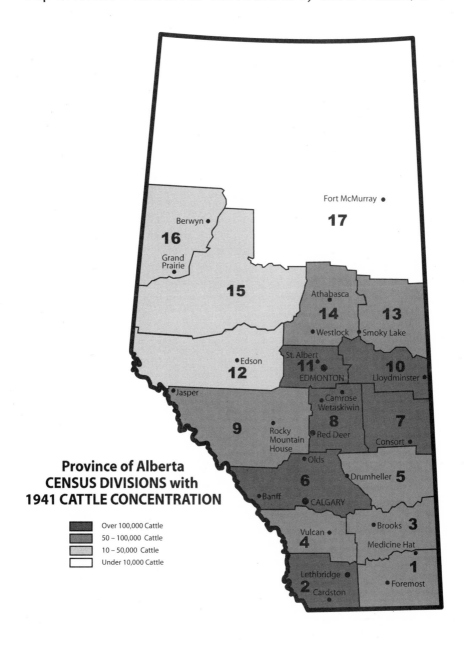

**Province of Alberta
CENSUS DIVISIONS with
1941 CATTLE CONCENTRATION**

Over 100,000 Cattle
50 – 100,000 Cattle
10 – 50,000 Cattle
Under 10,000 Cattle

# Notes

## Introduction

1. For discussion on this debate, see David H. Breen, *The Canadian Prairie West and the Ranching Frontier, 1874–1924* (Toronto: University of Toronto Press, 1983); Warren M. Elofson, *Cowboys, Gentlemen and Cattle Thieves: Ranching in the Western Frontier* (Montreal: McGill-Queen's University Press, 2000)

2. Evans has recently published an excellent article in *Prairie Forum* in which he discusses the significant challenges confronting the ranching industry in the new millennium. See, "Grazing the Grasslands: Exploring Conflicts, Relationships and Futures," *Prairie Forum* 26, no. 1 (spring 2001): 67–84.

# Chapter One
## The Legacy of the Ranching Era 1881–1907

1  For a comprehensive treatment of the ranching industry during this period, see Breen, *Canadian Prairie West*; with respect to public attitudes towards ranchers, see Debra L. Donahue, *The Western Range Revisited: Removing Livestock From Public Lands to Conserve Native Biodiversity* (Norman: University of Oklahoma Press, 1999), 23–25.

2  Breen, *Canadian Prairie West*, 7–8.

3  See William A. Waiser, *The Field Naturalist: John Macoun, the Geological Survey and Natural Science* (Toronto: University of Toronto Press, 1989), 33–34.

4  Quoted in "A Grazing Country Par Excellence," in *The Prairie West to 1905: A Canadian Sourcebook*, Lewis G. Thomas, ed. (Toronto: Oxford University Press, 1975), 230.

5  Thomas, "*Prairie West*," 43.

6  Canada, *Sessional Papers*, no. 4, 1888, annual report of the Department of the Interior.

7  For good discussion, see John Proskie, "Trends in Security of Tenure: Grazing Lands in Western Canada," *Canadian Cattlemen*, June 1939.

8  There were six such leaseholds totalling approximately 270,000 acres. Among the leaseholders were George Lane (43,736 acres), the Milk River Cattle Company (60,000 acres), the Grand Forks Cattle Company (47,218 acres and 7,615 acres), and the Matador Cattle Company in Saskatchewan. See Breen, *Canadian Prairie West*, 140.

9  *Farm and Ranch Review*, November 1905.

10  For example, see "Leases Tie Up the Land," *High River Times*, 15 February 1906.

11  See Simon Evans, "The Passing of a Frontier: Ranching in the Canadian West, 1882–1912" (Ph.D. diss., University of Calgary, 1976). Evans's study is a penetrating examination of the ranching industry during the period. For greater detail on the spectrum of American involvement in the western Canadian cattle industry during this entire period, see Evans's article, "American Cattlemen in the Canadian West, 1874–1914," *Prairie Forum* 4, no. 1 (1979): 121–33.

12  Evans, "Passing of a Frontier," 207.

13  Canada, *Sessional Papers*, no. 14, 1888; no. 25, 1903, annual reports of the Department of the Interior.

14  This notion prevailed even though there were several varieties of ranching in the United States. See the work of Terry Jordan-Bychkov in this regard.

15  Aside from climatic variables, ranchers had to contend with predators—especially wolves—and diseases such as mange that also exacted their toll on cattle numbers. For a discussion on environmental factors, see W. M. Elofson, "Adapting to the Frontier Environment: The Ranching Industry in Western Canada, 1891–1914," in *Canadian Papers in Rural History*, vol. 8, Donald H. Akeneson, ed. (Gananoque: Langdale Press, 1992), 307–27.

16  Quoted in "The Arithmetic of Vast Profits," in Thomas, *Prairie West*, 233.

17  These testimonials were among those detailed in a promotional publication by John R. Craig, *The Grazing Country of the Dominion of Canada: Reports of Tourists, Explorers and Residents of the Grazing Lands of the North-West Territory* (Edinburgh: Colston, 1882).

18  For an excellent account of climatic changes through time, see Alwynne B. Beaudon, "What They Saw: The Climatic and Environmental context for Euro-Canadian Settlement in Alberta," *Prairie Forum* 24, no. 1, (1999): 1–40.

19  The comment was made in the paper's inaugural edition, which may explain its booster tone. *Nanton News*, June 1903.

20  Elofson, "Adapting to the Frontier Environment."

21  D. H. Andrews, manager, to T. M. Richardson, 15 February 1893, Canadian Coal and Colonization Company Fonds, Stair Ranch Letterbook 1880–1893 (hereafter cited as Stair Letterbook), Glenbow Archives, Calgary.

22  For good discussion on the demise of the open-range era, see Simon Evans, "The End of the Open Range Era in Western Canada," *Prairie Forum* 8, no. 1 (1983): 71–85.

23  Evans, "Passing of a Frontier," 176, 183.

24  Ibid., 257.

25  Dora Dibney, "Pioneering in the Cochrane District," *Canadian Cattlemen*, June 1949.

26  Lloyd Carson and Gordon Carson, "The Houcher Story," *Canadian Cattlemen*, June 1949.

27  See article in *Lethbridge Herald*, 6 July 1948.

28  For examples, see correspondence dated 14 January 1891; 29 January, 4 June 1892, Stair Letterbook.

29  *Census of Canada*, 1911.

30  *Census of Canada*, 1901.

31  "Grazing Country Par Excellence."

32  "Bob Newbolt, Pioneer of 1884," as told to Angus McKinnon, *Canadian Cattlemen*, March 1960.

33  Claude Gardiner, *Letters from an English Rancher* (Calgary: Glenbow-Alberta Institute, 1988), 51–52. Half of Gardiner's home quarter was in crops. In 1895 he cropped 22 bushels of rye, 110 of barley, 27 of oats, and 145 of wheat.

34  Barry Potyondi, *Where the Rivers Meet: A History of the Upper Oldman Basin to 1939* (Pincher Creek: Southern Alberta Water Science Society, 1992), 79.

35  *Farm and Ranch Review*, March, April, October 1905; April 1906.

36  Canada, *Sessional Papers*, no. 13, 1896, 1899, annual reports of the Department of the Interior.

37  Canada, *Sessional Papers*, no. 13, 1896, 1899, annual reports of the Department of the Interior.

38  "Facts Regarding Western Canada's Feeding Materials, No. 1," *Farm and Ranch Review*, October 1905.

39  See G. W. Hervey, "Better Feeding Needed," *Farm and Ranch Review*, November 1907.

40  Canada, *Sessional Papers*, no. 13, 1899, annual report of the Department of the Interior.

41  Canada, *Sessional Papers*, no. 8, 1899, annual report of the Department of Agriculture. Both MacEachran and Pearce were ultimately proved wrong in assuming any deficiency in western Canada's ability to sustain a livestock industry. Yet paradoxically both were partly correct in their assessments, MacEachran in the short run, and Pearce in the long.

42  "Grazing Country Par Excellence."

43  *Lethbridge Herald*, 15 February 1944. The paper was referring to cattle belonging to Jim Pierce and gave the date of marketing as 29 May 1902.

44  *High River Times*, 24 May 1906.

45  *Macleod Advertiser*, 6 September 1909.

46  This belief was stated as late as 1915 by Alberta Livestock Commissioner W. F. Stevens. See *Farm and Ranch Review*, 16 December 1915.

47  "Expansion of the Cattle Feeding Industry," *Farm and Ranch Review*, 6 June 1912.

48  The doubts about the feasibility of growing corn in Alberta lasted well into the World War I period and into the subsequent expansion of irrigation. For sample opinion, see *Farm and Ranch Review* articles, "Can Alberta Grow Corn?" 20 March 1915, and "Corn Growing in Alberta," 6 October 1915. When Medicine Hat and Brandon rancher J. G. McGregor won several honours at the 1912 Chicago International, the above journal made the comment that "it dislodged the illusion that it was not possible to feed cattle to the highest point of perfection without corn." *Farm and Ranch Review*, 20 December 1912.

49  J. W. Robertson, *Experiments in the Feeding of Steers, 1875–1930* (Ottawa: Department of Agriculture, n.d.). It was found that the cost of feeding hay-based rations was 26.57 percent greater than feeding corn ensilage.

50  *Farm and Ranch Review*, April 1905.

51  Ibid., October 1905. This is undoubtedly true. The first scientific experiments in feeding were not carried out until the second half of the nineteenth century.

52  Ibid.

53  "Liberal Policy and Practice for Agriculture," *Farm and Ranch Review*, November 1907.

54  *Farm and Ranch Review*, May 1906; Potyondi, *Where the Rivers Meet*, 75.

55  *Farm and Ranch Review*, May 1906.

56  The figure given for average prices between 1899 and 1902 was 4.1 cents per pound. See *Farm and Ranch Review*, July 1906.

57  Robertson, *Feeding of Steers*.

58  Ibid.

59  D. H. Andrews to C. Akers, 4 January 1891, Stair Letterbook.

60  L. V. Kelly, *The Range Men* (Toronto: William Briggs, 1913), 391. This assertion was made by Dr. J. G. Rutherford, the Dominion Veterinary Director General in 1909.

61  *Farm and Ranch Review*, April, June 1905, September 1907.

62  Ibid., April 1905.

63 See comments by H. A. Mullen in *Farm and Ranch Review,* April 1908; also Evans, "Passing of a Frontier," 321.

64 Evans, "Passing of a Frontier," 309. Evans also notes that cattle ranked third among Canadian export items after 1892.

65 "Arithmetic of Vast Profits," in Thomas, *Prairie West,* 233.

66 Breen, *Canadian Prairie West,* 93–98.

67 Memo to the Minister of Agriculture, 3 November 1906, Papers of the Department of the Attorney General (hereafter cited as Attorney General's Papers), box 36, file 570, Provincial Archives of Alberta (PAA).

68 See Ian MacLachlan, *Kill and Chill: Restructuring Canada's Beef Commodity Chain* (Toronto: University of Toronto Press, 2001), 96–97.

69 "Ranchers Gave their Evidence to Commission," *High River Times,* 27 June 1907.

70 D. H. Andrews to John Clay, 1 May 1891, Stair Letterbook..

71 *Medicine Hat News,* 10 October 1901.

72 Canada, *Sessional Papers,* no. 7B, 1891, Export Cattle Trade in Canada.

73 See John Clay, "A Cattleman's View of Our Future," *Farm and Ranch Review,* September 1907.

74 *Farm and Ranch Review,* June 1905.

75 Ibid., July 1906.

76 Ibid., September 1907.

77 Ibid., September 1906.

78 Alex M. Campbell, *Report of the Beef Commission: The Purchase and Sale of Cattle, Hogs, Sheep, and Meat in the Provinces of Alberta and Manitoba* (Edmonton: King's Printer, 1906). It is interesting to note that the Winnipeg-based company of Gordon, Ironsides and Fares, which dominated the cattle trade in most of western Canada, made no marketing incursions into Alberta and was quite prepared to leave the area as Pat Burns's exclusive preserve.

79 Attorney General's Papers, box 36, file 570.

80 Campbell, *Report of the Beef Commission.*

81 Ibid. According to the commission, a twelve-hundred-pound two-year-old grain-fed animal netted the producer 3.5 cents per pound in Calgary. Offers of two cents per pound for other cattle were common.

82 "Ranchers Gave their Evidence."

83 See *High River Times,* 12 December 1905.

84 Evans, "Passing of a Frontier," 228.

85 Ibid., 314.

86 See *Farm and Ranch Review,* September 1942.

87 Evans has noted that Canadian cattle were used to help stock ranges in Wyoming and Montana during the large increase in American cattle inventories in the 1880s. Evans, "Passing of a Frontier," 325.

88 For good discussion on the Canadian cattle export trade to Britain during this period, see Simon Evans, "Canadian Beef For Victorian Britain," *Agricultural History* 53, no. 4 (October 1979): 748–62.

89 For full export numbers on cattle exports to Great Britain see Table 5.

90 Evans, "Canadian Beef," 757.

91 In sharp contrast to later periods, a heavier animal during this period had better marketing prospects. For example, the champion steer at the Winnipeg show in 1892 weighed 2,550 pounds. See "Steers of Yesteryear," *Canadian Cattlemen*, October 1951.

92 Argentina began eclipsing the United States as the chief supplier of chilled beef to Britain around 1905.

93 Evans, "Canadian Beef," 758.

94 William H. McIntyre Jr., "A Short History of the McIntyre Ranch," *Canadian Cattlemen*, September 1947.

95 Canada, Sessional Papers, no. 13, 1897, annual report of the Department of the Interior; also no. 15b, 1912, Health of Animals Branch. In his report on the cattle trade in Canada, Dr. J. G. Rutherford, Dominion Veterinary Director General, referred to the importation during this period of Mexican cattle, which he described as "degenerate descendants of an ancient Spanish breed."

96 "Store cattle" refers to animals not classified as "fat," and which therefore were not subject to immediate slaughter at the point of entry. Generally, they equated to the more popular term "feeder." It was very common for animals ready for slaughter upon leaving Canada not to be classed as "fat" when they reached Great Britain. It was estimated that 70 percent of Canadian store cattle were fattened in Scotland.

97 Canada, *Sessional Papers*, no. 50, 1893, Correspondence between Canada and the United Kingdom with Respect to the Scheduling of Canadian Cattle.

98 Ibid.

99 The first action was to trace the infected animals to their source. They were found to have come from Manitoba in the Minnedosa district. All animals in the surrounding area were subject to inspection. No evidence of the disease was located.

100 The inspection, which was continued well into 1893, was time-consuming and extensive. Up to eleven veterinarians visited each farm and ranch. In his final report, one inspecting veterinarian wrote, "In my opinion if Great Britain and the United States were as free from the disease as Canada, there would be no need for any inspection or quarantine."

101 The Canadians maintained, probably validly, that the diseased cattle did not have contagious pleuropneumonia but non-contagious bronchopneumonia, a condition induced by the rigours of their ocean voyage. However, it also could be argued that the Canadians only had themselves to blame. Knowing the British sensitivity towards any hint of disease, they had continued to export inferior cattle which were more prone to contacting bronchopneumonia.

102 See Great Britain, *Parliamentary Debates, House of Commons,* 6 February, 20 March 1893; 16 August 1895; 9 May 1896.

103 Ibid., 10 August 1895.

104 Canada, *Sessional Papers*, no. 13, 1893, annual report of the Department of the Interior, report of the Dominion Superintendent of Lands and Mines.

105 Canada, *Sessional Papers*, no. 13, 1894, annual report of the Department of the Interior, report of the Dominion Superintendent of Lands and Mines.

106 This view is shared by Simon Evans. See Evans, "Canadian Beef," 757.

107 Canada, *Sessional Papers*, no. 13, 1896, annual report of the Department of the Interior, report of the superintendent of Lands and Mines.

108 Letter from W. Waldron, assistant commissioner, Co-operation and Markets Branch, to H. Auld, 6 April 1923, Department of Agriculture Collection Ag. 8, file 39, Provincial Archives of Sasktchewan.

109 Canada, *Sessional Papers*, no. 7B, 1891, Export Cattle Trade in Canada.

110 Ibid.

111 See *Farm and Ranch Review*, January, June 1906; April 1908; *Grain Growers' Gazette*, April 1908.

112 *Farm and Ranch Review*, May 1906; January 1907.

# Chapter Two
## The Agricultural Frontier, 1900 – 13

1 Robert E. Ankli and Robert M. Litt, "The Growth of Prairie Agriculture: Economic Considerations," in *Canadian Papers in Rural History*, vol. I, Donald H. Akenson, ed. (Gananoque: Langdale Press, 1978), 43.

2 *Farm and Ranch Review,* 5 October 1911. William R. Motherwell, future federal Minister of Agriculture, referred to the ongoing attention needed for mixed farming as proving a real deterrent when compared to straight grain farming which at least offered some respite in winter. See Evans, "Passing of a Frontier," 281.

3 The stipulations respecting cattle raising in lieu of cultivation are defined in Section 133 of the *Revised Statutes of Canada*, 1906, vol. 2, "An Act Respecting Public Lands." The homestead purchase allowed those homesteaders who were unable to take advantage of adjacent vacant land to exercise their preemption rights to take out another homestead in a designated less fertile area for three dollars an acre. See *Statutes of Canada*, 1908, "An Act to Consolidate and Amend the Acts Respecting the Public Lands of the Dominion;" *Farm and Ranch Review,* 20 January 1913.

4 *Farm and Ranch Review,* 5 December 1909.

5 See "Economics of Steer Fattening," *Farm and Ranch Review,* November 1907.

6 *High River Times,* 4 October 1906.

7 See *High River Times,* 8 July 1910.

8 *Farm and Ranch Review,* 20 October 1909.

9 "Land of Diversified Resources," *High River Times,* 3 December 1908.

10 *High River Times,* 6 January, 4 April 1906. Ranch land was thirteen dollars per acre; crop land was twenty-five dollars per acre.

11 *Farm and Ranch Review,* 20 March 20, 1912.

12 *High River Times,* 15 November 1906.

13 *Farm and Ranch Review,* April 1909.

14 Ibid., 6 June 1910.

15 Ibid., 13 June 1909.

16 Breen, *Canadian Prairie West,* 141.

17 *Farm and Ranch Review,* 6 June 1910.

18 Ed Gould, *Ranching in Western Canada* (Sanichton: Harcourt House, 1978), 90.

19 Evans, "Passing of a Frontier." Evans was quoting the *Lethbridge Herald,* 11 December 1947.

20 *Farm and Ranch Review,* 20 April 1910.

21 *The Weekly Chronicle* (Fort Macleod), 8 June 1908. It was not so much that Harcourt was intent on criticizing the Macleod area's wheat production. Rather, he was trying to defend his decision not to include Macleod on a government-sponsored agricultural lecture series.

22  Canada, *Sessional Papers,* no. 16, 1907–08, report of director of Experimental Farms; also *Farm and Ranch Review,* September 1905.

23  Knowledge of dryland farming and the practice of summer fallowing had been present in Alberta since the mid-1880s. In fact, it was considered one of the prerequisites to successful agriculture on the prairies. However, it was not widely understood nor popularized until the land boom of the early twentieth century. See Ankli and Litt, "Growth of Prairie Agriculture," 39.

24  "Land Resources in Alberta," *Farm and Ranch Review,* October 1906.

25  *Farm and Ranch Review,* July 1909.

26  *The Advertiser* (Fort Macleod), 11 March 1910.

27  *Farm and Ranch Review,* 5 April 1912.

28  David C. Jones, *We'll All Be Buried Down Here: The Prairie Dryland Disaster, 1917–26,* Historical Society of Alberta, vol. 6 (Edmonton: Alberta Records Publication Board, 1986), xxxiv.

29  Potyondi, *Where the Rivers Meet,* 116.

30  *Farm and Ranch Review,* 5 June 1913.

31  *The Advertiser,* 30 November 1911.

32  *Farm and Ranch Review,* 20 May 1911.

33  Gould, *Ranching in Western Canada,* 84.

34  "Passed the Million Mark," *High River Times,* 8 April 1910.

35  C. H. McKinnon, *Events of LK Ranch* (Calgary: Phoenix Press, 1979), 59.

36  Evans, "Passing of a Frontier," 275. The Bar U lost half its herd of twenty-four thousand head. Even the efficiently run Matador experienced losses of 40–45 percent. In some areas losses were as high as 90 percent.

37  *Farm and Ranch Review,* 6 January 1913. The *Review* was referring to the general attitude of farmers in Manitoba but carried no smug comparisons to indicate that Alberta was superior.

38  See *Farm and Ranch Review,* 5 December 1912.

39  Ibid., 11 May 1910.

40  Alberta, *Sessional Papers,* no. 12, 1914.

41  Canada, *Sessional Papers,* no. 15a, 1909, annual report of the Department of Agriculture.

42  Alberta, *Department of Agriculture Annual Report,* 1910.

43  Canada, *Sessional Papers,* no. 15b, 1912, annual report of the Department of Agriculture.

44  For a good example of this attitude, see "The Beef Steer," *Farm and Ranch Review,* October 1907.

45  The practice of selling animals by the hundredweight rather than on a fixed price on the animal itself was related to the beginnings of the feeding industry.

46  Figures given to the 1934 Royal Commission on Price Spreads showed that the average boat rate between 1906 and 1913 was $6.50–7.50 per head while the average market price in Toronto was around $4.50.

47  "Ranchers Gave Their Evidence to Commission," *High River Times,* 27 June 1907.

48 Canada, *Sessional Papers*, no. 15b, 1913, report of the Veterinary General and Livestock Commissioner. The remark was made by a rancher at the general convention of the National Livestock Association, Ottawa, February 12–13, 1912.

49 *Farm and Ranch Review,* April 1908.

50 "Prices and Imports of Frozen and Chilled Beef, 1900–20," box 10, file 68, Western Stock Growers' Association Papers (hereafter cited as WSGA Papers), Glenbow.

51 See W. David Zimmerman, "Live Cattle Export Trade Between United States and Great Britain," *Agricultural History* 36, no. 1 (January 1962).

52 Canada, *Sessional Papers*, no. 5a, 1896, reports of the high commissioner. The other country was Argentina.

53 Canada, *Sessional Papers*, no. 8, 1898, annual report of the Department of Agriculture, Report by Chief Veterinarian, Dr. Alan MacEachran; also Max Foran, "The Politics of Animal Health: The British Embargo on Canadian Cattle, 1892–1932," *Prairie Forum* 23, no. 1 (1998): 1–17.

54 Canada, *Sessional Papers*, no. 7, 1887, annual report of the Department of the Interior.

55 F. Albert Rudd, "Production and Marketing of Beef Cattle From the Short Grass Plains Area of Canada" (master's thesis, University of Alberta, 1935), 105.

56 Canada, *Sessional Papers*, no. 6, 1891, annual report of the Department of Agriculture, Report of R. Evans on Fort Macleod cattle quarantine.

57 Rudd, "Production and Marketing," 105.

58 William Pearce had argued strenuously for this removal in his annual reports after the embargo was imposed, feeling that the freer movement of cattle across the line would augment the stocking of the Canadian ranges. Interestingly, however, the first resolution passed by the newly formed Western Stock Growers' Association in 1896 was one in favour of maintaining the present quarantine regulations. Clearly the southern Alberta ranchers were holding a narrower view than Pearce in that they feared American cattle would encroach on their leases.

59 Canada, *Sessional Papers*, no. 8, 1898, annual report of the Department of Agriculture.

60 Canada, *Sessional Papers,* no. 8, 1898, report on cattle quarantine in Canada from November 1896 to October 1897.

61 Abstracted from "Canadian Cattle Exports, 1867–1937," *Canadian Cattlemen,* June 1938.

62 Canada, *Sessional Papers*, no. 15, 1902, annual report of the Department of Agriculture.

63 Kelly, *Range Men*, 341.

64 Canada, *Sessional Papers*, no. 15a, 1909, report of Veterinary Director General and Livestock Commissioner. The Chicago market was huge. Covering some five hundred acres and with a capacity of handling seventy-five thousand head of cattle daily, the Chicago market transacted over half a billion dollars in 1916.

65 Lane's price in Chicago was $8.75 per hundredweight. See *The Advertiser,* 5 December 1912.

66  *Farm and Ranch Review,* September 1907; Canada, *Sessional Papers,* no. 15a, 1909, report of Veterinary Director General and Livestock Commissioner.

67  Canada, *Sessional Papers,* no. 15a, 1909, report of the Veterinary Director General and Livestock Commissioner.

68  Canada, *Sessional Papers,* no. 8c, 1898, report of commissioner of dairying and agriculture.

69  Alberta, *Department of Agriculture Annual Report,* 1912, report of Livestock Commissioner.

70  *Farm and Ranch Review,* 5 December 1912. The winning bull was two-year-old Glencarnock Victor, a 1,610-pound Aberdeen Angus. McGregor also won the herd championship, the herd bull championship for the breed, the two-year-old class, and the reserve championship in the female grand championship. The editor of the *Farm and Ranch Review* wrote, "such a clean up … has never before been recorded at any international show."

71  "George Lane Views Reciprocity," in *The Best of Times: Forging the Frontier, 1905–1911* (High River: *High River Times,* 1999), 454.

72  *The Advertiser,* 30 November 1911.

73  *Macleod Spectator,* 30 October 1913.

74  *Farm and Ranch Review,* 20 January 1913.

75  See Linda M. Young and John M. Marsh, "Integration and Interdependence in the U.S. and Canadian Live Cattle and Beef Sectors," *American Review of Canadian Studies* 28, no. 3 (Autumn 1998): 340.

76  McKinnon, *Events of LK Ranch,* 19.

77  *Farm and Ranch Review,* 5 December 1909.

78  John Clay, "A Cattleman's View of Our Future," *Farm and Ranch Review,* September 1907.

79  *Farm and Ranch Review,* 5 September 1910.

80  Ibid., April 1909.

81  Ibid., 20 February 1911.

82  Ibid., 5 August 1912.

83  Ibid., December 1908.

84  "Chilling, Packing and Exporting of Canada's Meat," *Farm and Ranch Review,* June 1908.

85  "The Chilled Meat Industry," *Farm and Ranch Review,* July 1908.

86  Ibid.

87  *Farm and Ranch Review,* December 1908.

88  Ibid., February, April 1909.

89  Jim Silver, "The Origins of Winnipeg's Packing Plant Industry: Transitions from Trade to Manufacture," *Prairie Forum* 19, no. 1 (Spring 1994): 28.

90  *Farm and Ranch Review,* 3 April 1910.

91  Ibid., 5 May 1910.

92  Ibid., July 1908.

93  Ibid., 5 November 1910.

94  "Dearth of Cattle," *High River Times,* 21 December 1911.

95  *The Advertiser,* 3 April 1912.

96 Ibid., 1 May 1913.

97 W. R. Fairfield, "Growing Forage Crops," *Farm and Ranch Review,* 5 May 1913.

98 Proskie, "Trends in Security."

99 Evans, "Passing of a Frontier," 293, 287.

100 Ibid., 298.

101 Ibid. Evans was quoting a *Calgary Herald* article, "Pre-emption Policy of 1908 Ruined Many Small Ranchers," 18 August 1949.

102 *Farm and Ranch Review,* 20 June 1910.

103 Ibid.

104 Ibid., September 1909.

105 Canada, *Sessional Papers,* no. 15b, 1912, report of the Veterinary Director General and Livestock Commissioner, appendix #12, "The Cattle Trade in Western Canada," submitted 31 march 1910.

106 Chester Martin, *Dominion Lands Policy,* edited by L. H. Thomas, the Carleton Library, no. 69 (Toronto: McClelland and Stewart, 1973), 180.

107 *Macleod Spectator,* 20 November 1913.

108 *Farm and Ranch Review,* 5 May 1911.

109 See Canada, *Sessional Papers,* no. 15b, 1913, report of veterinary general and Livestock Commissioner.

110 *Edmonton Journal,* 26 February 1913.

111 Potyondi, *Where the Rivers Meet,* 183.

112 *Red Deer Advocate,* 2 May 1913.

113 *The Advertiser,* 15 February 1912.

114 "Chance of Mixed Farming Further From Them Than Ever," *Edmonton Journal,* 27 February 1913.

115 *High River Times,* 4 August 1910.

116 Ibid., 24 August 1911.

117 *Farm and Ranch Review,* 5 December 1912.

118 S. E. Abel, "Coaxing An Arid Waste to Yield Luxuriantly," *Farm and Ranch Review,* 5 December 1913.

119 *The Advertiser,* 22 February 1912.

120 *Farm and Ranch Review,* 6 January 1913.

121 For information on the Ranch Inquiry Commission, see Breen, *Canadian Prairie West,* 188–94; for a copy of the 1913 grazing regulations, see box 70, file 554, A. E. Cross Family Fonds (hereafter cited as Cross Fonds), Glenbow; see also Canada, Order in Council, PC 296, 16 February 1914.

122 Cross Fonds, box 70, file 554.

123 Proskie, "Trends in Security," 201.

124 Canada, *Sessional Papers,* no. 15b, 1913, report of the veterinary director general and Livestock Commissioner.

125 *Farm and Ranch Review,* 20 October 1913. In addition to cattle, sheep and swine were also allowed free entry, as were beef, canned meat, hams, eggs, bacon and pork. Rye, corn and oats were also exempt with duties on barley dropping from thirty cents to fifteen cents a bushel. Wheat was subject to a 10 percent countervailing duty.

126 Ibid., 5 December 1914.

# Chapter Three
# Mixed Blessings, 1914 – 20

1  "Canadian Cattle Exports, 1867–1937," *Canadian Cattlemen*, June 1938.

2  "The Commercial Movement of Cattle and Calves, 1911–1937," (selected years), *Canadian Cattlemen*, June 1938.

3  For comment on the influence of the U.S. export market on Canadian domestic beef prices, see *Farm and Ranch Review*, 5 November 1913, 5 May 1916, 21 March 1921.

4  Canada, *Sessional Papers*, no. 21c, 1921, livestock and animal products statistics.

5  Abstracted from tables in C. W. Peterson, "The Livestock Situation," *Farm and Ranch Review*, 21 March 1921.

6  *High River Times*, 15 November 1917.

7  *Farm and Ranch Review*, 5 October 1915.

8  Ibid., 5 December 1916.

9  *High River Times,* 18 September 1917.

10  *Calgary Herald*, 6 September 1917; "Will Those Days Ever Return?" *Canadian Cattlemen*, December 1939.

11  Breen, *Canadian Prairie West*, 206.

12  Canada, *Sessional Papers*, no. 15, 1918, annual report of the Department of Agriculture, report of livestock branch.

13  Canada, *Sessional Papers*, no. 15, 1921, annual report of the Department of Agriculture.

14  *Farm and Ranch Review*, 20 September 1913.

15  Ibid., 5 May 1917.

16  Ibid., 20 October 1917, 5 December 1918.

17  Ibid., 3 July 1917.

18  *High River Times,* 6 September 1917. Others included the Nelson Trading Company in the Porcupine Hills and the Deer Creek Cattle Company.

19  *Farm and Ranch Review*, 20 September 1913.

20  The *Farm and Ranch Review* on 20 September 1917 advised the cessation of all veal production on the grounds that it reduced potential meat supplies.

21  *Farm and Ranch Review*, 5 March 1913.

22  Canada, *Sessional Papers*, no. 21c, 1921, livestock and animal products statistics.

23  *Farm and Ranch Review,* 20 September, 5 December 1917.

24  Ibid., 5 December 1918.

25  Canada, *Sessional Papers,* no. 15, 1920, annual report of the Department of Agriculture.

26  *Calgary Herald*, 3 October 1916.

27  Silver, "Winnipeg's Packing Plant Industry," 24.

28  See "Extracts from the Discussion at the Imperial War Conference, April 26, 1917," Canada, *Sessional Papers*, no. 42a, 1917, minutes of the proceedings of the Imperial War Conference, 1917. During the debate, Rogers also commented

that the embargo was a matter of policy for the development of British live cattle and that "we have no objection to a policy of protection."

29 "Extracts from Discussion," 3–4. Doubtless the British gratitude towards Canada for her significant contribution to the war effort contributed to their feelings of benevolence at the time.

30 U.K., *Parliamentary Debates, House of Lords*, 12 July 1922. Remarks by the Duke of Devonshire.

31 Ibid., 22 July 1922.

32 Ibid., 14 August 1919.

33 Ibid., 6 August 1919; vol. 121, 12 November 1919.

34 Ibid., quoted in embargo debate, 24 July 1922.

35 *Census of Canada*, 1931.

36 Ibid.

37 *Macleod News*, 6 September 1917.

38 *Farm and Ranch Review*, 20 February 1919.

39 Ibid., 21 August, 21 September 1916.

40 Alberta, *Department of Agriculture Annual Report*, 1911.

41 Alberta, *Department of Agriculture Annual Report*, 1917.

42 *Farm and Ranch Review*, 20 April 1917.

43 Ibid., 5 March 1918.

44 Alberta, *Department of Agriculture Annual Report*, 1917.

45 Ibid.

46 Ibid.

47 Probably the best example was the Livestock Encouragement Act (or Cow Bill) which granted loans to groups of farmers to purchase higher-quality stock.

48 For information on Collicutt's operations see Harold W. Riley, "Frank Collicutt, The Purebred Hereford King of Canada," *Canadian Cattlemen*, September 1941.

49 For information on the LK Ranch, see McKinnon, *Events of LK Ranch*.

50 Canada, *Sessional Papers*, no. 15b, 1912, "The Cattle Trade of Western Canada." The matter was put to the meeting of the Society of Animal Production in 1928 by the spokesman who said that "the domestic market should not function as a clearing house for beef below export standard."

51 *Calgary Herald*, 22 December 1915.

52 "Eastern Canadian Society of Animal Production: Reports Presented at First Annual General Meeting," *Scientific Agriculture* 8, no. 12 (August 1928).

53 "The Beef Solution," *Lethbridge Herald*, 10 April 1942.

54 Canada, *Sessional Papers*, no. 15, 1918, annual report of the Department of Agriculture. It could be argued that the policy did lead to some stabilization of western Canadian herd numbers. In the first two years of operation, the Car Lot Policy reduced the number of stockers and feeders shipped to the United States through the Winnipeg stockyards from 82 percent in 1915 to 42 percent in 1916 and 30 percent in 1917.

55 *Farm and Ranch Review*, 20 July 1918.

56 *Calgary Herald*, 14 September 1917.

57  Alberta, *Department of Agriculture Annual Report*, 1919.

58  Lane felt that Alberta could support 2 million head instead of the current six hundred thousand. He also believed that with feeding a two-pound-per-day gain would become commonplace. See *Calgary Herald*, 3 October 1916. Modern developments have vindicated Lane.

59  *Farm and Ranch Review,* 5 August 1915. The entire 6 March 1916 edition of the journal was devoted to the promotion of alfalfa.

60  Ibid., 6 December 1915.

61  *Calgary Herald*, 14 September 1917; *Farm and Ranch Review,* 20 January 1917.

62  See *High River Times,* 22 November 1917.

63  *Calgary Herald*, 19 September 1917.

64  See *Farm and Ranch Review*, "Can Alberta Grow Corn?" 20 March 1915; "Corn Growing in Alberta," 5 October 1915.

65  *Farm and Ranch Review,* 5 September 1916.

66  It was estimated that as late as 1936 that 70 percent of Alberta's cattle were marketed in an unfinished condition.

67  S. F. Tolmie, MP, "Livestock for Permanent Industry," Report by the chairman of the House of Commons Agricultural Committee to the House, 9 April 1919, *Appendices, Journals of the House of Commons*, 1919.

68  H. S. Arkell, "Markets for Livestock in 1919," *Appendices, Journals of the House of Commons*, 1919; also *Farm and Ranch Review*, 6 October 1918.

69  *Farm and Ranch Review,* 20 December 1918.

70  Tolmie, "Livestock for Permanent Industry."

71  For information on the WSGA see Alex Johnston, *Cowboy Politics: the Western Stock Growers' Association and Its Predecessors* (Calgary: Western Stock Growers' Association, 1971).

72  Meeting dated 11 May 1916, box 1, file folder 2, WSGA Papers.

73  A good discussion of this campaign is contained in a paper by Dan Balkwill, "Frontier vs. Metropolis: Early Attempts at Eradicating Mange on the Canadian Prairie" (graduate paper, History Department, University of Saskatchewan, 1997).

74  Annual general meeting, 30 January 1922, box 1, file folder 8, WSGA Papers.

75  "Monthly Average Price, Good Butcher Steers, Toronto, 1920–1938," *Canadian Cattlemen*, September 1938.

76  Canada, *Sessional Papers*, no. 5, 1923, thirtieth annual report of the Department of Trade and Commerce.

77  For a good discussion on the history of mixed farming in southwestern Alberta, see Warren M. Elofson, "Mixed and Dryland Farming Near Pincher Creek 1895–1914," *Prairie Forum* 19, no. 1 (1994): 31–51.

78  Department of Natural Resources, annual report of the Western Irrigation Block, 1916, Canadian Pacific Railway Fonds (hereafter cited as CPR Papers), Glenbow.

79  See *Edmonton Bulletin*, 14 March 1917; *Edmonton Journal*, 8 April 1924.

80  Tolmie, "Livestock for Permanent Industry."

81 David Spector, *Agriculture on the Prairies, 1870–1940*, History and Archaeology vol. 65 (Ottawa: Environment Canada, National Historic Parks and Sites Branch, 1983), 50–57.

82 See Paul Voisey, "A Mix-Up over Mixed Farming: The Curious History of the Agricultural Diversification Movement in a Single Crop Area of Southern Alberta," in *Building Beyond the Homestead*, David C. Jones and Ian MacPherson, eds. (Calgary: University of Calgary Press, 1985), 179–205.

83 Department of Natural Resources, annual report of the Agricultural and Animal Husbandry Branch, 1921, box 65, file folder 965, CPR Papers.

84 Canada, *Sessional Papers*, no. 25, 1917, annual report of the Department of the Interior, report of the inspector of ranches.

85 Abstracted from *Census of the Prairie Provinces*, 1926, 1946.

86 Ibid.

87 Potyondi, *Where the Rivers Meet*, 154.

88 *High River Times*, 6, 18 September 1917. Both men expected yields of at least thirty bushels to the acre.

89 Ibid., 1 November 1917.

90 *Edmonton Bulletin*, 12 March 1918.

91 Jones, *We'll All Be Buried*, liii. Using contemporary documents, Jones graphically describes the impact of drought and floundering cash-crop agriculture on the economic and social fabric of southern Alberta. One result was the increase in leasehold acreage by almost one-third between 1918 and 1930.

92 Canada, *Sessional Papers* no. 25, 1916, annual report of the Department of the Interior, report of inspector of ranches.

93 Department of Natural Resources annual report, 1918, report of Land Branch, box 60, file folder 582, CPR Papers.

94 *Macleod News*, 18 May 1916.

95 A. E. Cross to W. J. Roche, Minister of the Interior, 3 December 1913, box 69, file folder 544, Cross Fonds.

96 Department of Interior memorandum, 12 November 1919, RG 15, B2a, vol. 173, file 145330, part 7, Public Archives of Canada (PAC).

97 C. J. Christianson, *Early Rangemen* (Lethbridge: Southern Printing Co., 1973), 103.

98 *Edmonton Bulletin*, 21 March 1919.

99 Bert Sheppard, *Spitzee Days* (Calgary: John McAra, 1971), 215.

100 McKinnon, *Events of LK Ranch*, 96. The words are attributed to Lachlin McKinnon, noted early rancher in the Calgary area.

101 Kris Nielson and John Prociuk, *From Start to Finish: A History of Cattle Feeding in Alberta* (Calgary: Alberta Cattle Feeders' Association, 1999). Quote attributed to long-time rancher Fred Ings.

102 Department of the Interior, Orders in Council, vol. 42, order no. 15542, 4 November 1920, Provincial Archives of Alberta (PAA).

103 In 1920, Alberta was prepared to accept half the existing schedule of subsidies as compensation for lands already alienated. See Martin, *Dominion Land Policy*, 223.

104 Memorandum by B. L. York, head of Timber and Grazing Branch, 29 October 1918, RG, 15, B2a, vol. 172, file 1445330, part 8, PAC.

105 Department memo, 20 August 1915, RG 15, B2a, vol. 172, file 145330, part 7, PAC.

106 Correspondence dated 8 October 1918, RG 15, B2a, vol. 172, file 145330, part 8, PAC.

107 This is not to say the whole issue of taxation was not worrisome in this early period. In 1908 the federal inspector of ranches blamed some of the ranchers' abandonment of their leases as being due to "the dread of a provincial tax." See report of Albert Helmer in Canada, *Sessional Papers*, no. 25, 1908, annual report of the Department of the Interior. David Breen documents an incident whereby two homesteaders offered to sell their land to A. E. Cross, using as an inducement the fact that they could petition a school district which would then force him to pay school taxes. Breen, *Canadian Prairie West,* 161.

108 The source of this statement was Albert Helmer, federal Supervisor of Grazing. See C. Graham Anderson, grazing appraiser, Department of Lands and Mines, Province of Alberta in *Grazing Rates Report: Short Grass Area of Alberta*, compiled with the co-operation of the Short Grass Stock Growers' Association, (Edmonton: [Dept. of Lands and Mines], 1941), 71.

109 Department of the Interior, Orders in Council, no. 14840, 24 February 1919, PAA.

110 Cross Fonds, box 114, file folder 918.

111 Jones, *We'll All Be Buried,* 37–38. The farmer in question was giving evidence before the Board At Youngstown on 15 December 1921.

112 CPA Directors' Meeting, 24 June 1921, box 1, file folder 4, WSGA Papers.

# Chapter Four
## Change Out of Necessity, 1921 – 30

1 Alberta, *Department of Agriculture Annual Report*, 1925.

2 *Edmonton Journal*, 6 April 1923.

3 Glenbow, Canada Land and Irrigation Co. Ltd. Fonds, box 45, file folder 458.

4 *High River Times*, 27 October 1921.

5 Canada, *Sessional Papers*, no. 15b, 1922, annual report of the dominion veterinary general. Herd depletions were so great that the WSGA actually requested that the duty on American importations be removed to allow for herd build-up. See board of directors' meeting, 28 May 1920, box 1, file folder 4, WSGA Papers.

6 *Farm and Ranch Review*, 10 December 1925.

7 *Calgary Herald*, 27 June 1922.

8 *Farm and Ranch Review*, 25 September 1925.

9 T. W. Thomlinson, "The United States Tariff Act of 1922," *Farm and Ranch Review*, 10 June 1927.

10 *Farm and Ranch Review*, 3 May 1921. The value of cattle exports to the United States dropped by almost 90 percent from 1920 to 1921. See Canada, *Sessional Papers*, no. 5, 1923, annual report of the Department of Trade and Commerce.

11 Alberta, *Department of Agriculture Annual Report*, 1922.

12 Alberta, *Department of Agriculture Annual Report*, 1924.

13 Note dated 8 September 1922, box 115, file folder 926, Cross Fonds.

14 For example see *High River Times* issues from the autumn of 1921.

15 One such casualty was the well-known ranching business of McHugh Bros., which was sixty thousand dollars in debt by 1923. See Pat Burns Fonds, box 2, file folder 19, Glenbow.

16 *Edmonton Journal*, 6 April 1923.

17 Walters and Dunbar to Cross, 5 April 1921, box 113, file folder 905, Cross Fonds.

18 General meeting, 5 May 1920, box 1, file folder 4, WSGA Papers.

19 Directors' meetings, 28 January, 29 July 1921, box 1, file folder 4; W. F. Stevens, secretary, to S. F. Tolmie, federal Minister of Agriculture, 5 October 1920, box 12, file folder 105; executive meetings, 1, 25 February 1921, WSGA Papers.

20 Executive meeting, 20 January 1922, box 1, file folder 8, WSGA Papers.

21 *Farm and Ranch Review*, 5 December 1921.

22 Resolution passed 2 June 1922, box 1, file folder 8, WSGA Papers.

23 Executive meeting, 30 June 1922, box 1, file folder 8, WSGA Papers.

24 Knappen, of Knappen-Ulm Service Writing and Research, was familiar with Canadian conditions, having spent several years in the country. He had been recommended by J. H. Woods, editor of the *Calgary Herald*, and by Charles Mitchell of Medicine Hat, former Government of Alberta cabinet minister. See Dillon to Canadian Bankers' Association, 28 July 1922, box 9, file folder 65, WSGA Papers.

25 Knappen to J. F. Langan, 7 July 1922, box 9, file folder 65, WSGA Papers.

26  W. Dunbar to Dillon, 28 June 1922, box 9, file folder 65, WSGA Papers.

27  See WSGA Papers, box 12, file folder 104, for copy of circular dated 2 August 1922.

28  *Canadian Cattlemen*, June 1948.

29  WSGA Papers, box 12, file folder 104. This figure was used in the circular sent to the corn belt farmers.

30  Correspondence dated 8 September 1922, box 115, file folder 926, Cross Fonds.

31  Charles Robinson to Dillon, 3 July 1922, box 9, file folder 65, WSGA Papers.

32  Knappen to Dillon, 18 July 1922, box 9, file folder 65, WSGA Papers.

33  Dillon to the Canadian Bankers' Association, 28 July 1922, box 9, file folder 65, WSGA Papers.

34  Robinson to Cross, 28 August 1922, box 115, file folder 926, Cross Fonds.

35  Knappen to Langan, 6 July 1922, box 9, file folder 65, WSGA Papers. Knappen found it "amazing that the Alberta people had done nothing all the time the bill was under consideration."

36  Walters and Dunbar to Dillon, 28 June 1922, box 8, file folder 65, WSGA Papers.

37  Correspondence dated 6 September 1922, box 115, file folder 926, Cross Fonds.

38  Robinson to Cross, 22 September 1922, box 115, file folder 926, Cross Fonds.

39  Ibid. The lobbyist in question was Eugene Grubb, who had written to Robinson on 22 September 1922.

40  *Lethbridge Herald*, 14 October 1922.

41  Dillon to J. Mitchell, 31 July 1922, box 9, file folder 65; directors' meeting, 18 January 1923, box 1, file folder 8, WSGA Papers.

42  Directors' meeting, 14 December 1922, box 1, file folder 8, WSGA Papers.

43  Dillon to Dr. J. H. Grisdale, Deputy Minister of Agriculture, 16 December 1924, box 12, file folder 104, WSGA Papers.

44  Circular letter dated 17 August 1925, box 12, file folder 104, WSGA Papers.

45  Ibid. The typical Canadian feeder was described as "a big loose jointed framey calf with all the advantages nature can afford."

46  Dillon to J. Ingwerson, Swift and Co., Chicago, 9 January 1926, box 12, file folder 104, WSGA Papers. Ingwerson's reply was a polite but firm negative. Ingwerson to Dillon, 1 February 1926.

47  Correspondence dated 3 December 1925, box 12, file folder 104, WSGA Papers. The Tariff Commission's request was forwarded through the office of the American consulate in Calgary.

48  Knappen to Dillon, 1 January 1926, box 12, file folder 104, WSGA Papers.

49  *Farm and Ranch Review*, 10 August 1928.

50  Address by Senator Dan Riley, president, WSGA annual convention, 2 April 1929, box 19, file folder 178, WSGA Papers.

51  *Farm and Ranch Review*, 10 August 1928.

52  Address by Senator Dan Riley, president, WSGA annual convention, 2 April 1929, box 19, file folder 178, WSGA Papers.

53  Ibid.

54  Directors' meeting, 31 May 1929, box 2, file folder 11, WSGA Papers.

55 See Directors' meetings, 1 April 1929, 25 July 1930, box 2, file folder 11, WSGA Papers.

56 *Farm and Ranch Review*, 1 June 1929.

57 Dan Riley to William Lyon Mackenzie King, 27 September 1929, box 5, file folder 28, WSGA Papers.

58 Robinson to Cross, 3 October 1929, box 122, file folder 981, Cross Fonds.

59 Murray R. Benedict, *Farm Policies of the United States, 1790–1950: A Study of their Origins and Development* (New York: Octagon Books, 1966), 251. Benedict refers to Congressional tariff revisions almost always developing into "a log rolling spree."

60 President, Montana Stock Growers' Association to Dillon, 21 July 1922, box 9, file folder 65, WSGA Papers.

61 *Farm and Ranch Review*, 20 April 1923.

62 Directors' meeting, 22 July 1925, box 12, file folder 104, WSGA Papers.

63 Contained in WSGA Papers, box 9, file folder 65.

64 Canada, *House of Commons Debates*, 20 February 1925, 384–85.

65 Ruth Rogers to Dan Riley, 9 April 1923, box 5, file folder 27; Directors' meeting, 31 August 1923, box 1, file folder 8, WSGA Papers.

66 Directors' meeting, 22 July 1925, box 12, file folder 104; Dillon to Gray Silver, 25 August 1925; Gray Silver to Dillon, 7 November 1925, WSGA Papers.

67 Robinson to Cross, 13 September 1924, box 117, file folder 945, Cross Fonds. Part of Robinson's strategy had been a personal letter to President Coolidge in which he referred to the tariff as "taking money out of a man's pocket."

68 Benedict, *Farm Policies*, 250.

69 Referred to in Canada, *House of Commons Debates*, 8 May 1930, 1883.

70 John D. Black, *Agricultural Reform in the United States* (New York: McGraw Hill Book Co., 1929), 219.

71 Fred H. Brixby, secretary, American National Livestock Association to Dillon, 30 June 1922, box 9, file folder 65, WSGA Papers. Brixby wondered how the Canadians could be brash enough to want tariff relief when they were asking for the duty on U.S. stockers entering Canada to be doubled. Brixby had completely misread the WSGA correspondence to him. In it the WSGA had asked for the ANLA's co-operation on feeders, arguing that it was quite prepared to accept doubling the duty on *Canadian* stockers entering the U.S. This original stance on stockers was later changed to free entry for feeders only.

72 Thomlinson, "Tariff Act of 1922."

73 These organizations were the American Farm Bureau Federation, the National Grange, and the National Farmers' Educational and Co-operative Union. See James R. Connor, "National Farm Organizations and the United States Tariff Policy in the 1920s," *Agricultural History* 32, no. 1 (January 1958): 36–37. See also Alice M. Christensen, "Agricultural Pressure and Governmental Response in the United States, 1919–1929," *Agricultural History* 11, no. 1 (January 1937): 33–42; Martin L. Fausold, "President Hoover's Farm Policies, 1929–1933," *Agricultural History* 51, no. 2 (1977): 362–77.

74 Correspondences dated 25 August, 5 September 1925, box 12, file folder 104, WSGA Papers.

75 W. Coffey, Dean of Agriculture, University of Minnesota to Dillon, 16 September 1925, box 12, file folder 104, WSGA Papers.

76 For examples see references in Canada, *House of Commons Debates*, 31 May 1926, 24 February, 1 March 1927.

77 Knappen to Dillon, 26 January, 6 March 1926, box 12, file folder, 104, WSGA Papers.

78 Benedict, *Farm Policies,* 218.

79 Dillon to G. Coote, MP, 1 March 1926, box 12, file folder 104, WSGA Papers. Canada's Minister of Agriculture, W. R. Motherwell, gave the chances of Coolidge even considering a tariff commission recommendation for reduction as one in a hundred. Motherwell to Dillon, 2 September 1925, box 12, file folder 104, WSGA Papers.

80 Quoted in Canada, *House of Commons Debates*, 8 March 1929, 800.

81 *Farm and Ranch Review*, 26 January 1925. The speaker was Thomas King, a special correspondent in Washington who was addressing the Western Canada Livestock Union in Saskatoon; see also Canada, *House of Commons Debates*, 31 May 1926, 3383.

82 For examples, see *Farm and Ranch Review*, 6 September 1921, 20 May 1922, 11 February 1924, 10 November, 26 December 1925, 10 June 1926.

83 Directors' meeting, 24 February 1928, box 2, file folder 11, WSGA Papers.

84 *Farm and Ranch Review*, 5 August 1921, 26 July 1926.

85 Senator James A. Lougheed to A. E. Cross, 31 March 1921, box 113, file folder 908, Cross Fonds.

86 Canada, *House of Commons Debates,* 26 May 1921, 3905.

87 Ibid., 23 May 1922, 2112.

88 Ibid.

89 Ibid., 20 February 1925, 391; Directors' meeting, 3 April 1928, box 2, file folder 11, WSGA Papers.

90 Motherwell to Dillon, 2 September 1925, box 12, file folder 104, WSGA Papers.

91 Canada, *House of Commons Debates*, 20 February 1925, 386.

92 H. S. Arkell to A. E. Cross, vice president, WSGA, 21 August 1925, box 12, file folder 104, WSGA Papers.

93 Meeting between WSGA officials and Hon. Charles Stewart, 22 July 1922. See Dillon to J. Mitchell, 31 July 1922, box 9, file folder 65, WSGA Papers.

94 Duncan Marshall to Dillon, 30 June 1922, box 9, file folder 65, WSGA Papers. Agriculture Minister Motherwell referred to the tour as "a somewhat delicate undertaking to engage in." Motherwell to Dillon, 29 June 1922.

95 Canada, *House of Commons Debates*, 11 May 1923, 2649.

96 Ibid., 31 May 1926, 3902−03.

97 Ibid., 1 May 1930, 1630−31.

98 Thomlinson, "Tariff Act of 1922." He had a point. In the period 1920−22, the United States exported 21,000 cattle to Canada. In the same period, Canada exported 562,000 head to the United States.

99 Directors' meeting, 27 September 1929, box 2, file folder 11, WSGA Papers.

100 Some examples include the following items (U.S. tariff given first followed by Canadian): wheat: 42¢/bu., 12¢/bu.; corn: 15¢/bu., free; hay: $4.00/ton, $2.00/ton; wheat flour: $2.04/bbl, 50¢/bbl; eggs: 8¢/doz., 3¢/doz.; butter: 8¢/lb, 4¢/lb. Canada, *House of Commons Debates*, 12 February 1925, 1325–26.

101 Ibid., 23 May 1923, 3052–53, 24 February 1930, 27–29.

102 Figures quoted in Canada, *House of Commons Debates*, 22 April 1926, 2723.

103 *Report of National Beef Cattle Conference*, June 28–29, 1928, Alexandria Hotel, Winnipeg, Attorney General's Papers, PAA.

104 For example, see address given by R. B. Bennett, 20 August 1921, box 8, file folder 45, WSGA Papers.

105 United Grain Growers Livestock Superintendent to W. F. Stevens, 16 September 1921, box 8, file folder 45, WSGA Papers.

106 *Farm and Ranch Review*, 20 May, 5 October 1921.

107 W. F. Stevens to E. L. Richardson, secretary, Western Canadian Livestock Union, 12 October 1920, box 8, file folder 45, WSGA Papers.

108 Correspondence dated 23 July 1921, box 113, file folder 913, Cross Fonds.

109 Stevens to E. Watson, 30 November 1920, box 8, file folder 45, WSGA Papers.

110 The incident in the Dudley by-election was discussed at great length in the House of Commons Debate on the embargo in July 1922. Apparently, Beaverbrook's *Daily Express* flooded the electorate with leaflets. One MP was quoted as saying that "we were threatened with consequences should we dare oppose Lord Beaverbrook's will."

111 See *Royal Commission on the Importation of Live Cattle*, Report of His Majesty's Commissioners, 30 August 1921.

112 *Calgary Albertan*, 24 July 1921.

113 See *London Times*, 15 June 1922.

114 *Royal Commission on the Importation of Live Cattle*.

115 Ibid.

116 U.K., *Parliamentary Debates, House of Commons*, vol. 150, 9 February 1922.

117 U.K., *Parliamentary Debates, House of Lords*, vol. 53, 12, 26 July 1922.

118 U.K., *Parliamentary Debates, House of Commons*, vol. 157, 24 July 1922. Prominent cabinet ministers voting against the removal of the embargo included J. Austin Chamberlain, Lord Privy Seal and leader of the House, Stanley Baldwin, president of the boards of trade, and of course Arthur Griffith Boscawen, president of the Board of Agriculture.

119 The Royal Commission was right in its conclusions. Meat prices did not change appreciably with the lifting of the embargo.

120 Canada, *Sessional Papers*, no. 16, 1924, annual report of the Department of Agriculture.

121 "Canadian Agricultural Products and the British Market," *The Agricultural Gazette of Canada* 11, no. 1 (January–February 1924). Grisdale himself had considerable credentials, having succeeded Charles Saunders in 1911 as Chief Director of the federal Experimental Farm system. For most of his tenure (1911–19), he also headed up the field husbandry division.

122  Canada, *Journals of the House of Commons*, Appendices, report of Select Special Committee on Agricultural Conditions, January–June 1923.

123  *Farm and Ranch Review*, 20 April 1923.

124  See Arkell's address to the annual meeting of the Western Livestock Union in 1925 in *Farm and Ranch Review*, 26 December 1925.

125  D. Munro to W. F. Stevens, 18 May 1921, box 10, file folder 68, WSGA Papers.

126  *Shipping Cattle to Britain: Experiments in the Shipment of Live Cattle and Chilled Beef to England* (Ottawa: Department of Agriculture, Experimental Farms Branch, 1926).

127  See *Calgary Herald*, 7 January, 15 February 1921.

128  A Letter on Canadian Livestock Products, from the Industrial and Development Council of Canadian Meat Packers, February 1923, box 43, file folder 429, Canada Land and Irrigation Co. Ltd. Papers.

129  For a good account of these attempts see Canada, *House of Commons Debates*, 20 February 1925, 400–01.

130  Particularly given the fact that the ideal chilled beef animal was well finished, weighing about 1050 pounds and dressing out at around 61.5–62 percent, exactly the type of animal that was not being produced on western Canadian farms and ranches.

131  WSGA Papers, box 12, file folder 98.

132  James W. Robertson, *Report of Select Committee on Agricultural Conditions* (Ottawa: King's Printer, 1923), 233. McLean rightly held that Canadian cattle were not marketed early enough to appeal to the British consumer.

133  Canada, *House of Commons Debates*, 31 May 1926, 3888.

134  WSGA Papers, box 19, file folder 178.

135  Great Britain, *Parliamentary Debates, House of Commons*, vol. 171, 17 March 1924.

136  See comments by D. S. McIntosh, livestock dealer, Calgary, box 43, file folder 434, Canada Land and Irrigation Co. Ltd. Papers.

137  *Farm and Ranch Review*, 25 February 1927.

138  Cross Fonds, box 122, file folder 893.

139  Robertson, *Report of Select Committee*, 32.

140  *Farm and Ranch Review*, 25 August 1927.

141  For good example, see Charles Robinson to A. E. Cross, 24 October 1929, box 122, file folder 981, Cross Fonds.

142  Cross Fonds, box 114, file folder 914.

143  *Farm and Ranch Review*, 10 November 1927.

144  "Monthly Average Price of Good Butcher Steers, Toronto, 1920–38," *Canadian Cattlemen*, September 1938; Charles Robinson to A. E. Cross, 14 August 1925, box 118, file folder 954, Cross Fonds; *Farm and Ranch Review*, 11 July 1927.

145  *Farm and Ranch Review*, 20 January 1925.

146  *Farm and Ranch Review*, 26 November 1928.

147  Quoted in *Farm and Ranch Review*, 5 January 1923.

148  "A Half Century of Service," *Canadian Cattlemen*, September 1938.

149  Alberta, *Sessional Papers*, no. 39, 1925, "Cattle Shipments to Japan."

150  See "William Mackenzie of Southern Alberta Co-op. Resigns Post," *Lethbridge Herald*, 8 January 1947.

151  Glenbow, Pat Burns Fonds, box 2, file folder 27. The feeding agreements covered the period December through March or April, and involved batches of from 150 head up to 300. The farmers were also feeding their own cattle at the same time. The feed used was hay and threshed timothy. One farmer who fed 150–200 head used 140 tons of hay and 30 tons of threshed timothy.

152  *Farm and Ranch Review*, 26 April 1926.

153  "Eastern Canadian Society of Animal Production: Reports Presented at First Annual General Meeting," *Scientific Agriculture* 8, no. 12 (August 1928): 775. Remarks made by R. S. Hamer on behalf of the Beef Cattle Production Committee.

154  For information on each, see *Farm and Ranch Review*, 26 December 1924; *Canadian Cattlemen*, February 1950; *Lethbridge Herald*, 12 June 1942.

155  *Farm and Ranch Review*, 26 December 1924.

156  Alberta, *Department of Agriculture Annual Report*, 1932.

157  Correspondence dated 27 April 1923, box 1, file folder 9, WSGA Papers.

158  G. Muir and S. Chagnon, *The Winter Feeding of Beef Cattle in Ontario* (Ottawa: Department of Agriculture, Animal Husbandry Division, 1922); also see evidence by H. S. Arkell before the Select Committee on Agricultural Conditions, 1923.

159  Canada, *Sessional Papers*, no. 16, 1924, annual report of the Department of Agriculture, report of Livestock Branch.

160  "A Case for Canada," *Farm and Ranch Review*, 26 October 1925.

161  Alberta, *Department of Agriculture Annual Report*, 1921, report of the College of Agriculture.

162  Alberta, *Department of Agriculture Annual Report*, 1923.

163  For example, experiments showed that corn silage was better than sunflower silage but that beet pulp was an excellent substitute.

164  *Farm and Ranch Review*, 25 March 1925. Under this policy, farmers who bought feeders at regional stockyards were reimbursed for the cost of freighting the animals back to their farms. Originally designed to keep cattle in the country during the era of free trade with the Americans 1914–20, the policy was continued into the 1920s and beyond as an incentive to promote a home-grown feeder industry.

165  *Farm and Ranch Review*, 26 November 1928. The U.S. prices justified this high number in spite of the tariff and evince the irresistible pull of the American market.

166  Gavin Jack Commission Co. Ltd., Calgary, 13 December 1923, box 43, file folder 434, Canada Land and Irrigation Co. Ltd. Papers.

167  *Farm and Ranch Review*, 10 November 1926.

168  E. L. Fitzimmons to A. E. Cross, 26 March 1924, box 117, file folder 945, Cross Fonds.

169  C. Robinson to A. E. Cross, 20 November 1925, box 118, file folder 958, Cross Fonds.

170  *Farm and Ranch Review*, June 1941.

171  Edmonton Board of Trade, *The Edmonton District in Central Alberta: Canada's Richest Mixed Farming Country* (Edmonton: The Board, 1917).

172  W. F. Stevens to D. Munro, 21 April 1921, box 10, file folder 69, WSGA Papers.

173  Interview, December, 1971, by author with Dr. J. W. Grant MacEwan, livestock authority of the period (hereafter cited as MacEwan interview). In addition to being from a farming homestead family, head of the Department of Animal Husbandry at the University of Saskatchewan 1928–46, Dean of Agriculture at the University of Manitoba 1946–51 and manager of the Canadian Council of Beef Producers, Western Section, MacEwan was a recognized cattle judge and had been an assistant editor with the *Canadian Cattlemen*. MacEwan argued that the later attempt by Senator Harry Hays to develop a true Canadian breed, the Hays Converter, represented the first serious effort to incorporate Holstein size into a beef breed.

174  *Edmonton Journal*, 24 February 1922.

175  See *Census of Canada*, 1921, 1931, 1941; *Census of the Prairie Provinces*, 1926; *Census of Alberta*, 1936.

176  Dairy numbers dropped in the late 1920s with the rise in beef prices, only to rise again amid collapsing beef prices in the early 1930s. In 1936 the number of cows being milked stood at an all-time high of 348,773, about 140,000 more than in 1921. Beef cattle numbers, although still swollen by the marketing uncertainties, showed nowhere near the same level of increase. By 1941, when beef prices were on the rise, dairy numbers had dropped 30,000 below the 1936 figure.

177  *Farm and Ranch Review*, 25 February 1927.

178  Ibid., 4 November 1922.

179  M. J. Timlin, "Finishing Steers for Market in North-Western Saskatchewan," Pamphlet 17 (Ottawa: Experimental Farms Branch, Department of Agriculture, 1922). For example, the pamphlet emphasized the importance of shelters in spite of the cost, and was very vague in its recommendations.

180  Grant MacEwan interview; also *Farm and Ranch Review*, 26 March 1928.

181  *Farm and Ranch Review*, 2 December 1929.

182  Address to WSGA by J. H. Woods, 16 August 1934, box 126, file folder 1012, Cross Fonds.

183  *Farm and Ranch Review*, 26 September 1920.

184  Marshall, a longtime Minister of Agriculture, had a strong interest in livestock and was the author of many publications on livestock management.

185  *Farm and Ranch Review*, 6 October 1916, 20 January 1917.

186  MacEwan interview.

187  "Proceedings of the Fourth Annual Meeting of the Western Canadian Society of Animal Production, June 6–7, 1931," *Scientific Agriculture* 11 (March 1931): 435.

188  "Eastern Canadian Society of Animal Production. Reports Presented at First Annual General Meeting," *Scientific Agriculture* 8 (August 1928): 774–78. The conference was told that "for the past two or three years however, American

competition for the best of our western feeders has been so keen that only the more optimistic of our eastern cattle feeders have felt justified in paying the price."

189   Muir and Chagnon, "Winter Feeding."

190   General Manager to F. W. Hanna, 9 February 1924, box 45, file folder 457, Canada Land and Irrigation Co. Ltd. Papers.

191   See CPR Fonds, box 65, file folder 595.

192   Rudd, "Production and Marketing of Beef Cattle," 62.

193   *Farm and Ranch Review*, 26 November 1928, 2 January 1929.

194   Ibid., 25 June 1925.

195   "A Letter on Canadian Livestock Products, April 1923," box 43, file folder 429, Canada Land and Irrigation Co. Ltd. Papers.

196   Canada, *House of Commons Debates*, 31 May 1926, 3398.

197   Canada, *House of Commons Debates*, 12 April 1927, 2342.

198   *National Beef Cattle Conference*, Attorney General's Papers.

199   Ibid.

200   Cross Fonds, box 122, file folder 983. Commissioner H. S. Arkell made the comments in supporting the formation of a national council of beef producers, 16 December 1929.

201   "Livestock Statistics," *Canadian Cattlemen*, December 1940.

202   *National Beef Cattle Conference*, Attorney General's Papers.

203   *Farm and Ranch Review*, 25 January 1927.

204   One has only to note the newsletters circulated by the packing companies during this period. Based in Toronto, these newsletters devoted over 90 percent of their space to pork and bacon.

205   See *Brooks Bulletin*, 29 April 1937.

206   See *Census of the Prairie Provinces*, 1946.

207   "Livestock Statistics: Per Capita Consumption of Meats, 1920–1939," *Canadian Cattlemen*, December 1940.

208   See remarks by the president of the National Livestock Union in *Farm and Ranch Review*, 26 December 1925.

209   One wonders whether the Australians ever heard of or took heart from this effusive compliment from C. W. Peterson, editor of the *Farm and Ranch Review*. See issue, 25 June 1925. As for dietary value, meats were being trumpeted by the meat packers as early as 1921 as being a newly discovered source of Vitamin B.

210   See *National Beef Cattle Conference*, Attorney General's Papers.

211   Todd, S. L., "Functions of the Meat Packer," *Farm and Ranch Review*, July 1939.

212   "Where the Money Comes from in Meat Packing: A Letter on Canadian Livestock Products from the Industrial and Development Council of Canadian Meat Packers, May 1923," box 43, file folder 429, Canada Land and Irrigation Co. Ltd. Papers.

213   "Co-operative Cattle Selling: A System of Marketing Cattle for the Benefit of Producers," *United Grain Growers Publication*, 15 March 1924.

214 For good discussion, see *Farm and Ranch Review*, 20 May 1911.

215 "Sherm Ewing: Transcripts of Interviews" (hereafter cited as Sherm Ewing Interviews), vol. 1, Bert Sheppard Library and Archives, Western Heritage Centre, Cochrane. Interview with Marshall Copithorne, 14 June 1986. The comment was made by Ewing himself, and while probably referring specifically to a later period, doubtless could be applied to this period as well.

216 Jack Byers, "Developments in Beef Grading," *Canadian Cattlemen*, March 1939.

217 Department of the Interior, Orders in Council, vol. 41, 1919, no. 14840, 24 February 1919, PAA.

218 R. A. Gibson, Acting Deputy Minister, Department of the Interior, Timber and Grazing Branch to B. L. York, Head, Timber and Grazing Branch, 7 October 1920, RG 15, B2a, vol. 175, PAC.

219 W. F. Stevens to A. M. Frith, 27 June 1921, box 11, file folder 84, WSGA Papers.

220 B. L. York to Deputy Minister, 5 October 1920, RG 15, B2a, vol. 175.

221 Department of the Interior, Orders in Council, vol. 42, 1920, no. 14452, 4 November 1920.

222 For an excellent account of these and subsequent proceedings, see WSGA summary statements dated 15 May 1922, RG 15, B2a, vol. 175. The delegation consisted of E. D. Hardwick of Gleichen, E. V. Bennis of High River, and J. Lafferty of Calgary as a legal advisor.

223 E. Hardwick, Grazing Committee chairman to James A. Lougheed, 16 May 1921, box 11, file folder 84, WSGA Papers.

224 Department of the Interior, Orders in Council, vol. 43, 1921–23, no. 15767, 23 September 1921; no. 15570, 3 October 1921.

225 R. A. Gibson to B. L. York, 26 September 1921, RG 15, B2a, vol. 175.

226 See WSGA document dated 15 May 1922 in RG 15, B2a, vol. 175.

227 WSGA Papers, box 11, file folder 84. Lougheed's response to Stewart was evasive. He wanted the whole matter left in abeyance pending the result of the provincial election. Clearly he expected Stewart to lose. See James Lougheed to Charles Stewart, 25 July 1921.

228 These were: *(a)* A few old open leases granted in 1887; *(b)* About 8 – 10 irrevocably closed twenty-one-year leases covering about 282,000 acres granted under regulations dated 15 February 1905; *(c)* A good number of twenty-one-year leases containing the two-year cancellation clause, granted 27 July 1905; *(d)* A large number of ten-year closed leases granted under the 1913 regulations, with a few containing a three- or four-year cancellation clause; *(e)* A small number covering lands more than forty miles from a railroad subject to cancellation upon one year's notice after a railroad has been built.

229 See *Canada Gazette*, 13 May 1922, vol. 55, no. 46. Copy also contained in RG 15, B2a, vol. 175.

230 RG 15, B2a, vol. 175. The main difference was that York had suggested a rental rate of four cents per acre.

231 See "Report and Recommendations of the Southern Alberta Survey Board," *Calgary Herald*, 6 February 1922. The Board recommended on the need for water storage areas, insect pest control through legislation, accelerated soil surveys, and adequate financial support for irrigation projects.

232 Magrath to Cross, box 114, file folder 918, Cross Fonds.

233 *Statutes of Alberta*, 13 George V, 1923, chap. 16, An Act Respecting Private Grazing Associations; chap. 17, An Act Respecting Community Grazing.

234 See *Alberta Gazette*, 15 February 1924.

235 C. M. Hamilton, Minister of Agriculture, Province of Saskatchewan to the deputy minister, Department of the Interior, 23 February 1922, RG 15, B2a, vol. 175.

236 *Edmonton Bulletin*, 17 March 1922.

237 A. Mitchner, "The Bow River Scheme: CPR's Irrigation Block," in *The CPR West: The Iron Road and the Making of a Nation*, Hugh A. Dempsey, ed. (Vancouver: Douglas and McIntyre, 1984), 270–71.

238 Cross Fonds, box 118, file folder 955.

239 Letter dated 5 May 1925, box 118, file folder 954, Cross Fonds.

240 A. E. Cross to C. A. Magrath, member of the Southern Alberta Survey Board, 7 March 1922, box 114, file folder 918, Cross Fonds.

241 *Census of the Prairie Provinces*, 1926, table 88.

242 See Jones, *We'll All Be Buried.*

243 S. E. Clarke, "Pasture Investigations in the Short Grass Plains of Saskatchewan and Alberta," *Scientific Agriculture* 10, no. 10 (June 1930): 731–49.

244 One has only to read the Sessional Papers during the period. Heavy emphasis was placed on crop experiments. In fact, all forage experimentation was discontinued during the First World War.

245 Clarke, "Pasture Investigations," 733.

246 See S. E. Clarke, J. A. Campbell and J. B. Campbell, *An Ecological and Grazing Capacity Study of the Native Grass Pastures in Southern Alberta, Saskatchewan and Manitoba.* Publication 738, Technical Bulletin 44, Dominion Experimental Station, Swift Current, Saskatchewan (Ottawa: Department of Agriculture, Division of Forage Crops, 1942), 4; resolution passed at Thirty-first Annual Conference, Calgary, 30 March 1927, box 1, file folder 9, WSGA Papers.

247 The station was on a lease held by R. Gilchrist, who supplied the cattle and the winter feed for the experiments. The federal government was responsible for the staffing and buildings.

248 See Clarke, "Pasture Investigations." Clarke was the agrostologist at Manyberries at the time he wrote the article; also L. B. Thomson, superintendent of Manyberries Research Station, "Carrying Capacities and Beef Production," address to Canadian Society of Animal Production, eighth annual meeting, June 1936, in *Farm and Ranch Review*, August 1936.

249 Of particular interest in the area of forage and regrassing was the nutritious and palatable crested wheat grass. For good contemporary discussion on the origins of the use of crested wheatgrass in western Canada, see W. Moore, "Our Experience With Crested Wheat Grass," *Canadian Cattlemen*, June 1939.

250 *Edmonton Bulletin*, 1, 5 April 1920.

251 *Edmonton Bulletin*, 24 February 1923.

252 Alberta, *Department of Municipal Affairs Annual Report*, 1921–29. Leases were generally located in areas designated for taxation purposes as municipal or improvement districts. Arrears on dominion lease rentals alone amounted to $39,771.44 at the time of transfer of natural resource to the provinces. See *Canadian Cattlemen*, June 1938.

253 See *Edmonton Bulletin*, 26 February 1924; also A. E. Cross to George Hoadley, Minister of Agriculture, Province of Alberta, 7 June 1924, box 117, file folder 943, Cross Fonds.

254 WSGA Papers, box 2, file folder 11. The resolution was passed at a meeting in Medicine Hat on 30 June 1928.

255 Rudd, "Production and Marketing of Beef Cattle," 63.

256 L. B. Thomson, "Costs of Beef Production," *Canadian Cattlemen*, June 1938, 42. Thomson at the time of writing was superintendent of the experimental station at Swift Current, but was referring to experiments undertaken at Manyberries during his tenure there as superintendent. The survey represented cattle numbers in excess of fifty thousand. Thomson, according to Grant MacEwan, was a no-nonsense, very capable, and highly respected administrator. MacEwan remembers him as the only Western agriculturalist "who Jimmy Gardiner (federal Agriculture Minister) would ever listen to."

# Chapter Five
## The Depression Years, 1930 – 39

1 "Cattle Survey in Alberta, December 1940," *Canadian Cattlemen*, March 1941.

2 *Census of Canada*, 1941.

3 Gross leasehold acreage had been steadily rising since the formation of the province in 1905, partly as a result of farm abandonments after 1920 but mostly because of the increasing amount of marginal land being sought after for grazing purposes. In 1906, 1.551 million acres were under lease, 1.737 million acres in 1910, 2.563 million acres in 1918, and 2.925 million acres in 1923.

4 "High Tariff Walls," *Nanton News*, 28 July 1932.

5 John Cross to George Porter, 24 July 1933, box 125, file folder 1009, Cross Fonds. John Cross was A. E. Cross's son, who took over ranching operations upon the death of his father.

6 For good discussion of this tariff within a Canadian context, see Richard Kottman, "Herbert Hoover and Hawley-Smoot Tariff: Canada, a Case Study," *Journal of American History* 62 (1975 – 76): 609 – 36.

7 W. Eastwood, Co-operative Wholesalers Society Ltd., to W. Wieland, Montreal, 21 May 1935, box 13, file folder 116, WSGA Papers.

8 Department of Natural Resources annual reports, 1935, 1936, box 76, file folder 625, 626, CPR Papers.

9 WSGA Papers, box 2, file folder 10.

10 *Farm and Ranch Review*, September 1936.

11 Cross to Rice Whaley, St. Boniface, 11 Sept 1930, also Cross to C. Robinson, Chicago, 25 August 1930, box 122, file folder 987, Cross Fonds.

12 Alberta, *Department of Agriculture Annual Report*, 1930.

13 *Census of Canada*, 1946, table 16.

14 "Monthly Price Good Butcher Steers, Toronto, 1920 – 1938," *Canadian Cattlemen*, September 1938. The average price of $19.59 in 1920 dropped dramatically the following year to $7.58, and fell below $7.00 in 1923 and 1924 before recovering slightly and then exceeding $10.00 in 1928 – 29. In sharp contrast, the average price between 1931 and 1938 was $5.50. These Toronto prices were higher than what would have been realized in regional markets like Calgary.

15 Alberta, *Department of Agriculture Annual Report*, 1931, report of the Livestock Supervisor.

16 Ibid., 1932.

17 Ibid., 1933.

18 Canada, *Sessional Papers* no. 238, 1932 – 33, "Correspondence Between G. G. Serkau and Department of Agriculture Respecting the Exchange of Canadian Cattle for Russian Oil Products," Harry Vosper to Robert Weir, 11 January 1933.

19 The low prices received for agricultural products during the depression has spawned a host of stories, most apocryphal, but all making a tragic point about the economic miseries of a world gone crazy. The story is told about a farmer who, after bringing his wheat to the elevator, received less than the cost of getting it there. He resolved the situation by promising the elevator operator a turkey to make up the difference. A month later he brought in two turkeys as payment. When reminded by the elevator operator that he only owed one turkey, the farmer replied that the other turkey was to cover the second load of wheat he had just brought in.

20 Interview with Dr. J. W. Grant MacEwan, Calgary, 20 August 1997. MacEwan himself was heavily involved in animal nutrition research during the period under discussion, and frequently published his findings in *Scientific Agriculture* in the early 1930s. He later published extensively in *Canadian Cattlemen,* where he served for a time as associate editor. "Canner cow" was used to describe those low-grade animals whose meat was to be used for canning purposes.

21 Canada's five-year agreement with Great Britain signed on 20 August 1932 was later extended to 1940. Beef products from the non-empire countries were subject to a duty of seventy-five cents per pound. *Canada Year Book*, 1937.

22 Department of Natural Resources annual report, 1935, box 76, file folder 626, CPR Fonds.

23 Canada, *Royal Commission on Price Spreads and Mass Buying: Proceedings and Evidence,* 1934 (hereafter cited as *Price Spreads Commission*), 608.

24 *Brooks Bulletin*, 15 August 1935, 11 November 1937. In 1936 Canada's hog production was 147.68 million pounds. of which Alberta's share was 25.1 million pounds.

25 *Brooks Bulletin*, 10 March 1938.

26 *Statutes of Canada*, George VI, chap. 17, "The United Kingdom Trade Agreement," referring to original agreement of 20 August 1932.

27 *Farm and Ranch Review*, January 1934; *Canada Year Book*, 1937. This figure compares unfavourably to the 150,000 annual average 1902–06, and the average of over 80,000 in the four years following the lifting of the embargo, 1923–26.

28 "The Livestock Industry of Alberta," prepared by the Alberta Department of Agriculture for presentation to the Stevens Parliamentary Committee and presented by Agriculture Minister George Hoadley, box 133, file folder 112, WSGA Papers.

29 See remarks made by Dominion Livestock Commissioner G. B. Rothwell in *Farm and Ranch Review*, July 1936.

30 *Brooks Bulletin*, 27 May 1937.

31 *Price Spreads Commission,* 741.

32 Hon. George Hoadley, "Agricultural Diversification," *Farm and Ranch Review*, 1 October 1930.

33 J. Latimer, "Intra-Empire Trade: the Opportunity for Agriculture," *Scientific Agriculture* 13, no. 5 (January 1933): 281–303.

34 H. S. Arkell, "Competition for the United Kingdom Meat Market," *Canadian Cattlemen*, September 1939. As early as 1932 Arkell had told the fourth annual

general meeting of the Eastern Society of Animal Production that the solution to Canada's marketing problem was to decide on the exportable surplus, send it to Great Britain thus establishing domestic prices at acceptable levels, and pay any loss on the export through a levy on total marketings.

35  WSGA Papers, box 13, file folder 111.

36  Ibid.

37  "Canadian Imports of Beef," *Canadian Cattlemen*, June 1938.

38  *Nanton News*, 14 April 1933. This federal initiative was a response to stockmen's allegations that speculators were tying up boat space to Britain.

39  See *Nanton News*, 9 June, 6 October 1932. With respect to the export cattle, the Eastern feeder would apply for the 50 percent rebate when his animals were ready to export.

40  WSGA Annual Convention, 1936, box 2, file folder 10, WSGA Papers.

41  "Need Aggressive Selling Policy," *Brooks Bulletin*, 3 September 1936.

42  *Farm and Ranch Review*, January 1938.

43  *Canadian Cattlemen*, March 1939.

44  WSGA Annual Convention, 1939, box 2, file folder 10, WSGA Papers.

45  The figures given by R. A. Wright, president of the Western Canada Livestock Union, were $505.25 to Melfort, $283.00 to Montreal. See Brief of Western Canada Livestock Union to Price Spreads and Mass Buying Committee, Ottawa, 19 April 1934, box 13, file folder 112, WSGA Papers.

46  "Conditions of the Export Trade in Canada and the Cattle Industry Generally," brief for presentation to the Standing Committee on Agriculture and Forestry, Senate of Canada, 1934, box 13, file folder 111, WSGA Papers.

47  *Price Spreads Commission*, 742.

48  "The Livestock Industry in Alberta," brief presented by the Department of Agriculture to the Stevens Parliamentary Committee, April 1934, box 13, file folder 112, WSGA Papers. The study showed that the average gross price in Britain per animal was $61.01 less $37.61 for the marketing expenses associated with transportation.

49  "Conditions of the Export Trade," WSGA Papers.

50  The federal government did try to shore up exports to Britain by guaranteeing an exchange rate of $4.60 to the British pound. The pound had slumped to below $3.75. According to estimates, this translated into a 10 percent increase, or one cent per pound live weight.

51  As the *Farm and Ranch Review* put it in September 1932, "The British want two year olds and smaller, cuts not suitable to Canadian conditions."

52  See *Nanton News*, 30 November 1933; *Brooks Bulletin*, 25 October 1934.

53  *Nanton News*, 21 December 1933.

54  Ibid., 12 October 1933.

55  A. M. Shaw, "Report on the Experiments of Chilled Beef to Britain," *Scientific Agriculture* 15, no. 1 (November 1934): 158–64.

56  E. C. Hope, "The Significance of Demand in the Determination of Prices of Beef and Pork in Canada, 1920–1932," *Scientific Agriculture* 15, no. 2 (October 1934): 72.

57 Todd, "Functions of the Meat Packer."

58 A. M. Shaw, "Phases of Beef Cattle Markets," *Canadian Cattlemen*, June 1938; "The Council of Western Beef Producers: What Is It?" *Canadian Cattlemen*, December 1943.

59 *Farm and Ranch Review*, June 1932.

60 Jack Byers to A. B. Claypool, 17 February 1934, box 13, file folder 117, WSGA Papers.

61 George Ross to A. E. Cross, 31 January 1933, box 125, file folder 1007, Cross Fonds.

62 *Price Spreads Commission*, 611.

63 See Max Foran, "Hooves for Gallons: The Canada/Russia Barter Deal of 1932–33," *Alberta History* 49, no. 2 (Spring 2001): 12–19.

64 *Farm and Ranch Review*, December 1935; E. L. Kendall, "The U.S. Duty on a Definite Quota of Canadian Cattle Should be Eliminated," *Canadian Cattlemen*, December 1939.

65 See "Canadian Cattle Exports," *Canadian Cattlemen*, June 1938, June 1942; *House of Commons Debates*, 29 April 1942, 1977–78.

66 *Farm and Ranch Review*, July 1939.

67 *Canadian Cattlemen*, June 1942, March 1946.

68 *Lethbridge Herald*, 18 April 1939.

69 Alberta, *Department of Agriculture Annual Reports*, 1936–40.

70 For good comment here, see "Farm Marketing Livestock Faulty Declares Burrell," *Edmonton Bulletin*, 9 March 1931. A. W. Burrell was the manager of the Edmonton stockyards.

71 "Per Capita Consumption of Meats, 1920–1939," *Canadian Cattlemen*, December 1940. In 1929 the figure was 51.1 pounds per person; in 1939 the figure was 49.0 pounds.

72 *Brooks Bulletin*, 24 January 1934. The 1929 figure was 66.57 pounds; the 1932 figure, 56.02 pounds.

73 J. Walters to Jack Byers, 24 March 1938, box 4, file folder 25, WSGA Papers.

74 Jack Byers to J. Walters, 18 March 1938, box 4, file folder 25, WSGA Papers.

75 Ibid.

76 "The Livestock Industry of Alberta," box 13, file folder 112, WSGA Papers.

77 L. B. Thomson, "Economics of the Ranching Industry in Alberta and Saskatchewan," box 13, file folder 112, WSGA Papers.

78 L. B. Thomson, "An Economic Study of Beef Cattle Raising on the Range Areas of Alberta and Saskatchewan," preliminary report, 1932, box 13, file folder 112, WSGA Papers.

79 *Edmonton Bulletin*, 9 March 1932.

80 See L. B. Thomson, "Costs of Beef Cattle Production," *Canadian Cattlemen*, June 1938; also "Monthly Average Price of Good Butcher Steers, Toronto, 1920–38," *Canadian Cattlemen*, September 1938.

81 Sherm Ewing Interviews, vol. 1, interview with Wes Alm, 29 December 1988. Alm was referring to the experience of his father Albert during the Depression.

82 Cross Fonds, box 125, file folder 1007.

83 "WSGA Annual Convention, 1936," *Farm and Ranch Review*, July 1936.

84 The idea of insurance against diseased animals dated to 1912 and an agreement between Ontario producers and the packing industry. The original levy of twenty cents for steers and bulls and fifty cents for cows was later extended Canada-wide and changed to 0.5 percent of the selling price. Western stockmen always argued that they were no part of the 1912 "gentlemen's agreement," and that the deduction was not really applicable to the healthier Western cattle. The 1940 carcass condemnation figure was 1.7 percent. Alberta's was 0.47 percent. See "Condemnation Insurance," *Canadian Cattlemen*, December 1941.

85 *Edmonton Bulletin*, 6 March 1938. This levy became a tax when it was taken over by the provincial government. The reason for its imposition was associated with the loss of carcass value due to bruising in the stockyards.

86 *Price Spreads Commission*, 558–59.

87 Ibid., 622.

88 G. C. Hay, "The Livestock Marketing Problem," box 13, file folder 112, WSGA Papers.

89 "Packing House Facilities and Practices," *Canadian Cattlemen*, December 1938. This article was based on the *Price Spreads Commission*.

90 *Price Spreads Commission*, 56.

91 Ibid.

92 The figure given was after all costs and covered a total slaughter of 84.47 million animals. See *Farm and Ranch Review*, August 1941.

93 *Price Spreads Commission*, 5290.

94 Ibid., 56, 5093.

95 Ibid., 56.

96 *Edmonton Bulletin*, 9 March 1931.

97 *Brooks Bulletin*, 24 January 1934.

98 "Meats Costing Consumers Too Much Declares Expert to Agricultural Committee," *Edmonton Journal*, 27 February 1931.

99 "Essay on the Cow," *Brooks Bulletin*, 7 April 1938.

100 E. J. Lyne, "The Retail Meat Dealer," *Canadian Cattlemen*, December 1938. The term used by Lyne was "any Tom Dick or Harry."

101 *Price Spreads Commission*, 1836, 1868, 2052–53.

102 Ibid., 167.

103 Alberta, *Department of Agriculture Annual Report*, 1932.

104 Alberta, *Department of Agriculture Annual Report*, 1933, Report of Feeding Supervisor.

105 Ibid.

106 Movement of feed to cattle: free freight on a maximum of three cars of forage and one of grain shipped to producers' foundation herds. Movement of cattle to feed: a maximum of ten cars free to and from winter feeding locations.

107 Jack Byers, "Recent Activities of the Western Stock Growers' Association," *Canadian Cattlemen*, June 1938.

108 See C. A. Lyndon, "Feeding Associations in Alberta," *Canadian Cattlemen*, December 1938.

109  Brief presented by R. A. Wright of the Western Canadian Livestock Union before the Special Committee on Price Spreads and Mass Buying, 19 April 1934, box 13, file folder 112, WSGA Papers.

110  *Brooks Bulletin*, 1 December 1938, 2 February 1939.

111  Ibid., 20 July 1939.

112  Alberta, *Department of Agriculture Annual Report*, 1940.

113  *Brooks Bulletin*, 3 August 1939.

114  Alberta, *Department of Agriculture Annual Report*, 1932, report of the Livestock Commissioner.

115  WSGA Papers, box 2, file folder 10.

116  *Farm and Ranch Review*, January 1936.

117  Alberta, *Department of Agriculture Annual Report*, 1938, report of the Livestock Commissioner.

118  Address by Hon. D. B. Mullen to WSGA, *Farm and Ranch Review*, July 1939.

119  Total beef cattle marketings from Alberta in 1930 were 116,859; in 1940, 248,748. See *Canadian Cattlemen*, June 1942, March 1946; also Alberta *Department of Agriculture Annual Reports*, 1930, 1940.

120  C. W. Vrooman, "Coast Markets for Canadian Cattle," *Canadian Cattlemen*, March 1946; *Lethbridge Herald*, 12 June 1942.

121  Brief to Mackenzie King, 18 November 1929, box 13, file folder 111, WSGA Papers.

122  "Economics of the Ranching Industry in Alberta and Saskatchewan," brief given before the Special Agricultural Committee, Regina, 16 January 1932, box 13, file folder 112, WSGA Papers.

123  See J. B. Cross to J. M. McKay, CPR Agent, 17 October 1933, box 125, file folder 1008, Cross Fonds.

124  Ibid.

125  Ibid. The company even supplied a booklet advising farmers how to take advantage of Russian thistle as stock feed.

126  *Canadian Cattlemen*, September 1938.

127  Brief presented by R. A. Wright of the Western Canadian Livestock Union before the Special Committee on Price Spreads and Mass Buying, 19 April 1934, box 13, file folder 112, WSGA Papers.

128  See *Edmonton Bulletin*, 9 March 1931.

129  George E. Rothwell, "Western Canada and Eastern Cattlemen," *Canadian Cattlemen,* September 1938; *Farm and Ranch Review*, November 1937.

130  Jack Byers, Dominion Livestock Commissioner, made an interesting observation on the mindset of the stock grower when he said in 1939 that the main reason influencing Eastern cattle shipments was the previous year's price. *Canadian Cattlemen*, December 1939.

131  Council of Western Beef Producers to A. E. Claypool, MLA Didsbury, 17 February 1934, box 13, file folder 117, WSGA Papers.

132  Jack Byers to H. Henderson, 9 September 1937, box 4, file folder 23, WSGA Papers.

133 WSGA Papers, box 2, file folder 12; also, Jack Byers to H. Henderson, 9 September 1937, box 4, file folder 23, WSGA Papers.

134 The University of Alberta and the CPR farm at Strathmore also had some excellent high-quality commercial herds.

135 *Farm and Ranch Review*, 25 February, 25 July 1927.

136 *Census of Canada*, 1931. The figure was 0.88 percent.

137 Address by Hon. D. B. Mullen, Alberta Minister of Agriculture, WSGA annual convention, 1939, in *Farm and Ranch Review*, July 1939.

138 Alberta, *Department of Agriculture Annual Report*, 1936, reports of the district agriculturalists.

139 *Farm and Ranch Review*, January 1936.

140 Alberta, *Department of Agriculture Annual Report*, 1936.

141 *Farm and Ranch Review*, 5 February 1919.

142 Alberta, *Department of Agriculture Annual Report*, 1931, reports of district agriculturalists.

143 Annual Report of the Department of Agriculture and Animal Husbandry, 1934, box 76, file folder 625, CPR Papers.

144 Alberta, *Department of Agriculture Annual Reports*, 1935, 1936, 1937, 1938, reports of district agriculturalists. These included: St. Paul, Grande Prairie, Thorsby, Wetaskiwin, Red Deer, Claresholm, Lethbridge, Cardston.

145 Ibid.

146 See *Lethbridge Herald*, 15, 16 June 1939.

147 K. D. Smith, R. T. Berg, M. H. Hawkins, M. E. Stiles, and S. C. McFadyn, *The New Beef Grades* (Edmonton: University of Alberta, Faculty of Agriculture and Forestry, 1975), 6–9.

148 "Livestock Industry of Alberta," box 133, file folder 112, WSGA Papers.

149 "Findings Submitted to Convention," *Canadian Cattlemen*, September 1942.

150 Lyne, "Retail Meat Dealer."

151 Brief dated April 1934, box 13, file folder 112, WSGA Papers.

152 *Statutes of Canada*, chap. 57, 1934, An Act to Improve the Methods and Practices of Marketing of the Natural Products of Canada in the Export Trade, and to Make Further Provision in Connection Therewith.

153 *Statutes of Alberta*, chap. 34, 1934.

154 See *Brooks Bulletin*, 22 November, 12 December 1934.

155 *Canada Law Reports*, 1936, Supreme Court of Canada, 399.

156 *Canada Law Reports*, 1937, Appeal Cases, House of Lords, Judicial Committee of the Privy Council, 368–90.

157 *Statutes of Alberta*, chap. 3, assented to 3 April 1939.

158 *Edmonton Journal*, 28 March 1939.

159 WSGA Papers, box 2, file folder 12.

160 For good example of the tenor of outrage, see Board of Directors' meeting, 12 June 1939, box 2, file folder 12, WSGA Papers.

161 See *Lethbridge Herald*, 3, 5, 8, 10 April 1939.

162 *Alberta Gazette* 35, no. 8, 29 April 1939.

163 *Lethbridge Herald*, 17 June 1939.

164  See remarks by L. B. Thomson to the forty-second annual convention of the WSGA, box 2, file folder 12, WSGA Papers.

165  See remarks made by A. W. Burrell, Manager of the Edmonton stockyards, in the *Edmonton Bulletin*, 9 March 1931.

166  Frank M. Baker, "The Meat Packer and the Cattle Industry," *Canadian Cattlemen*, June 1938.

167  Lyne, "Retail Meat Dealer."

168  Todd, "Functions of the Meat Packer."

169  For excellent discussion on demand and price variables, see, Hope, "Significance of Demand," 65–79.

170  For a discussion on the development of the community auction, see "Community Cattle Sales Profitable For Ranchers," *Farm and Ranch Review*, January 1946.

171  Directors' meeting, 12 June 1939, box 2, file folder 12, WSGA Papers.

172  The fall auctions were held in Cardston, Lundbreck, Bain, Pincher Creek, Vermilion and Marwayne. Directors of the company included Rube Gilchrist of Medicine Hat and George Ross. See *Canadian Cattlemen*, September 1939. For information on the community auctions, see MacLachlan, *Kill and Chill*, 91–92.

173  "Yearly Average Prices, Toronto and Edmonton, 1932–44," *Canadian Cattlemen*, December 1945.

174  UFA Fonds, box 2, file folder 3c; "Federal Survey of Living Conditions on Alberta Farms," *Brooks Bulletin*, 23 April 1936.

175  Abstracted from Alberta, *Department of Municipal Affairs Annual Reports*, 1927–42.

176  *Canadian Cattlemen*, September 1938.

177  Alberta, *Department of Agriculture Annual Report*, 1936, report of the Grazing Supervisor.

178  *Nanton News*, 6 October 1932.

179  Directors' meeting, 1 November 1940, WSGA Papers.

180  *Calgary Albertan*, 27 November 1933. The editorial gave a selling price of 2.5 cents per pound and a production cost of six cents per pound.

181  Thomson, "Costs of Beef Cattle Production," 42. Thomson at the time was superintendent of the dominion experimental farm at Swift Current, Saskatchewan. It was felt that profits were assured only when ranchers had over 50 percent of their equity in cattle.

182  Discussion on range rehabilitation, 4 July 1937, box 4, file folder 23, WSGA Papers.

183  Thomson, "Costs of Beef Cattle Production."

184  See address by L. B. Thomson, then superintendent of Manyberries Research Station, 11 May 1935, box 2, file folder 11, WSGA Papers. According to Thomson, land costs on producing a hundred pounds of beef represented 12 percent of total costs; a similar figure for grain was 6 percent.

185  See "Brief on Grazing Lands," Short Grass Stock Growers' Association, 1937, box 13, file folder 121, WSGA Papers. Another economic survey in 1938–39 put

land charges and rentals as 19 percent of production in the shortgrass country. See *Canadian Cattlemen,* December 1940, 485.

186 Figures abstracted from the Department of Lands and Mines annual reports suggest that well over one thousand leases were cancelled between 1935 and 1940. One result of these cancellations was the establishment of provincial grazing reserves. By 1944 there were three such reserves totalling 223,500 acres running 3,933 head of cattle plus another ten reserves run by approved grazing associations.

187 *Census of the Prairie Provinces,* 1936, table 112.

188 *Brooks Bulletin,* 13 August 1936.

189 WSGA Papers, box 13, file folder 112.

190 Alberta, *Annual Report of the Department of Lands and Mines,* reports of Grazing Supervisors, 1931, 1935, 1936. It was held that overgrazing could reduce the market weight of a yearling by as much as fifty-five pounds.

191 Alberta, *Department of Lands and Mines Annual Report,* 1944.

192 Ibid., 1936.

193 Alberta, *Department of Agriculture Annual Report,* 1937, reports of district agriculturalists.

194 Correspondence dated 6 September 1934, box 126, file folder 1012, Cross Fonds. See also *Farm and Ranch Review,* October 1935, 4.

195 See circular to membership, 25 January 1937, box 13, file folder 121, WSGA Papers; also J. Harvie, Deputy Minister, Department of Lands and Mines, "Alberta's Grazing Policy," *Canadian Cattlemen,* September 1938. In typical fashion, the WSGA was self-congratulatory over its role in securing these arrangements. See *Farm and Ranch Review,* June 1937, 9.

196 Not all leasehold areas in the province had the same rates. Generally the maximum of four cents an acre was paid in the foothills area while rates in the more arid shortgrass country were lower.

197 Harvie, "Alberta's Grazing Policy."

198 A good example occurred in 1937 when the WSGA board of directors' meeting referred to "the shocking figures supplied by the Department of Lands and Mines on 30 January as to the number and proportion of leaseholders in arrears of rentals and taxes." See minutes of board of directors' meeting, 30 March 1937, box 2, file folder 11, WSGA Papers.

199 At the time of the transfer of natural resources to the province, the several long-term leases granted by the dominion government continued to operate as such. As late as 1936, 1,790 dominion leases covered 2.029 million acres in comparison to 992 provincial leases on 1.122 million acres. By the mid-1940s all long-term grazing leases in Alberta were under provincial control.

200 "Regulations Governing the Leasing of Grazing Lands," Orders in Council, 18 June 1931, 656–31, PAA.

201 E. D. Hardwick, chairman of the WSGA Grazing and Taxation Committee to the directors of the WSGA, 15 April 1932, box 2, file folder 11, WSGA Papers.

202 L. B. Thomson, "Economics of the Ranching Industry in Alberta and Saskatchewan," box 13, file folder 112, WSGA Papers.

203 WSGA Papers, box 2, file folder 10. Thomson's words were echoed by Clarke in an address to the 1937 convention.

204 Ross is a fascinating figure. The son of a rancher, Ross learned to fly during the First World War and afterwards became one of the first, if not the first, cattlemen to use his own plane for business activities. He served for several years on the executive of the WSGA, including a term as president. He was also chairman of the Canadian Council of Beef Producers and a member of the federal advisory Wartime Prices and Trade Board. Ross died at his Milk River ranch in 1956.

205 In the late 1920s, Ross conducted what many thought was a foolish experiment when he shipped several feeders to farms around Saskatoon to be tended by rural children. The success of the experiment confounded his critics. One carload sold at seventeen cents per pound, well over the current market price.

206 See *Farm and Ranch Review*, July 1936; Also *Canadian Cattlemen*, July 1939, for SGSGA president George Ross's statements regarding founding reasons.

207 George Ross to N. E. Tanner, 20 January 1937, box 2, file folder 11, WSGA Papers.

208 Proceedings of WSGA forty-first convention, May 25–27 1937, box 2, file folder 10, WSGA Papers.

209 N. E. Tanner to WSGA, 16 November 1937, box 2, file folder 11, WSGA Papers.

210 See Anderson, *Grazing Rates Report,* 10–11; George Ross, "New Approach to the Economics of Lease Rentals and Taxes," *Canadian Cattlemen*, September 1938.

211 "Brief on Grazing Lands," compiled by the Short Grass Stock Growers' Association, 1937, box 13, file folder 121, WSGA Papers.

212 See *Canadian Cattlemen*, September 1939; also Anderson, *Grazing Rates Report,* 9–12.

213 Annual convention, 1938, box 2, file folder 11, WSGA Papers; the WSGA also commented that the results of the investigation were "awaited with keen interest." See *Canadian Cattlemen*, March 1940.

214 Annual convention, 1938, box 2, file folder 11, WSGA Papers.

215 "Keep Politics Out," *Brooks Bulletin,* 23 March 1939. The issue in this case involved the relocation of Saskatchewan farmers to federal lands in Alberta. It is also interesting that in their excellent biography of James Gardiner, *Jimmy Gardiner: Relentless Liberal* (Toronto: University of Toronto Press, 1990), Norman Ward and David Smith write that "from first to last, Gardiner's Alberta venture was a striking demonstration of how a politician well-schooled in the Liberalism he had grown up with in Saskatchewan and Manitoba found himself all but helpless in the context of another community as close as Alberta" (220).

216 Canada, *Sessional Papers*, no. 99a, 1939.

217 Canada, *Sessional Papers,* nos. 99, 99b, 1939. Acreage under drought, 1937: Saskatchewan, 67.4 million; Alberta, 18.04 million. Population of drought areas: Saskatchewan, 594,028, Alberta, 85,378. Total federal expenditures, 1934–38: Saskatchewan, $28.7 million, Alberta, $2.4 million.

218 For information here see Dan Balkwill's excellent study of community pastures, "The PFRA Community Pasture Program, 1937–41," master's thesis, University of Saskatchewan (2002).

219  C. M. Williams, "Always the Bridesmaid: the Development of the Saskatchewan Beef Production System, Part One," *Saskatchewan History* XLII, no. 3 (Autumn 1989): 110.

220  *Census of Canada, 1931, 1941.*

221  G. H. Craig and J. Coke, *An Economic Study of Land Utilization in Southern Alberta.* Publication 610, Technical Bulletin 16 (Ottawa: Department of Agriculture, 1938).

222  In 1937, sixteen community pastures were created in Saskatchewan, ranging in size from six thousand to twenty-five thousand acres. These pastures were controlled by local grazing associations under the direction of a federally appointed manager, and were subject to regulations respecting grazing rates and bull placement. See George Spence, "Land Utilization Under the Prairie Farm Rehabilitation Program," *Canadian Cattlemen*, June 1938.

223  For good information on the Special Areas, see R. S. Rust, "An Analysis and Evaluation of Land Use in the Special Areas of Alberta," master's thesis, University of Alberta, 1956. Grazing associations in Special Areas were governed through yearly permits with priority being given to nearby residents and payment being not less than ten cents per head per month. See *Alberta Gazette*, 31 August 1939.

224  James Gardiner to W. J. Patterson, 22 September 1937, box 42, file folder 367, William Levi Jacobsen Papers, PAS.

225  *Brooks Bulletin*, 7 September 1939. The comment was made by J. R. Sweeney, Deputy Minister of Agriculture.

226  "The Trend in Farming," *Brooks Bulletin*, 27 August 1936.

227  *Brooks Bulletin*, 21 March 1934.

228  Ibid., 13 September 1934.

229  Ibid., 13 August 1936.

230  Ibid., 11 November 1937.

231  Alberta, *Department of Agriculture Annual Report*, 1936, report of the Grazing Supervisor.

232  See chapter 4, note 256.

233  L. B. Thomson, "Costs of Production and Land Charges," 1935, "Carrying Capacities and Beef Production," 1936; S. E. Clarke, "A Study of Our Range Pastures," 1929, "The Differences Between Grass in the East and in the Foothills," 1932, "Providing Feed For Range Livestock," 1935, "Leaseholds and Production Costs," 1937.

234  For example, experiments began at Brandon in 1933 to see if fall rye or oats would provide continuous pasture. See *Brooks Bulletin*, 6 September 1933.

235  *Farm and Ranch Review*, December 1939. The cultivated grasses used in the experiment at Scott Experimental Station in Saskatchewan were western rye, crested wheatgrass, brome, and alfalfa; see also "Abandoned Lands Regrassed," *Farm and Ranch Review*, November 1941.

236  S. Smoliak and A. Johnson, Lethbridge Research Station, *Managing Crested Wheatgrass Pastures*, Publication 1473/E (Ottawa: Department of Agriculture, revised edition, 1981).

237 Crested wheatgrass came to Canada from the United States via the University of Saskatchewan in 1915 where, over a period of years, scientists at the university manufactured a sizeable seed base. See *Brooks Bulletin*, 16 December 1937, 10 March 1938.

238 D. H. Henrichs and T. Lawrence, *Russian Wild Ryegrass for Western Canada*, publication 991 (Ottawa: Department of Agriculture, 1956).

239 H. G. Hargrave, Chief, PFRA Agricultural Services, "Land, Water and the Farmer," paper presented at the fifteenth annual convention of the Saskatchewan Rivers Development Association, 27 October 1962.

240 Unpublished paper prepared by Spence explaining his rehabilitation policies, Prairie Farm Rehabilitation Administration Papers (hereafter cited as PFRA Papers), PAS.

241 *Statutes of Alberta*, chap. 10, An Act to Amend and Consolidate the Provincial Lands Act, assented to 3 April 1939.

242 See comments of L. E. Kirk, a district agriculturalist, in *Nanton News*, 7 January 1932.

243 Alberta, *Department of Agriculture Annual Report*, 1940, report of the District Agricultural Service.

# Chapter Six
## Extraordinary Times, 1939–48

1 See Canada, *Sessional Papers*, no. 165, 1949, annual production, 1940–48; "Record Slaughter in 1945," *Canadian Cattlemen*, March 1946.

2 Ibid.

3 "Cattle Price Floors," editorial, *Lethbridge Herald,* 24 October 1942.

4 The ceilings were adjusted upwards 0.5¢ per pound every two to three months until May when they were moved up 0.25¢. Upward annual revisions of these ceilings occurred throughout the war period. The original ceiling prices on commercial cattle for western Canada at $16.50 per hundredweight were the lowest in the country. Special quality beef was 0.5¢ per pound more, plain beef 1–1.5¢ less, cutter beef 1–3¢ less, and cow beef 2.5¢ less. See *Canadian Cattlemen*, December 1942.

5 See *Canadian Cattlemen*, December 1942.

6 Cattle numbers and production levels increased steadily throughout the war period. Between 1940 and 1945, Canada sent a carcass weight of 223 million pounds of beef to Britain. In the same years, the average beef consumption in Canada rose from a five-year average 1935–39 of 54.4 pounds to 70.4 pounds in 1944. At the outbreak of the war the inspected mature cattle slaughter was 872,574. In 1944 it was 1,354,194. Total Canadian cattle numbers increased from 8.475 million head in 1939 to 10.346 million head in 1944. See *Canadian Cattlemen*, March 1945, March 1946; Canada Packers Ltd., "Facts Regarding Canada's Cattle Industry, *Canadian Cattlemen*, March 1945.

7 Resolutions of forty-fourth annual convention, June 1940, box 2, file folder 12, WSGA Papers.

8 *Farm and Ranch Review,* October 1942.

9 Many cattlemen doubted the reality of this "shortage." Some blamed the packers for refusing to buy; others saw the shortage as a smokescreen for an attack on price. Others attributed the shortage to a temporary disequilibrium caused by increased consumer capacity to purchase beef.

10 See E. W. Brunsden, "Beef Shortage," *Canadian Cattlemen*, June 1942.

11 Board of Directors' meeting, 31 March 1942, box 2, file folder, 12, WSGA Papers.

12 Kenneth Coppock, "Record of Industry Controls 1941–44," *Canadian Cattlemen*, March 1948.

13 Brunsden, "Beef Shortage."

14 "U.S. Cattle Imports," *Canadian Cattlemen*, September 1948.

15 Coppock, "Record of Industry Controls."

16 Ibid.

17 Special meeting to discuss embargo possibility, 31 March 1942, box 2, file folder 12, WSGA Papers.

18 Report of WSGA delegates Jim Cross and George Ross of Winnipeg, meeting 23 April 1942, box 2, file folder 12, WSGA Papers.

19 Coppock, "Record of Industry Controls."

20 WSGA annual convention, June 1942, box 2, file folder 12, WSGA Papers.

21 Ibid.

22 Ibid.

23 Directors' meeting, 9 July 1942, box 2, file folder 12, WSGA Papers; Coppock, "Record of Industry Controls."

24 Directors' meeting, 9 July 1942, box 2, file folder 12, WSGA Papers.

25 Coppock, "Record of Industry Controls."

26 The criticism that producers were holding back cattle in anticipation of better prices was oft-repeated during 1942. For a good example see *Farm and Ranch Review*, October 1942.

27 Proceedings of special meeting, 25 August 1942, box 2, file folder 12, WSGA Papers.

28 In August, this differential was two dollars per hundredweight. See "The Food Corporation," *Canadian Cattlemen,* September 1942.

29 See *Farm and Ranch Review,* September 1942, for commentary.

30 Canada, *House of Commons Debates,* 18 February 1943, 847. Figures given were an increase of 78.6 percent in cattle shipments and an actual decrease of 5.9 percent in inspected killings.

31 Coppock, "Record of Industry Controls."

32 Ibid.

33 Directors' meeting, 16 November 1942, box 2, file folder 12, WSGA Papers.

34 See remarks made by R. S. Hamer, director, production services, Department of Agriculture in *Lethbridge Herald*, 18 June 1943.

35 The twelve-month policy maintained a flat ceiling and set floors influenced by the previous year's ceilings. From 27 May to 14 August, the floor price was 0.25¢ under the ceiling; from 15 August to 18 September, 1¢; from 19 September to 1 December, 2¢; from January to April, 0.5¢.

36 Rationing was applied to all meats and limited buyers to two pounds per week per person.

37 "Wanted Fair Prices," *Canadian Cattlemen,* September 1942.

38 *Lethbridge Herald*, 20 July 1945.

39 Report of delegates to Ottawa, 4 April 1944, box 2, file folder 12, WSGA Papers.

40 *Farm and Ranch Review*, September 1946.

41 *Lethbridge Herald*, 25 April 1947.

42 Ibid., 10 December 1947.

43 Ibid., 3 June 1943.

44 Ibid., 12 June 1943.

45 Ibid., 27 January 1944; "Keeping Informed," *Canadian Cattlemen*, March 1944.

46 The ceilings were lifted for one month between June and July. See *Lethbridge Herald*, 12 July 1946.

47 For examples, see "Cattle and Lambs Fat But Buyers Not Interested," *Lethbridge Herald,* 17 August 1945; "Packers Stand Creates Meat Crisis," *Lethbridge Herald,* 17 April 1946.

48 This occurred in early 1944 when the value of cows and feeders fell well below the floor price. See "Keeping Informed," *Canadian Cattlemen*, March 1944. See also testimony before the House of Commons Prices Committee in the *Lethbridge Herald*, 6 May 1948.

49 *Edmonton Bulletin*, 22 February 1944.

50 "The Packers Answer," *Lethbridge Herald*, 28 August 1945.

51 "How the Editor Views It," *Farm and Ranch Review*, May 1944.

52 In March 1947, beef ceilings were raised from two to four cents per pound. According to the *Lethbridge Herald*, 3, 12 March 1947, the increase to producers was twenty-eight cents per hundredweight.

53 "Keeping Informed," *Canadian Cattlemen*, March 1944.

54 For statistics on numbers and values see Canada, *Sessional Papers*, no. 155d, 164c, 1948; 155c, 165, 1949.

55 Coppock, "Record of Industry Controls"; *Lethbridge Herald*, 30 June 1943. Italics added.

56 *Farm and Ranch Review*, September 1944.

57 Canada, *House of Commons Debates*, 4 March 1944.

58 *Farm and Ranch Review*, September 1944.

59 *Canadian Cattlemen*, December 1944. It was not only cattle which were clogging the processing facilities. Hog marketings were up by almost 2 million and sheep by eighty-six thousand.

60 See resolutions of Western Canadian Council of Beef Producers in *Canadian Cattlemen*, December 1944. At its meeting in November the council called for restoration of the U.S. live cattle export market.

61 "Protest Livestock Situation," *Farm and Ranch Review*, April 1944.

62 *Farm and Ranch Review*, April 1944; directors' meeting, 4 April 1944, box 2, file folder 12, WSGA Papers.

63 *Farm and Ranch Review*, May 1945.

64 *Farm and Ranch Review*, July 1945.

65 "Address before Canadian Society of Animal Production (Western Section), Monday, June 25, 1945," *Canadian Cattlemen*, September 1945.

66 *Farm and Ranch Review*, October 1945. McLean repeated his assertion in 1946 and 1947. In the former year he said that "Canadian beef cannot hold a permanent place in the British market." See *Canadian Cattlemen*, September 1946.

67 Canada Packers Ltd., "Report to Shareholders," *Canadian Cattlemen*, September 1947.

68 J. P. Sackville, "Livestock Men Served World Well in 1945," *Farm and Ranch Review*, February 1946.

69 "Observations Re Floor Prices," *Canadian Cattlemen*, September 1944.

70 "Give Producers a Break," *Lethbridge Herald*, 29 August 1945.

71 "Keeping Informed," *Canadian Cattlemen*, September 1944; "Cattlemen's Future Uncertain," *Farm and Ranch Review*, May 1944; "New Price Policy," *Farm and Ranch Review*, September 1944.

72 The beef equivalent of 202,390 head of cattle was shipped to Britain in the first four and a half months of 1945. *Canadian Cattlemen,* June 1945.

73 "Chips and Chatter," *Canadian Cattlemen,* June 1944.

74 *Lethbridge Herald,* 27 August 1947.

75 In 1946, J. S. McLean, president of Canada Packers Ltd., said in his annual report that wheat and bacon were the only two food products Canada can produce in competition with the rest of the world. See note 67; also, *Canadian Cattlemen,* September 1946.

76 *Canadian Cattlemen,* March 1948. Italics added.

77 *Lethbridge Herald,* 11 February 1948.

78 Board of directors' meeting, 4 April 1944, box 2, file folder 12, WSGA Papers. Gardiner often couched his mistrust of the American market by maintaining that any resumption of shipments to the U.S. would only mean an increase in her Lend-Lease shipments, and that Canada was better suited to utilize her own like programme to ship more cattle to needy areas.

79 *Farm and Ranch Review,* December 1945, November 1946; See "With Your Editor," and "National Beef Council Meets in Four Day Session in Toronto," *Canadian Cattlemen,* December 1946.

80 *Lethbridge Herald,* 17 January 1947; "With Your Editor," *Canadian Cattlemen,* March 1948.

81 Secretary's address, annual convention, January 1948, box 3, file folder 13, WSGA Papers.

82 The duty was cut to $1.25 per hundredweight. Indeed, the movement was so great that Mexico herself placed a limit of five hundred thousand exportable head in order to protect her own herds. "The Outlook for the Beef Cattle Industry," *Canadian Cattlemen,* March 1947.

83 See board of directors' meeting, 23 August 1947, box 3, file folder 13, WSGA Papers; "Northern Alberta Breeders Urge Opening of U.S. Cattle Markets," *Farm and Ranch Review,* January 1947.

84 *Canadian Cattlemen,* December 1947. The duty on animals over the quota was reduced from three to two cents per pound, the duty on animals two hundred to seven hundred pounds removed completely, and the quota on calves below two hundred pounds was raised from one hundred thousand to two hundred thousand.

85 The Geneva Trade Agreement's Boon to Prairie Agriculture," *Canadian Cattlemen,* December 1947. The optimism was further increased by the fact that Mexico, Canada's only rival for the U.S. market, was currently under embargo for foot and mouth disease.

86 Text of Hon. James Gardiner's address to the fifty-second annual convention of the Western Stock Growers' Association, Lethbridge, 15 January 1948, box 3, file folder 13, WSGA Papers. See also "Canada's Agricultural Policy and the Beef Cattle Industry," *Canadian Cattlemen,* March 1948.

87 Lorne Stout, "Historic Convention," *Canadian Cattlemen,* March 1948.

88 Ibid.

89 *Lethbridge Herald,* 16 April 1948.

90 For a good account of these deliberations see Robert Cuff and J. L. Granatstein, "The Rise and Fall of Canadian-American Free Trade, 1947–48," *Canadian Historical Review* 58, no. 4 (December 1977): 459–82; *For Better or For Worse: Canada and the United States to the 1990s*, J. L. Granatstein and Norman Hillmer, eds. (Toronto: Copp Clark Pitman, 1991), 163–75.

91 Canada raised its dollar to parity with the U.S. dollar in July 1946.

92 "What Will Britain Do?" editorial, *Lethbridge Herald*, 16 June 1948. Three years later in 1951, Britain found herself in a deadlock with Argentina over the price of beef contracts. The British apparently were refusing to pay the equivalent of seventeen cents a pound dressed weight. The irony was not lost on Canadian Cattlemen editor Ken Coppock, who let the fifty cents per pound retail price of beef in Calgary stores speak for itself. "With Your Editor," *Canadian Cattlemen*, February 1951.

93 "U.S. Cattle Export Embargo Lifted," *Lethbridge Herald*, 13 August 1948.

94 Fred Kennedy, "Cattle Drives Revived," *Canadian Cattlemen*, December 1948.

95 *Canadian Cattlemen*, December 1948; By 1951, the value of export cattle to the United States totalled over $300 million.

96 "Cattle to U.S.," editorial, *Lethbridge Herald*, 8 June 1948.

97 "The Importance of Alberta Agriculture to Canada's Export Trade," *Canadian Cattlemen*, March 1949.

98 "Western Stock Growers' Convention," *Canadian Cattlemen*, March 1949.

99 Ken Coppock, "The Beef Cattle Outlook." Text of speech given over CJCJ, Calgary, 12 October 1949, reproduced in *Canadian Cattlemen*, November 1949. Coppock was reiterating remarks he had made in a press release on 13 August 1948 following the announcement of the lifting of the embargo.

100 "With Your Editor," *Canadian Cattlemen*, March 1948.

101 "With Your Editor," *Canadian Cattlemen*, September 1948.

102 Alberta, *Department of Agriculture Annual Report*, 1948.

103 Charles McKinnon compared American and Canadian cattleman at the Calgary Bull Sale. A good bull cost the American the equivalent of three two-year-old steers, whereas the Canadian had to pay the equivalent of five two-year-old steers.

104 *Farm and Ranch Review*, April 1945.

105 Quoted in the *Farm and Ranch Review*, June 1947.

106 *Canadian Cattlemen*, March 1951, July 1953.

107 Canada, Department of Labour, *Annual Report on Wage Rates and Hours of Labour in Canada*, report no. 32, table II, October 1949, 9.

108 *Canada, Royal Commission on Prices*, booklet no. 41, 14 December 1948, 2137. Quoting Canadian Bureau of Statistics.

109 Ibid., 2179.

110 Ibid., 2163.

111 Ibid., 2172.

112 Ibid., 2171.

113 "Better Beef Cattle," Canadian Cattlemen, March 1946.

114 H. J. Maybee, *Beef and Veal Grading in Canada*, publication 962 (Ottawa: Department of Agriculture, Livestock Division, 1964), 37.

115 "Better Beef Cattle," *Canadian Cattlemen*, March 1946.

116 Canada, *Royal Commission on Prices*, booklet no. 38, 7 December 1948, 2005.

117 *Lethbridge Herald*, 17 August 1948.

118 "Have Beef Producers a Job to Do?" *Canadian Cattlemen*, March 1946. Among the small operators, quality stock remained a problem. Unable to afford quality sires, they were criticized in 1945 for "making no attempt towards definite herd improvement."

119 See J. P. Sackville, "The Economics of Cattle Finishing," *Farm and Ranch Review*, November 1945.

120 See *Federal Marketing and Price Legislation in Canada*, 1930–50, Economics Division, Marketing Service, Department of Agriculture, 1950.

121 British Columbia was also included in this feeder freight policy.

122 *Farm and Ranch Review*, October 1945.

123 "Federal Marketing and Price Support Legislation in Canada," *Journal of Farm Economics* November 1947; also House of Commons *Debates*, comments by the Minister of Trade and Commerce, 27 February 1948, 1677–78.

124 *Canadian Cattlemen*, March 1950.

125 Canada Packers Ltd., "Report to Shareholders," *Canadian Cattlemen*, September 1946.

126 *Farm and Ranch Review*, February 1942.

127 "Cattle Finishing in Alberta," *Farm and Ranch Review*, December 1942.

128 *Farm and Ranch Review*, April 1945.

129 "Finishing Beef With Home-Grown Feeds," *Farm and Ranch Review*, December 1945.

130 "Feed Values and Prices," *Lethbridge Herald*, 2 January 1948. The swing from wheat to barley was enhanced in the post-war period by sawfly infestations in wheat.

131 *Farm and Ranch Review*, April 1945. At the sale 799 bulls were sold for a total price of $364,845.

132 H. J. Hargrave, "Improving Range Livestock," *Canadian Cattlemen*, March 1946.

133 Sherm Ewing, *The Ranch: A Modern History of the North American Cattle Industry* (Missoula: Mountain Press, 1995), 36.

134 Ibid., 35.

135 Ibid.

136 For an excellent discussion on "dwarfism," see Frank Jacobs, *Cattle and Us, Frankly Speaking: Or, Cattle Come in Five Sexes* (Calgary: Detselig, 1993), 131–39.

137 Maybee, *Beef and Veal Grading*, 8.

138 Hugh Horner, *A Review of the Meat Industry in Alberta* ([Edmonton]: Alberta Economic Development, 1981), 19.

139 "Record Crowd at Feeder Day Hears Cover Crop Discussed," *Lethbridge Herald*, 29 June 1945.

140 "Scientists Have Produced Perennial Grasses that Will Be a Boon to Western Canada," *Taber Times*, 19 March 1942.

141 *Lethbridge Herald*, 21 February, 13 June 1947.

142 Ibid., 23 November 1946.

143 V. A. Wood, "Alberta's Land Policy Past and Present," *Journal of Farm Economics* 34, no. 4, part 2, 743.

144 The figure given for the winter of 1954–55 was sixty thousand. See F. Whiting, *Feedlot Finishing of Cattle in the Irrigated Districts of Alberta*, publication 786 (Ottawa: Department of Agriculture, 1955).

145 The Grassland Investigations Report was published in four issues in *Canadian Cattlemen*, 1942; Also Clarke, Campbell and Campbell, *Ecological and Carrying Capacity Study*; C. W. Vrooman, G. D. Chattaway and Andrew Stewart, *Cattle Ranching in Western Canada*. Publication 776, Technical Bulletin 778 (Ottawa: Department of Agriculture, Marketing Services, Economic Division in co-operation with the Experimental Farm Service, 1946).

146 H. E. Clements to J. A. Anot, 3 October 1945, file 176, PFRA Papers.

147 See W. D. Willms, S. Smoliak, and G. B. Schallje, "Cattle Weight Gains in Relation to Stocking Rate on Rough Fescue," *Journal of Range Management* 39, no. 2 (March 1986): 182–87.

148 Cattle, like other grazers, feed selectively with the result that they create an imbalance in the range plant community. Some plants that are grazed intensively tend to decrease with time, leaving others to increase in their stead.

149 Wood, "Alberta's Land Policy," 751.

150 Alberta, *Department of Lands and Mines Annual Report*, 1943.

151 *Canadian Cattlemen*, September 1941.

152 See J. A. Campbell and J. B. Campbell, "Grasslands Investigations in Alberta, Saskatchewan and Manitoba," in *Canadian Cattlemen*, March, June, September, December 1942.

153 N. E. Tanner to WSGA board of directors, 14 January 1944, box 2, file folder 12, WSGA Papers.

154 See Anderson, *Grazing Rates Report*, 10–11; also, George Ross, "New Approach to the Economics of Lease Rentals and Taxes," *Canadian Cattlemen*, September 1938.

155 The government made a half-hearted effort to secure a 12.5 percent royalty, but certainly the popular opinion among stockholders was that the royalty should be set at a maximum of 10 percent.

156 Brief on grazing lands, compiled by the Short Grass Stock Growers' Association, 1937, box 13, file folder 121, WSGA Papers.

157 Board of directors' meeting, 22 October 1941, WSGA Papers.

158 Resolution passed at forty-second Convention, 2–3 June 1938, box 2, file folder 11, WSGA Papers.

159 See "Revised Alberta Lease Regulations," *Canadian Cattlemen*, March 1940; Alberta, *Department of Lands and Mines Annual Report*, 1940. It is interesting that while the three-year cancellation clause remained in effect, this long-contentious issue had ceased to be of concern. The soil surveys which had

followed the provisions of the new Land Act in 1939 had clearly classified the true agricultural potential of land.

160 See "Revised Alberta Lease Regulations," *Canadian Cattlemen*, March 1940; WSGA Papers, box 2, file folder 11.

161 Abstracted from Anderson, *Grazing Rates Report,* 178.

162 On 3 April 1939, the Legislature of the Province of Alberta had assented to an important new act, An Act to Amend and Consolidate the Provincial Lands Act, chapter 10, *Statutes of Alberta,* 1939. This act abolished the old homestead system and replaced it with an agricultural leasing policy. The act also directed the minister of Lands and Mines to divide the province for land utilization purposes.

163 Later a forty-acre-to-one-animal zone was added to include most of the area north of Edmonton. See "Alberta, Grazing Capacity and Grazing Rates, 1951," Map, Glenbow.

164 Tanner to chairman of WSGA Grazing Committee, 14 January 1944, box 2, file folder 12, WSGA Papers.

165 N. E. Tanner, "Alberta's Grazing Policy," *Canadian Cattlemen*, March 1944.

166 Ibid.

167 Report of Grazing Committee, WSGA annual convention, 15–16 June 1944, box 2, file folder 13, WSGA Papers.

168 For details see meeting with government and Grazing Committee, 12 October 1944, box 2, file folder 13, WSGA Papers.

169 *Canadian Cattlemen*, December 1944.

170 Ibid.

171 Alberta, *Department of Lands and Mines Annual Report,* 1946.

172 Directors' meeting, 19 March 1945, box 3, file folder 13, WSGA Papers.

# Conclusion

1  Anthropologist John Bennett refers to a process he calls behavioural selection which suggests that over a long period of time certain traits survive and predominate in a well-defined group. Interestingly, he used the ranching community in south-west Saskatchewan as a possible example. See John W. Bennett, "Adaptive Strategy and Processes in the Canadian Plains," in Richard Allen ed., *A Region of the Mind* (Regina: Canadian Plains Research Centre, 1973), 193–94.

2  Terry G. Jordan-Bychkov, *North American Cattle Ranching Frontiers: Origins, Diffusion and Differentiation* (Albuquerque: University of New Mexico Press, 1993). The other systems were called the "Texas" and "California."

3  See Terry G. Jordan-Bychkov, "Does the Border Matter? Cattle Ranching and the 49th Parallel," in Evans, Carter, and Yeo, *Cowboys, Ranchers and the Cattle Business*, (Calgary: University of Calgary Press, 2001), 1–10.

# Select Bibliography

## Manuscript Sources

Public Archives of Canada, Ottawa. RG 15. Department of the Interior Papers.
Provincial Archives of Alberta, Edmonton. Papers of the Department of the Attorney General.
PAA. Premiers' Papers.
Glenbow Archives, Calgary. Pat Burns Fonds.
Glenbow. Canada Land and Irrigation Company Ltd. Fonds.
Glenbow. Canadian Agricultural, Coal and Colonization Company Fonds, Stair Ranch Letterbook 1890–1893.
Glenbow. Canadian Pacific Railway Fonds.
Glenbow. Cathro, Matthews Family Fonds.
Glenbow. Cochrane Ranche Company Ltd. Fonds, W. F. Cochrane Diary and Letterbook.
Glenbow. A. E. Cross Family Fonds.
Glenbow. Gilbert and Luella Goddard Fonds, Bow River Horse Ranch Papers.
Glenbow. Ella Inderwick Fonds, Diary and Personal Letters from North Fork Ranch.
Glenbow. United Farmers of Alberta Fonds.
Glenbow. Western Stock Growers' Association Papers.
Provincial Archives of Saskatchewan, Department of Agriculture Collection.
PAS, Prairie Farm Rehabilitation Administration Papers.
PAS, William Levi Jacobsen Papers.
University of Alberta Archives, Edmonton. William Pearce Papers.
Government Sources
Alberta. Royal Commissions and Commissions of Inquiry. *Report of the Beef Commission.* 1908.
Alberta. Department of the Attorney General. *Report of National Beef Cattle Conference, Winnipeg, June 28–29, 1928.*
Alberta. Post-War Reconstruction Committee. *Report of the Subcommittee on Agriculture.* March 1943.
Canada. Department of Labour. Report no. 32. Table II. *Annual Report on Wage Rates and Hours of Labour in Canada,* October 1949.
Canada. Report of His Majesty's Commissioners. *Royal Commission on the Importation of Live Cattle,* 30 August 1921.

Canada. *Royal Commission on Price Spreads and Mass Buying: Proceedings and Evidence,* 1934.

Canada. *Royal Commission on Prices,* 1948.

## Books, Articles, and Pamphlets

Anderson, C. Graham. Compiled with the co-operation of the Short Grass Stock Growers' Association. *Grazing Rates Report: Short Grass Area of Alberta.* Edmonton: [Dept. of Lands and Mines], 1941.

Ankli, Robert E. and Robert M. Litt. "The Growth of Prairie Agriculture: Economic Considerations." In *Canadian Papers in Rural History,* vol. I. Donald H. Akenson, ed. Gananoque: Langdale Press, 1978.

Anstey, T. H. *One Hundred Harvests,* 1886–1986. Research Branch, Agriculture Canada, Historical Series no., 27, 1986.

Archibald, E. S. "A National Cattle Policy," *Scientific Agriculture* 15, no. 3, (November 1934).

Arkell, H. S. "Competition for the United Kingdom Meat Market." Canadian Cattlemen, September 1939.

Balkwill, Dan. "Frontier vs. Metropolis: Early Attempts at Eradicating Mange on the Canadian Prairie." Graduate paper, History Department, University of Saskatchewan, 1997.

———. "The PFRA Community Pasture Program, 1937–41." Master's thesis, University of Saskatchewan, forthcoming.

Beaudon, Alwynne B. "What They Saw: The Climatic and Environmental Context for Euro-Canadian Settlement in Alberta." *Prairie Forum* 24, no. 1 (1999).

Benedict, Murray R. *Farm Policies of the United States,* 1790–1950: *A Study of Their Origins and Development.* New York: Octagon Books, 1966.

Bennett, John W. "Adaptive Strategy and Processes in the Canadian Plains." In *A Region of the Mind.* Richard Allen, ed. Regina: Canadian Plains Studies Centre, 1973.

Black, John D. *Agricultural Reform in the United States.* New York: McGraw Hill, 1929.

Brado, Edward. *Cattle Kingdom: Early Ranching in Alberta* . Vancouver: Douglas and McIntyre, 1984.

Breen, David H. *The Canadian Prairie West and the Ranching Frontier,* 1874–1924. Toronto: University of Toronto Press, 1983.

Butler, W. F. *The Great Lone Land: A Narrative of Ttravel and Adventure in the north-West Land of America.* London: Sampson, Low, Marston, Low and Searle, 1872.

Campbell, Alex M. *Report of the Beef Commission: Purchase and Sale of Cattle, Hogs, Sheep and Meat in the Provinces of Manitoba and Alberta.* Edmonton: King's Printer, 1906.

Campbell, J. A., and J. B. Campbell. "Grasslands Investigations in Alberta, Saskatchewan and Manitoba." *Canadian Cattlemen,* March, June, September, December 1942.

"Canadian Agricultural Products and the British Market." *Agricultural Gazette of Canada* 11, no. 1 (January–February 1924).

"Canadian Cattle Exports, 1867–1937." *Canadian Cattlemen*, June 1938.

Carson, Lloyd, and Gordon Carson. "The Houcher Story." *Canadian Cattlemen*, June 1949.

Christensen, Alice M. "Agricultural Pressure and Governmental Response in the United States, 1919–1929." *Agricultural History* 11, no. 1 (January 1937).

Christianson, C. J. *Early Rangemen*. Lethbridge: Southern Printing Co., 1973.

Clarke, S. E. "Pasture Investigations in the Short Grass Plains of Saskatchewan and Alberta." *Scientific Agriculture* 10, no. 10 (June 1930).

Clarke, S. E., J. A. Campbell, and J. B. Campbell. *An Ecological and Grazing Capacity Study of the Native Grass Pastures in Southern Alberta, Saskatchewan and Manitoba*. Publication 738, Technical Bulletin 44. Ottawa: Department of Agriculture, Division of Forage Crops, 1942.

Clawson, Marion. *The Western Range Livestock Industry*. New York: McGraw Hill, 1950.

Collins, J. L. "Genetics and Breeding." *Scientific Agriculture* 7 (August 1927).

Connor, James R. "National Farm Organizations and the United States Tariff Policy in the 1920s." *Agricultural History* 32, no. 1 (January 1958).

"Co-Operative Cattle Selling: A System of Marketing Cattle for the Benefit of Producers." *United Grain Growers Publication*, 15 March 1924.

Coppock, Kenneth. "Record of Industry Controls 1941–44." *Canadian Cattlemen*, March 1948.

Craig, G. H. and J. Coke. *An Economic Study of Land Utilization in Southern Alberta*. Publication 610, Technical Bulletin 16. Ottawa: Department of Agriculture, 1938.

Craig, John R. *Ranching with Lords and Commons*. Toronto: William Briggs, 1903.

———. *The Grazing Country of the Dominion of Canada: Reports of Tourists, Explorers and Residents of the Grazing Lands of the North-West Territory*. Edinburgh: Colston, 1882.

Cuff, Robert, and J. L. Granatstein. "The Rise and Fall of Canadian-American Free Trade, 1947–48." *Canadian Historical Review* 58, no. 4 (December 1977).

Dale, Edward Everett. *The Range Cattle Industry: Ranching on the Great Plains From 1865 to 1925*. Norman: University of Oklahoma Press, 1960.

Dibney, Dora. "Pioneering in the Cochrane District." *Canadian Cattlemen*, June 1949.

Donahue, Debra L. *The Western Range Revisited: Removing Livestock From Public Lands to Conserve Native Biodiversity*. Norman: University of Oklahoma Press, 1999.

"Eastern Canadian Society of Animal Production: Reports Presented at First Annual General Meeting." *Scientific Agriculture* 8 (August 1928).

Edmonton Board of Trade. *The Edmonton District in Central Alberta: Canada's Richest Mixed Farming Country*. Edmonton: The Board, 1917.

Elofson, Warren M. "Adapting to the Frontier Environment: The Ranching Industry in Western Canada, 1891–1914." In *Canadian Papers in Rural History*, vol. 8. Donald H. Akenson, ed. Gananoque: Langdale Press, 1992.

————. *Cowboys, Gentlemen and Cattle Thieves: Ranching on the Western Frontier.* Montreal: McGill-Queen's University Press, 2000.

————. "Mixed and Dryland Farming Near Pincher Creek 1895–1914." *Prairie Forum* 19, no. 1 (1994).

Evans, Simon. "American Cattlemen in the Canadian West, 1874–1914." *Prairie Forum* 4, no. 1 (1979).

————. "Canadian Beef For Victorian Britain." *Agricultural History* 53, no. 4 (October 1979).

————. "The End of the Open Range Era in Western Canada." *Prairie Forum* 8, no. 1 (1983).

————. "Grazing the Grasslands: Exploring Conflicts, Relationships and Futures." *Prairie Forum* 26, no. 1 (Spring 2001).

————. "The Origins of Ranching in Western Canada: American Diffusion or Victorian Transplant?" *Great Plains Quarterly* 3, no. 2 (Spring 1983).

————. "The Passing of a Frontier: Ranching in the Canadian West, 1882–1912." Ph.D. diss., Department of Geography, University of Calgary, 1976.

Evans, Simon, Sarah Carter, and Bill Yeo, eds. *Cowboys, Ranchers and the Cattle Business: Cross-Border Perspectives on Ranching History.* Calgary: University of Calgary Press, 2000.

Ewing, Sherm. *The Range.* Missoula: Mountain Press, 1990.

————. *The Ranch: A Modern History of the North American Cattle Industry.* Missoula: Mountain Press, 1995.

Fausold, Martin L. "President Hoover's Farm Policies, 1929–1933." *Agricultural History* 51, no. 2 (1977).

*Federal Marketing and Price Legislation in Canada, 1930–50,* Economics Division, Marketing Service, Department of Agriculture, 1950.

"Federal Marketing and Price Support Legislation in Canada." *Journal of Farm Economics* November 1947.

Fisher, J. R. "The Economic Effects of Cattle Disease in Britain and Its Containment, 1850–1900." *Agricultural History* 54 (April 1980).

Foran, Max. "Calgary and Its Hinterlands: Ranching, Farming, Oil and Gas." *Centennial City: Calgary 1894–1994.* Donald Smith, ed. Calgary: University of Calgary Press, 1994.

————. "The Politics of Animal Health: The British Embargo on Canadian Cattle, 1892–1932." *Prairie Forum* 23, no. 1 (1998).

————. "Mixed Blessings: The Second 'Golden Age' of the Alberta Cattle Industry, 1914–20." *Alberta History* 46, no. 3 (1998).

————. "A Forced Solution: the Depression and the Province of Alberta's Grazing Leasehold Policy, 1931–45." In *Cowboys, Ranchers and the Cattle Business: Cross-Border Perspectives on Ranching History.* Simon Evans, Sarah Carter, and Bill Yeo, eds. Calgary: University of Calgary Press, 2000.

————. "Fighting a Losing Battle: Canadian Stockmen and the American Tariffs, 1920–30." *Agricultural History* 74, no. 4 (Fall 2000).

————. "Hooves For Gallons: The Canada/Russia Barter Deal of 1932–33." *Alberta History* 49, no. 2 (Spring 2001).

————. "The Price of Patriotism: Alberta Cattlemen and the Loss of the American Market, 1942–48." *Great Plains Quarterly* 21, no. 1 (Winter 2001).

Kottman, Richard. "Herbert Hoover and Hawley-Smoot Tariff: Canada, a Case Study." *Journal of American History* 62 (1975–76).

"Fourth Annual General Meeting of the Eastern Canadian Society of Animal Production." *Scientific Agriculture* 13 (November 1932).

Fowke, Vernon C. *Canadian Agricultural Policy: the Historical Pattern.* Toronto: University of Toronto Press, 1946.

Gardiner, Claude. *Letters From an English Rancher.* Calgary: Glenbow Museum, 1988.

Gould, Ed. *Ranching in Western Canada.* Sanichton: Harcourt House, 1978.

Graber, Stan. *The Last Roundup: Memories of a Canadian Cowboy.* Saskatoon: Fifth House, 1995.

Granatstein, J. L., and Norman Hillmer, eds. *For Better or For Worse: Canada and the United States to the 1990s.* Toronto: Copp Clark Pitman, 1991.

"Grazing Country Par Excellence, A." In *The Prairie West to 1905: A Canadian Sourcebook.* Lewis G. Thomas, ed. Toronto: Oxford University Press, 1975.

Hamer, R. S. "Report of Beef Cattle Production Committee." *Scientific Agriculture* 8 (August 1928).

Hargrave, H. C. "Land, Water and the Farmer." Paper presented at the Fifteenth Annual Convention of the Saskatchewan Rivers Development Association, 27 October 1962.

Harvie, J. "Alberta's Grazing Policy." *Canadian Catllemen*, September 1938.

Henrichs, D. H., and T. Lawrence. *Russian Wild Ryegrass for Western Canada.* Publication 991. Ottawa: Department of Agriculture, 1956.

Hind, Henry Youle. *Reports of Progress Together with a Preliminary and General Report on the Assiniboine and Saskatchewan Exploring Expedition.* Toronto: John Lovell, 1859.

Hope, E. C. "The Significance of Demand in the Determination of Prices of Beef and Pork in Canada, 1920–1932." *Scientific Agriculture* 15, no. 2 (October 1934).

Horner, Hugh. *A Review of the Meat Industry in Alberta.* [Edmonton]: Alberta Economic Development, 1981.

Ings, Fred W. *Before the Fences: Tales from the Midway Ranch.* Calgary: McAra Press, 1980.

Jacobs, Frank. *Cattle and Us, Frankly Speaking: Or, Cattle Come in Five Sexes.* Calgary: Detselig, 1993.

Jameson, Sheilagh S. *Ranches, Cowboys and Characters: the Birth of Alberta's Western Culture.* Calgary: Glenbow Museum, 1987.

Johnston, Alex. *Cowboy Politics: The Western Stock Growers' Association and Its Predecessors.* Calgary: Western Stock Growers' Association, 1971.

————. *To Serve Agriculture: The Lethbridge Research Station 1906–76.* Historical Series no. 9. Ottawa: Research Branch, Department of Agriculture, 1977.

Jones, David C., ed. *We'll All Be Buried Down Here: The Prairie Dryland Disaster, 1917–26.* Historical Society of Alberta vol. 6. Edmonton: Alberta Records Publication Board, 1986.

Jones, David C. *Empire of Dust: Settling and Abandoning the Prairie Dry Belt.* Edmonton: University of Alberta Press, 1987.

Jordan-Bychkov, Terry G. "Does the Border Matter? Cattle Ranching and the 49th Parallel." In *Cowboys, Ranchers and the Cattle Business: Cross-Border Perspectives on Ranching History.* Simon Evans, Sarah Carter, and Bill Yeo, eds. Calgary: University of Calgary Press, 2000.

———. *North American Cattle-Ranching Frontiers: Origins, Diffusion and Differentiation.* Albuquerque: University of New Mexico Press, 1993.

Kelly, L. V. *The Range Men: The Story of the Ranchers and Indians of Alberta.* Toronto: William Briggs, 1913.

Klassen, Henry. "Entrepreneurship in the Canadian West: The Enterprises of A. E. Cross, 1886–1920." *Western Historical Quarterly* 22, no. 3 (August 1991).

———. "A Century of Ranching at the Rocking P and Bar S." In *Cowboys, Ranchers and the Cattle Business: Cross-Border Perspectives on Ranching History.* Simon Evans, Sarah Carter, and Bill Yeo, eds. Calgary: University of Calgary Press, 2000.

Latimer, J. "Intra-Empire Trade: The Opportunity for Agriculture." *Scientific Agriculture* 13, no. 5 (January 1933).

Lyne, E. J. "The Retail Meat Dealer." *Canadian Cattlemen*, December 1938.

MacLachlan Ian, *Kill and Chill: Restructuring Canada's Beef Commodity Chain.* Toronto: University of Toronto Press, 2001.

MacEwan, Grant. *Blazing the Old Cattle Trail.* Saskatoon: Western Producer Prairie Books, 1962.

MacInnes, C. M. *In the Shadow of the Rockies.* London: Rivingtons, 1930.

Maybee, H. J. *Beef and Veal Grading in Canada.* Publication 962. Ottawa: Department of Agriculture, Livestock Division, 1964.

McAlla, Alex F. "Protectionism in Inter national Trade, 1850–1968." *Agricultural History* 63, no. 3 (July 1969).

McIntyre, William H. Jr. "A Short History of the McIntyre Ranch." *Canadian Cattlemen*, September 1947.

McKinnon, Charles H. *Events of LK Ranch.* Calgary: Phoenix Press, 1979.

Macoun, John. *Manitoba and the Great North-West.* Guelph: World Publishing, 1882.

Marchildon, Gregory P. "Canadian-American Agricultural Trade Relations: A Brief History." *American Review of Canadian Studies* 28, no. 3 (Autumn 1998).

Martin, Chester. *Dominion Lands Policy.* Edited by L. H. Thomas. The Carleton Library no. 69. Toronto: McClelland and Stewart, 1973.

McElroy, L. W. *Cattle Finishing in Alberta.* Edmonton: University of Alberta, Faculty of Agriculture, Department of Animal Science, 1958.

Mitchner, A. "The Bow River Scheme: CPR's Irrigation Block." In *The CPR West: The Iron Road and the Making of a Nation.* Hugh A. Dempsey, ed. Vancouver: Douglas and McIntyre, 1984.

Muir, G. and S. Chagnon. *The Winter Feeding of Beef Cattle in Ontario.* Ottawa: Department of Agriculture, Animal Husbandry Division, 1922.

Nielson, Kris, and John Prociuk. *From Start to Finish: A History of Cattle Feeding in Alberta.* Calgary: Alberta Cattle Feeders' Association, 1999.

Potyondi, Barry. *Where the Rivers Meet: A History of the Upper Oldman Basin to* 1939. Pincher Creek: Southern Alberta Water Science Society, 1992.

"Proceedings of the Second Annual General Meeting of the Eastern Canadian Society of Animal Production." *Scientific Agriculture* 11 (January 1930).

"Proceedings of the Fourth Annual General Meeting of the Western Canada Society of Animal Production." *Scientific Agriculture* 11 (January 1930).

"Proceedings of the Fourth Annual Meeting of the Western Canadian Society of Animal Production, June 6–7, 1931." *Scientific Agriculture* 11 (March 1931).

Proskie, John. "Trends in Security of Tenure: Grazing Lands in Western Canada." *Canadian Cattlemen*, June 1939.

Robertson, James W. *Experiments in the Feeding of Steers,* 1875–1930. Ottawa: Department of Agriculture, n.d.

———. *Report of Select Committee on Agricultural Conditions.* Ottawa: King's Printer, 1923.

Rudd, F. Albert. "Production and Marketing of Beef Cattle from the Short Grass Plains Area of Canada." Master's thesis, University of Alberta, 1935.

Rust, R. S. "Land Use in the Special Areas of Alberta." Master's thesis, University of Alberta, 1956.

Rutherford, W. J. *The Feeding Value of Corn and Its Comparison With Other Grains for Feeding Purposes.* Regina: W. J. Reid, [1915?].

Sheppard, Bert. *Spitzee Days.* Calgary: John McAra, 1971.

Skaggs, Jimmy M. *Prime Cut: Livestock Raising and Meatpacking in the United States,* 1607–1983. College Station: Texas A&M University Press, 1986.

Slatta, Richard W. *Comparing Cowboys and Frontiers.* Norman: University of Oklahoma Press, 1997.

Shaw, A. M. "Report on the Experiments of Chilled Beef to Britain." *Scientific Agriculture* 15, no. 1 (November 1934).

———. "Phases of Beef Cattle Markets." *Canadian Cattlemen*, June 1938.

*Shipping Cattle to Britain: Experiments in the Shipment of Live Cattle and Chilled Beef to England.* Ottawa: Department of Agriculture, Experimental Farms Branch, 1926.

Silver, Jim. "The Origins of Winnipeg's Packing Plant Industry: Transitions From Trade to Manufacture." *Prairie Forum* 19, no. 1 (Spring 1994).

Smith, K. D., R. T. Berg, M. H. Hawkins, M. E. Stiles, and S. C. McFadyn, *The New Beef Grades.* Edmonton: University of Alberta, Faculty of Agriculture and Forestry, 1975.

Smoliak, Sylvester, and Alexander Johnston. *Managing Crested Wheatgrass Pastures.* Publication 1473/E. Ottawa: Department of Agriculture, 1981.

Soule, George, and Vincent P. Carosso. *American Economic History.* New York: Dryden Press, 1957.

Spector, David. *Agriculture on the Prairies,* 1870–1940. History and Archaeology, vol. 65. Ottawa: Environment Canada, National Historic Parks and Sites Branch, 1983.

Spence, George. "Land Utilization Under the Prairie Farm Rehabilitation Program." *Canadian Cattlemen*, June 1938.

Thomas, L. G. "The Rancher and the City: Calgary and the Cattlemen, 1883–1914." *Transactions of the Royal Society of Canada*, 4th series, vol. 6. Ottawa: Royal Society of Canada, 1968.

Thomas, Lewis G., ed. *The Prairie West to 1905: A Canadian Sourcebook.* Toronto: Oxford University Press, 1975.

Thomlinson, T. W. "The United States Tariff Act of 1922." *Farm and Ranch Review*, 10 June 1927.

Thomson, L. B. "Costs of Beef Cattle Production." *Canadian Cattlemen*, June 1938.

Tinline, M. J. *Finishing Steers for Market in North-Western Saskatchewan.* New Series. Pamphlet 17. Ottawa: Department of Agriculture, 1922.

Todd, S. L. "Functions of the Meat Packer." *Farm and Ranch Review*, July 1939.

Voisey, Paul. "A Mix-Up over Mixed Farming: The Curious History of the Agricultural Diversification Movement in a Single Crop Area of Southern Alberta." In *Building Beyond the Homestead*. David C. Jones and Ian MacPherson, eds. Calgary: University of Calgary Press, 1985.

Vrooman, C. W., G. D. Chattaway, and Andrew Stewart. *Cattle Ranching in Western Canada.* Publication 776, Technical Bulletin 778. Ottawa: Department of Agriculture, Marketing Services, Economic Division in co-operation with the Experimental Farm Service, 1946.

Waiser, William A. *The Field Naturalist: John Macoun, the Geological Survey and Natural Science.* Toronto: University of Toronto Press, 1989.

Ward, Norman, and David Smith. *Jimmy Gardiner: Relentless Liberal.* Toronto: University of Toronto Press, 1990.

Whiting, F. *Feedlot Finishing of Cattle in the Irrigated Districts of Alberta.* Publication 786. Ottawa: Department of Agriculture, 1955.

Williams, C. M. "Always the Bridesmaid: The Development of the Saskatchewan Beef Production System, Part One." *Saskatchewan History* XLII, no. 3 (Autumn 1989).

Willms, W. D., S. Smoliak, and G. B. Schallje. "Cattle Weight Gains in Relation to Stocking Rate on Rough Fescue." *Journal of Range Management* 39, no. 2 (March 1986).

Wilson, C. F. *A Century of Canadian Grain: Government Policy to 1951.* Saskatoon: Western Producer Prairie Books, 1978.

Wood, V. A. "Alberta's Land Policy Past and Present." *Journal of Farm Economics* 34, no. 4, part 2.

Young, Linda M., and John M. Marsh. "Integration and Interdependence in the U.S. and Canadian Live Cattle and Beef Sectors." *American Review of Canadian Studies* 28, no. 3 (Autumn 1998).

Zimmerman, W. David. "Live Cattle Export Trade Between United States and Great Britain." *Agricultural History* 36, no. 1 (January 1962).

# Index